A Quick
Overview
of *the*
BIBLE

Douglas A. Jacoby

HARVEST HOUSE PUBLISHERS

EUGENE, OREGON

Cover by Dugan Design Group, Bloomington, Minnesota

Cover photo © Mele Avery / Fotolia

Maps by Michael Brumagin

A QUICK OVERVIEW OF THE BIBLE
Copyright © 2012 by Douglas A. Jacoby
Published by Harvest House Publishers
Eugene, Oregon 97402
www.harvesthousepublishers.com

Library of Congress Cataloging-in-Publication Data
    Jacoby, Douglas A.
    A quick overview of the Bible / Douglas Jacoby.
       p. cm.
    Includes bibliographical references.
    ISBN 978-0-7369-4424-3 (pbk.)
    ISBN 978-0-7369-4425-0 (eBook)
    1. Bible—Introductions. I. Title.
    BS475.3.J33 2012
    220.6'1—dc23

                               2011033505

Printed in the United States of America

      14 15 16 17 18 19 20 21 22 / LB-SK / 11 10 9 8 7 6 5 4 3 2

To my brother, Steve

CONTENTS

Part 1

GETTING
STARTED

THE BIG PICTURE

The law from your mouth is more precious to me
than thousands of pieces of silver and gold.

PSALM 119:72

M any people value the word of God so highly that they will go to great lengths to hear it. They cherish it. I'm thinking of a man whose black eyes were alight and whose handshake was firm as he thanked me for a Bible lesson. Who would have known he had walked for three hours on dusty desert roads and through the heart of a dangerous Muslim city just to hear God's word?

I'm thinking of a Brazilian woman who greeted me with a bright smile and a joyful embrace as she told me how God's word had transformed her marriage and family. Who would have known she had been up all night working before coming to hear a Bible exposition that morning?

I'm thinking of an entire Vietnamese congregation who took a day off work—not a member was missing—and assembled early for a full day of biblical teaching.

In Saddam Hussein's Iraq, Christians (especially converts from Islam) were persecuted. Two prisoners' Bibles had been confiscated, so they had to make do. One used chicken bones to scribble Scripture on the walls of his cell. The other, who was forced to clean the latrine, found that the guards were using Bible pages for toilet paper. He cleaned them and treasured them. Both men risked beatings for the sake of the word that sustained them in their darkest hour.

I could tell countless stories like these of people all around the world who make extraordinary sacrifices—missing sleep, skipping work, defying their governments, and even risking their lives—just to hear the word of God. Are these people crazy? A little too obsessed? Or have they discovered something worth all these sacrifices and more?

I deeply admire people like this, people whom I have the honor of meeting through my international teaching ministry. They are truth seekers. And they are willing to invest significant time and energy for a wonderful eternal payoff. They are not alone, for through the course of history many have paid with their very lives for the privilege of reading God's word.

Seekers

Today I am writing in Paraguay. I am here to teach the Bible. In one respect, this South American nation is no different from the dozens of other lands in which I've taught in the past year—places like Switzerland, Haiti, Egypt, Trinidad, Israel, and Canada. People everywhere are looking for answers to the fundamental questions of life: Who are we, and how did we get here? Is there an afterlife? How should I relate to other people? What is meaningful? Who decides what is right and wrong? What is my purpose during the few decades of my earthly existence? My experience leads me to believe that the only place to go for answers to these questions is the Holy Bible.

No Other Book Even Comes Close!

The Bible is my all-time favorite book. I've read thousands of books but none as often as the Bible (50 times and counting). No other book is remotely as deserving of a lifetime of study. The Bible has been my daily companion since I came to faith in Christ in 1977. I continue to learn from it and am amazed by its depth. This book led me to God, transforming my thinking and living. Even now it challenges me to the core. The Bible is the most exciting book in the world, standing uniquely as divine revelation amid its rivals—works of human wisdom that invariably fall short. I urge you to read it, preferably every day, in order to hear God's voice.

Fears and Hopes

"Sounds great," you may be thinking, "but aren't there many interpretations of the Bible and endless church denominations? What hope
do we really have of understanding the Bible?" Perhaps you're a newcomer to the Scriptures, and you fear, "I'll never finish 1000 pages!" I
can assure you that with the benefit of an *overview*—an introduction
to the Scriptures—length is no object. Or you may be afraid of what
you'll find when you do begin to explore. Confusion? Disappoint-
ment? Unbearable demands? To the contrary, I believe you'll be profoundly encouraged. Or perhaps your faith has withered—possibly
under the critique of a college religion professor—and you long to
rediscover what is true in the Bible. Most readers aren't quite sure how
all the pieces fit together: the books, chapters, and verses; prophets,
priests, and kings; history, geography, and archaeology. *A Quick Overview of the Bible* makes your task easier, clarifying the sometimes puz-
zling structure of God's word.

Most people who simply pick up a Bible and start reading do not
feel completely at home. They aren't familiar with the lands, empires,
and issues around which the biblical story revolves. Even many Christians, if not most of them, don't grasp the big picture. They're puzzled.

Further, an enormous gulf separates us from the people in biblical times. Society, dress, customs, language, attitudes—all are different. We may *think* we understand what we're reading, yet the chasm
between our time and theirs, our culture and theirs, is considerable.
To cite one example among hundreds, in Bible times, as in the Middle East today, people greeted each other with a holy kiss. The practice
is not explained; it's assumed. But we shouldn't think this means men
were at liberty to kiss random women—which could have led to fights!
Men kissed men, and women kissed women.

A Puzzle

My family likes to work on puzzles, usually the 1000-piece kind. We
spread one out on the table, a jumble of cardboard pieces that should
fit together but are as yet unconnected. They aren't self-assembling—
we have to do the work. We find the straight edges and complete the

border. Then we match up pieces with the same colors, taking cues from the picture on the puzzle box. Piece by piece it comes together. Though every family member vies for the privilege of setting in the final piece, the endeavor is a group project.

The Bible is a bit like that. Until we grasp its outlines and contours, it is an amorphous mass of puzzle pieces. But as it comes together, what was a scrambled pile is transformed into a striking and compelling image.

A Guidebook

Have you ever traveled to another country? We consult maps and surf the web to find out as much as we can before we step off the plane. Outsiders can easily miss something basic—perhaps something important. So it is when we approach the Bible, when we travel from our world to an ancient one. Babylonians, cubits, apostles, psalms—these are not part of the average modern person's world. When we jump into the Scriptures without any orientation, one of three outcomes normally results:

1. We give up. We stop reading. Our spiritual roots remain shallow; they are not strong enough to keep us upright when the storms of life assail us.

2. We pick and choose. We force ourselves to wade through the Bible even though so much belongs to an alien world. As in a treasure hunt, we search for bits of Bible that speak to us, hoping we're not wasting our time. Most of the verses seem extraneous until we find our favorite promise or uncover a biblical truth. Yet all of the Scriptures are there for a reason. When we read with adequate preparation, they come to life.

3. We deceive ourselves. In the worst of the three outcomes, we imagine we understand what we have read, but in fact, we do not. Joining with others, perhaps in a group discussion, does not help because many group leaders have never been properly oriented to the Scriptures, and we end up only pooling our ignorance.

A Map

When I was 22, I moved to London with a small group of Americans and Britons to plant a new church. I needed to learn my way around this colossal city, so I began with a map of the Underground (subway), first teaching myself the stations, in sequence, between my flat and my workplace. The truth is, I didn't do it all by myself; I asked for lots of help. In time I developed a grasp of the entire system. I didn't know the location of every station, but I certainly learned to get around. In other words, it wasn't a cinch, but neither was it impossible. So it is with the Scriptures. In time, anyone who determines to give it a go will learn—especially when he or she is humble enough to receive help from others.

Light

One reoccurring biblical image of God's word is *light*. The word is a lamp for our feet, helping us to see where we're going (Psalm 119:105). It illuminates the path of God's commands (and our lives). God's light provides security and freedom. "I run in the path of your commands, for you have broadened my understanding" (Psalm 119:32; also see John 8:31-32). We don't idolize the Bible as an end in itself (that is called *bibliolatry*), but we view it as a tool for living in God's world, for staying on the straight path.

Overview

The purpose of an overview (or Bible survey) is to acquaint us with the world of the Bible, to help us to hear the message as it was heard originally. Orientation, whether for a new job, a new school, or new software, provides us with the necessary information, putting us at ease. So it is with a Bible survey. It demystifies the Bible, giving us fresh eyes for examining the Scriptures. The Bible will always have some element of mystery, but *that* mystery has nothing to do with one's confusion between chapter numbers and verse numbers or ignorance about ancient Babylon! A Bible overview builds a bridge that enables us to visit the world of the Bible.

Here's how *A Quick Overview of the Bible* is structured.

Part 1, "Getting Started," introduces the Bible. What is it? How did it come to be? How can you get the most out of your time in the Scriptures?

Part 2, "The First Testament," sets the Old Testament (the first three quarters of the Bible) in perspective. What are we supposed to learn? What still applies today?

Part 3, "The Second Testament," elucidates the New Testament (the Gospels, Acts, the epistles [or letters], and the Apocalypse) and shows how and why Jesus Christ is the central character not only of the New Testament but also of the Old Testament—in fact, he is Lord of history. As others have said, "History is *his story.*"

You can find appendixes to this book online*—further information and strategies to help you optimize your efforts to learn from the Scriptures.

A Special Word to Bible Teachers

Do you lead Sunday school classes, Bible discussions, small groups, or large congregational seminars? If you do, this book is for you. Of all people, we who teach need to grasp the big picture of God's word. When we see how the pieces fit together, three benefits accrue.

1. Our competence grows. We become proficient in helping others with God's word because we are being trained to handle it correctly (2 Timothy 2:15).

2. Our confidence follows. Godly and humble confidence (not arrogant bluster) results from knowing the difference between what we do know and what we don't know.

3. Our credibility is enhanced. Our listeners realize that we're not speaking theoretically, but from personal transformation.

Bible teachers *must* become diligent students of God's word, and this includes aiming for proficiency in the history, geography, sociology, and theology of the Scriptures. As your knowledge grows, Bible reading becomes an adventure. When we are able to translate its images, symbols, and culture into terms we relate to, we see in color instead of black and white. We also see stereoscopically, with the depth perception that comes from historical perspective and appreciation of biblical culture.

---

* www.douglasjacoby.com/view_article.php?ID=6264.

Let's Begin

And now I invite you to join the Paraguayans and Pakistanis, Kenyans and Koreans, Croatians and Canadians, Indians and Iraqis, and all earnest seekers across the planet in the quest for truth, love, and meaning. Only through the lens of biblical truth, with Christ Jesus at the center, does reality come into focus. We see our need and his initiative, and we understand why so many have suffered so much for the Bible. It is a true treasure.

Once the pieces fit together, the Bible is no longer a fragmented book—an unsolvable puzzle with missing pieces—but an integral whole, a beautiful and complete picture. "All Scripture is God-breathed and is useful for teaching, rebuking, correcting and training in righteousness" (2 Timothy 3:16).

2

A STORY IN
FOUR DIMENSIONS

After this I looked, and there before me was a great multitude
that no one could count, from every nation, tribe, people and
language, standing before the throne and before the Lamb.

REVELATION 7:9

The people pictured in the verse above loved truth and sought it, and in the process they came to know God. They knew they didn't have the answers themselves, but they knew the one who has the answers.

How might such an image be realized—the ultimate biblical vision of a mass of humanity humbly and worshipfully assembled before the throne of God? God created man in a state of sinlessness, in the paradise of Eden, but something has obviously gone terribly wrong. What is the biblical story?

The Plot

The story begins with a picture of God's will for humanity. Adam and Eve are living in a state of grace, tasked to exercise responsible dominion over the planet in communion with him and with each another. But sin spoils the picture. Again and again throughout the biblical record, God rescues humanity from the consequences of our rebellion (recall the stories of Adam, Cain, Noah, and Abraham, for example). Rather than write off humanity, God chooses a single man, Abraham, calling him from the darkness of idolatry to a relationship with God himself.

17

Three generations later, Abraham's descendants form the nucleus of what will one day become the nation of Israel. Several centuries later these 12 tribes inherit a small but crucial plot of land in the Middle East at the convergence of Africa and Asia—the crossroads of the ancient world. If only God's people will follow his voice, they will be a light to the nations (Exodus 19:6). Yet interminable cycles of rebellion, humiliation, repentance, and rescue run their course through the patriarchal period (Genesis), the Exodus and desert wanderings (Exodus–Deuteronomy), the conquest of the Promised Land (Joshua), and the period of the Judges (Judges and Ruth). The cycle continues through the period of the monarchy (1 Samuel–2 Chronicles) and even the exile and return (Ezra–Esther). Some figures come closer than others to embodying the righteous ideals of the Messiah, such as Abraham, Moses, David, and Solomon, but all are marred by self-will and sin.

When the Old Testament ends a few hundred years before the birth of Christ, God's people are still living in confusion, enjoying neither national sovereignty nor the rule of Yahweh (the personal name of God in the Old Testament). Then something unexpected happens: Christ comes to Earth. This was predicted in many Old Testament passages, including Ezekiel 34 and Malachi 3, but hardly anyone seems prepared for what ensues. (The foreign magi and two elderly Jews, Simeon and Anna, are notable exceptions.)

Deity enters our human condition, taking on flesh (this is called the *incarnation*). Jesus Christ is born and grows up to be the teacher of Israel. Moreover, he not only talks about the way but also shows us the way through his righteous life and loving relationships with his Father and with the people he met.

Yet the Scriptures boldly declare even more: Jesus *is* the way (John 14:6), which means that Christianity is not a religion, but a relationship. It's not so much about a path as it is about a person. The disparity between sinful man and a holy God is enormous, and not surprisingly, the light is rejected by the darkness (John 1:11-13; 3:19-20). Christ is scorned and executed. And yet his death brings us life as he takes our sin upon himself at the cross. Emerging from the tomb on the third day, the Lord of life guarantees that he is also the Lord over death.

And so the story will conclude, one day, when we join him. Though now we can begin to taste the glory of the kingdom of God, in that day our joy will be consummated. We were created for relationship, for love. The Bible speaks of a time when sin will no longer destroy all that is precious. We will have arrived at our destination.

But Until Then...

As we await that day, we know that God himself has visited our planet in Jesus Christ, and the Bible recounts the story. (Had sin not entered the world, the Scriptures would be a slim four chapters—Genesis 1–2 and Revelation 21–22—instead of a whopping 1189 chapters!) The Bible is a story in four dimensions. It takes place in both space (three dimensions) and time (one). This is not to say the Bible is only a story, as if it weren't true. Although the Bible incorporates many genres of literature, including figurative language and poetry, it is a true and epic story of creation, fall, redemption, and restoration. And because God's storyline is anchored in space and time, history and geography are not extraneous to the plot, for apart from them it is impossible to understand the way the pieces of the story fit together.

Many of the chapters in *A Quick Overview of the Bible* will outline and explore the action and flow of this spiritual narrative, but we're getting ahead of ourselves. Let's first turn our attention to the physical book in which we find God's narrative.

The Meaning of *Bible*

The word *Bible* comes from the Greek *biblion* (book). *Ta biblia* means "the books," as in the English word *bibliography*. The Bible is a library of 66 life-giving volumes. You may have heard this acronym: Basic Instructions Before Leaving Earth. Yet the purpose of the Bible is not just to relay information, but to bring about transformation.

The Hebrew Bible contains the same books as our Old Testament, but the books are arranged in a different order into three groups: the Law, the Prophets, and the Writings. In most Christian Bibles, Malachi is the final book, but in the Hebrew Bible, the canon concludes with 1–2 Chronicles instead. In the original Hebrew order, the Prophets include the former prophets (Joshua, Judges, Samuel, Kings) and the latter prophets (Isaiah, Jeremiah, Ezekiel, and the 12 minor prophets). The Writings, the third division of the Hebrew canon, consists of Psalms, Proverbs, Job, Song of Songs, Ruth, Lamentations, Esther, Ecclesiastes, Daniel, Ezra–Nehemiah, and Chronicles.

The Hebrew Bible	The Christian Old Testament
Torah (5 books of the Law)	the Law (same 5 books)
Nevi'im (21 books of the prophets)	history and poetry (17 books, from Joshua to Song of Songs)
Kethuvim (13 books of writings)	the prophets (17 books, from Isaiah to Malachi)

The New Testament is laid out in four parts: the Gospels, Acts, the epistles (or letters), and the Apocalypse, with 4, 1, 21, and 1 book(s) in each section, respectively. In some ancient copies, the letters from James to Jude follow Acts; in others, Hebrews follows Romans. But this hardly matters. The *order* isn't inspired, but the *content* is.

The Bible was written, for the most part, between 1000 BC and AD 95. Genesis 36:31 suggests that the final version of Genesis was written after the monarchy was established in Israel. (Saul was anointed as Israel's first king around 1050 BC.) And the New Testament books were written in the half-century between AD 45 and 95. Thus the entire Bible was written during a span of about 1000 years.

Inspiration

Inspired means more than just "true." It also means more than "inspiring." Many documents are substantially true (including an invoice, a magazine article, or a police report), but they don't qualify as Scripture. Others are uplifting or motivating (such as a poem, a piece of sports journalism, or a war story) but not divinely inspired. Inspiration refers to the *function* of revelation—its ability to guide, shape, and direct our lives toward God. As for the nature of biblical inspiration, one helpful viewpoint asserts that the Bible is "reliable in all that it genuinely affirms, and authoritative for guidance in doctrine and behavior."[1]

Second Timothy 3:16-17 states that *all* Scripture is both inspired and useful. But what does this mean? Some people imagine that Scripture somehow addresses every area of knowledge, both human and divine. They believe every verse has a profound meaning—nothing is incidental—and that the Bible contains comprehensive knowledge about every conceivable topic: history, physics, biology, psychology, and so on. But this turns out to be a restrictive, flat theology; it presses the Scriptures into unnatural service, making them a textbook of science, medicine, or philosophy. Some go even further, using the Bible as a kind of sanctified Ouija board, flipping through its pages in search of patterns, codes, or clues to God's will for their lives. This misguided approach ignores the textured nature of God's word.

Ten Major Characters in the Bible	
Old Testament	*New Testament*
Abraham, the father of all believers	Jesus, Lord and Christ
Jacob, the patriarch of the 12 tribes	John the Baptist, the forerunner of Jesus Christ
Moses, the lawgiver	Mary, a paragon of faith
David, king, poet, and musician	Peter, the apostle to the Jews
Solomon, king and sage	Paul, the apostle to the Gentiles

The Bible does not interpret itself, just as a puzzle does not assemble itself and a map is not a magic carpet that takes you where you want to go. Bible study is more than simply reading and obeying without the middle step of interpretation. Some piously intone, "Don't interpret the Bible, just obey it." Of course, the *basic* truths of the Bible may be plain for all to see, yet most Scriptures require disciplined study in order to be understood. Interpretation reveals the meaning of a passage, first in its original context and then today. The Bible never claims that every part is easy to understand (quite the opposite—2 Peter 3:14-16), although it urges us to meditate diligently on the word (Joshua 1:8;

Psalm 1:2; 19:7-11; 119), applying ourselves in hope that the Lord will give insight (2 Timothy 2:7,15).

Perhaps you have heard people argue about whether the Scriptures are meant to be taken literally. So what is the answer? Should we take the Scriptures literally? My response: Take each passage as it was meant to be taken. When a passage is written in straightforward language, we may take it literally; when a passage employs figurative language, we should read it from that perspective.

Is it really raining cats and dogs when heavy precipitation falls to the earth? Of course not. We recognize figures of speech in everyday conversation, and the Bible employs its share of figurative language. Rivers clap their hands, stones cry out, and stars plummet to the earth—all in a poetic way, not literally (Psalm 98:8; Luke 19:40; Revelation 6:13). As with any book we read, we need to distinguish the medium from the message. Sometimes the medium is colorful and poetic, and at other times it is prosaic. Once we discern the type of literature we are reading—and usually this is not too difficult—we can take the passage at face value. That is the way to fully appreciate the inspired word of God.

Reliability

The Bible is reliable and trustworthy in three essential ways.

1. It is *accurate* in its content and message. In its pages we find an accurate diagnosis of the human condition. The story takes place in history, and many of the facts it relates are verifiable.

2. Its preservation through the millennia is *adequate*. Though minor changes have entered into the thousands of ancient biblical manuscripts, the contents remain unaffected. No other ancient book has been so well preserved. We can have confidence that the Bible you are reading is not substantially different from the original documents that came together as Scripture. (More on this in the next chapter.)

3. It is *practical*. Like an instruction manual, it is designed to show us how life works. When we follow its precepts, life makes sense. We relate harmoniously to our fellow man and, more vitally, to our Creator. The Bible equips us to meet the challenges of life with equipoise and grace.

A Quick Review

The Bible is a story that takes place in space and time, for God has entered our world in the person of Jesus Christ. Christ is the central figure of history, "the way, the truth, and the life" (John 14:6). The story is encapsulated in the Hebrew and Greek Scriptures, delivered to God's people millennia ago yet surviving untarnished to this day. Our lives originate in the creative activity of God, and we are made for loving relationship, so God's will is that we become his people, a vast international family. All are invited to share in the destiny for which we were created. From Genesis to Revelation, the story line develops, attesting to God's faithful love and earnest desire for all who are willing to enjoy a relationship with him forever.

3

TONGUES, TRANSLATION, AND TRANSMISSION

We hear them declaring the
wonders of God in our own tongues!

ACTS 2:11

If the Bible originally came to us as the word of God but then was corrupted through centuries of copying, it wouldn't do us much good. Moreover, the Bible wasn't delivered to us in English, and especially not in King James English. In what languages was it originally written? Do we have adequate translations of the biblical material? And have these manuscripts been copied and recopied without error?

Tongues

Think of the Bible as a library, not a single document. Its constituent books were written and edited over a period of many centuries, and they originate from many countries. So we should not be surprised that these documents were written in different languages. Though many words from other languages found their way into the Bible, the Bible is written in three principal tongues.

1. Almost all of the Old Testament (99 percent) was written in Hebrew. The Old Testament contains most of the pages of the Bible, so Hebrew is the principal language of Scripture.

2. Of the approximately 23,000 verses in the Old Testament, 271 were written in Aramaic. Aramaic is closely related to Hebrew and uses the same writing system. A few Aramaic words and phrases are also

found in the New Testament, as this was the language of Jesus and the other first-century Jews of the Near East.[1]

3. All of the New Testament was written in Greek.

Latin is not one of the original languages of the Bible, though a fourth-century Latin translation (called the Vulgate) became standard among the Western church in the early Middle Ages and reigned for longer than a millennium—long after Latin functioned as a living language.

Translation

Translation is not the same thing as interpretation. Translation takes us from the original tongue to another language, such as from Hebrew to Egyptian (Genesis 42:34) or from Persian to Hebrew (Esther 8:9). Interpretation, on the other hand, involves how we *understand* the text once we've read it in a language we understand. (What does it mean? How do we apply it to our lives?) Of course, translation involves some degree of interpretation. For example, in going from Spanish to English, the translator must decide whether *señor* means mister, sir, lord, or Lord. Usually the context resolves any ambiguity.

Hebrew, Aramaic, and Greek are well understood by scholars, so we can be confident that we are reading accurate translations of the original biblical documents. Modern translations are made from ancient copies. As a case in point, the original Greek Gospel of John was probably written at the end of the first century. Handwritten copies have survived from the second century onward. (I have enjoyed the privilege of holding the oldest copy in my hand!) English Bibles today are translated from these ancient copies. So your Bible is a translation, but it is not a translation of a translation, as is often alleged by those ignorant of the actual process. Scholars work from the oldest manuscripts available in the original languages.

Hebrew, the principal language of the Bible, is not as precise as such modern languages as English, Russian, or German. And even the original Greek of the New Testament, though more precise than Hebrew, often permits more than one way to translate a word or phrase. English is constantly changing and evolving, so every generation requires fresh translations.

When I became a Christian, many believers were reading either the rather formal KJV or RSV, the NASB, or the overly paraphrased Living Bible or Phillips New Testament. The NIV (New Testament only) had only recently been completed (1973). Later in the 1970s, the NIV translators finished the Old Testament. It was a breath of fresh air. Though it is still popular, today's Bible readers are finding help in more up-to-date versions, such as the ESV (2001), NET (2005), and the increasingly popular HCSB (1999).[2]

---

12 MAJOR BIBLE TRANSLATIONS IN ENGLISH

English Standard Version (ESV)

Holman Christian Standard Bible (HCSB)

Jerusalem Bible (JB)

King James Version (KJV)

New American Standard Bible (NASB)

New English Bible (NEB)

New English Translation (NET)

New International Version (NIV)

New King James Version (NKJV)

New Living Translation (NLT)

New Revised Standard Version (NRSV)

Revised Standard Version (RSV)

There are more than 120 English versions of Scripture! As English readers, we are spoiled for choice. Most major languages of the world have the Bible available in only a handful of versions, and some of the minor languages have only the New Testament.

We should be profoundly grateful for those who have done the laborious work of Bible translation, including past generations of missionaries, linguistic pioneers, and copyists. And perhaps we should be a little suspicious of those preachers who habitually refer to the Greek or Hebrew yet no longer study these languages.

Transmission

Manuscripts are by definition handwritten. (*Manuscript* comes from the Latin words *manus* ["hand"] and *scriptum* ["written"].) The original manuscripts of the Bible are long lost. At first, this might seem to be a strike against the Bible, but it's not. The original manuscripts were not carelessly lost, but read so many times that they literally fell apart. I have worn out numerous Bibles, not from neglect, but from daily study. And many manuscripts were confiscated and burned in the Roman persecutions (from about AD 95 to about 311). Fortunately, multiple copies were made, so the message was widely disseminated. The Scriptures of the Jews were translated into Greek, Aramaic, and other languages in the Jewish community and scattered throughout the Mediterranean world. The Scriptures of the Christians, which included the former, were in time translated into Latin, Syriac, Coptic, Ethiopic, Armenian, Georgian, Arabic, and other tongues current in the ancient world.

Because the number of manuscripts is so large, especially for the New Testament—at least 25,000 before the invention of the printing press—scholars are able to compare documents and work backward where necessary in order to correct the small errors that were invariably made. Some of these errors are simply spelling mistakes and omissions of words. An illustration may help. Jesus found the demon-possessed man (Mark 5:1) in the region of the Gerasenes—or was it the Gadarenes? Or the Gergasenes? Geographical confusion on the part of an ancient scribe would be understandable. (Similarly, people today might confuse Newark and New York, or New York City and New York State.) Scholars are not sure which reading is original. But does it matter where the demoniac was cured? Nothing essential is lost regardless of which variant is correct.

No surviving manuscript is an exact copy of the original New Testament or Old Testament writings, although many ancient manuscripts are extremely close. The alternative readings listed in the footnotes of your Bible are not contradictions. They are simply instances in which translators were unsure. This is the important principle to remember: Inspiration applies to the original text, not to copies. Most Bible believers do not hold the modern translations to be perfect; only the original *autographs* (as scholars call them) are held to be pristine. However, most differences are so minor that listing them would be tiresome. No biblical doctrine is affected.

As most Scriptures were copied onto perishable materials, such as papyrus and parchment, they were subject to destruction by fire, water (humidity is the perennial enemy of books), and even confiscation by enemies. We are fortunate for the survival of so many manuscripts, such as the papyri found in Oxyrhynchus, Egypt, in the first through sixth centuries AD, and the massive trove discovered in the Dead Sea caves beginning in 1947.

Could Something Be Missing?

The message of the Bible is presented multiple times and in various ways. Even if a few books of the Bible were removed or further words of the prophets or apostles were discovered, no substantive revision to the faith would be necessary. Fear that something might be missing is similar to a fear that the *Mona Lisa* would be forever lost if a couple of brush strokes were undone or an extra one added. It would make little, if any, difference. Everyone knows the original wasn't bearded or horned. And so through the ages she smiles at her admirers.

Canon

Indeed, the subject of canonization (how the books of the Bible came together) is perhaps one of the most complex subjects in all of Christian history. Though most of the 66 books of the Bible were originally written as individual documents, in time they were recognized as authoritative. Believers confessed that the Scriptures of the Old and New Testaments were the vehicle through which God spoke to them. What the Scriptures contained resonated with their faith experience; in these Scriptures they discerned the voice of the Lord.

Of course, believers have always liked to write down their thoughts and convictions, and the Scriptures are only a small portion of the total literature generated by the ancient Jews and Christians. To distinguish between the general body of religious literature and those works understood to be vehicles of God's voice, the concept of *canon* was employed. This has nothing to do with armaments; *kanon* is a Greek word meaning measuring rod, limits, sphere, area, principle, rule. Canon is the yardstick against which Scripture is measured. Following is an outline of the process of canonization.

The Old Testament Canon

- The Old Testament was written and edited over the period of a thousand years, from the middle of the second millennium to the middle of the first millennium BC.

- The New Testament confidently assures that the Old Testament is inspired (Romans 15:4; 1 Corinthians 10:11; 2 Timothy 3:14-17) and that the Scriptures are ultimately fulfilled in the ministry of Jesus Christ (Matthew 5:17-20; Acts 1:16; 3:18).

- Jesus himself affirmed the inspiration of the Old Testament Scriptures (Luke 24:25-27,44). He accepted them as divinely inspired, and we have come to know him as the Lord of history, so it is logical that we too accept them.

- The old covenant anticipates the new, particularly in such books as Isaiah (59:19-21), Jeremiah (31:31-34), and Ezekiel (36:24-27). In other words, the Old Testament prophesied that it would be replaced by the New Testament.

- Scholars believe that sometime between AD 70 (the date of the destruction of Jerusalem by the Romans in the First Jewish War) and AD 135 (the end of the Bar-Kochba Revolt), rabbis discussed the limits of the canon. And yet every legitimate Old Testament book had been written centuries before this council.

The New Testament Canon

- The New Testament was written over the period of about 50 years, from AD 48 to 95.

- The New Testament documents are *apostolic*. That is, they were written by apostles or by their close associates. These 27 works reflect genuine apostolic teaching.

- The inspiration of the New Testament is also guaranteed by its apostolic connection to Jesus Christ (John 14:26; 16:12-13; Galatians 1:11-12; 2 Peter 1:12-18). Jesus explained that the Spirit would enable his followers to relay the gospel message and its implications.

- Multiple copies could be disseminated quickly throughout the Roman Empire. On the other hand, despite the efficiency of the Roman postal system, not all Christian communities would have necessarily ended up with the same documents.

- Use of secretaries was widespread.[3] It is possible that several scribes were listening and writing during a single reading of a biblical document.

- Though the early church discussed the emerging canon, and at times did not agree on its exact limits, in time unanimity was reached.[4]

- The writings penned later than the close of the Old Testament canon, or in the case of Christianity, generations after the apostolic period, were never part of the Bible. Nothing has been removed. In fact, the mainstream vigorously rejected the numerous apocryphal gospels (and stories and letters and apocalypses) created by the heretics in later centuries and often attributed to apostles. (More on this in chapters 15 and 19.)

Ultimately, we understand that the canonization process took place through the inspiration and guidance of the Holy Spirit. The early church recognized the authority of these documents; they were not approved on the basis of a democratic vote. And if the canon is complete, it is closed.

A Quick Review

The original tongues of the Bible are Hebrew, Aramaic, and Greek. As the Scriptures spread geographically, they were promptly translated into numerous other languages. Holding the Scriptures in high regard, God's people carefully copied the books of the Bible generation to generation. The copies were not perfect yet were more than adequate. The variation between modern Bibles and the ancient manuscripts is therefore minimal. No matter of faith has been altered. The translation and transmission of the documents is a simple matter compared to the history of how the Scriptures came together, the process scholars call canonization. Believers understand that this complex process evolved under the superintendence of the Holy Spirit. Hearing the word of God in our own tongue is a great privilege indeed.

Having taken a few chapters to lay a foundation, we are now ready to study these Scriptures. With open eyes and a good strategy, we will soon see how they all fit together.

Part 2

THE FIRST TESTAMENT

INTRODUCING THE OLD TESTAMENT

For everything that was written in the past was written to teach
us, so that through the endurance taught in the Scriptures
and the encouragement they provide we might have hope.

ROMANS 15:4

W e've surveyed the land. In chapters 4 through 15, we'll explore
the world of the Old Testament more thoroughly. In chapters 16
through 23, we'll visit the New Testament.

About Testaments

Testament is another word for a covenant, or an agreement based on
mutual commitments. The first book of the Bible, Genesis, includes a
number of covenants. For example, God made covenants with Adam,
Noah, and Abraham. Yet for purposes of simplicity, this book will discuss only the two principal covenants of the Bible. The first of these two
was enacted at Sinai between God and the Jews and is expressed in the
Law of Moses. The other principal covenant in the Bible was enacted
at Calvary and replaced the first.

The Books of the Old Testament

Jews call the Old Testament *Tanakh*. This is an acronym for the
three divisions of the Hebrew Bible.

Torah (the Law, or instruction)

Nevi'im (the Prophets)

Khethuvim (the Writings)

Interestingly, when Jesus explained his identity to his dumbstruck followers after his resurrection, he made use of all three sections of the Hebrew Scriptures (Luke 24:27,44). The early church, like the Jews from whose ranks most of the first Christian leaders came, believed that the entire Jewish Bible pointed to the Messiah (John 5:39,46; Acts 3:22-25).[1]

The Books of the Old Testament	
Law	*Genesis* is the Greek word for *origin*. The book lays out the origins of the cosmos, mankind, and the major human institutions.
	Exodus is a Latin word from the Greek *exodos* (exit). Exodus records Israel's deliverance from Egyptian slavery.
	Leviticus is a Latin word that means "pertaining to Levi," who was one of the 12 sons of Jacob. His descendants were responsible for worship and sacrifice, which are important topics of this book.
	Numbers includes two censuses, or numberings, of the men in Israel who were 20 or older and able to go to war.
	Deuteronomy is from the Greek word *deuteronomion* (second law). This book restates the Law shortly before the Israelites enter Canaan.
History (Before the Exile)	*Joshua* was Moses' successor, the military commander who led God's people into the Promised Land. In Hebrew, Joshua means "savior." The names Joshua and Jesus are identical in Hebrew as well as in Greek.
	Judges is named after the leaders, or judges, who led God's people before Israel's first king (approximately from 1300 to 1050 BC). The judges led only a handful of tribes at a time, and their periods of leadership overlap somewhat.
	Ruth (Hebrew for "companion" or "friend") is the heroine of this book, which describes life in the period of the judges and ends with a genealogy of David that leads in to the ensuing history of Israel's monarchy.
	1 and *2 Samuel* are named after Israel's last judge, a prophet who is a major character through much of 1 Samuel but not 2 Samuel. His name means "God has heard."
	1 and *2 Kings* describe Israel's history under the monarchy. During most of this period, Israel was divided into two kingdoms, Israel in the north and Judah in the south. (In the Hebrew Bible, the books from Joshua to 2 Kings were known as "the former prophets.")

The Books of the Old Testament
History (During the Exile) These books were written after the Babylonians had broken down the wall around Jerusalem, destroyed the temple and many of the buildings, and taken the people of Judah (the southern kingdom of the original nation of Israel) into captivity.
1 and *2 Chronicles* record the reigns of the kings, particularly those of Judah. These were the last of the Old Testament books to be written and date from the fifth century BC.
Ezra and *Nehemiah* were perhaps originally one book. They are named after two of the key figures in the rebuilding of Israel after the exile. Ezra's name is similar to the Hebrew word for *help*, and Nehemiah's name sounds like the Hebrew phrase "God is my comfort."
Esther (from *Ishtar*, a Babylonian love goddess) was a Jewess providentially made queen by the Persian King Ahasuerus. This book recounts the miracle of Purim, when God saved the deported Jews from extinction by the hands of the Persians. Esther's Hebrew name was Hadassah ("myrtle").
Poetry *Job* is a man whose world and theology were thrown into confusion as he personally confronted the problem of suffering.
Psalms were originally prayers and hymns sung to the accompaniment of stringed instruments. *Psallo* is old Greek for "pluck," as in plucking the strings of instruments.
Proverbs is a collection of hundreds of wise sayings from Solomon and other contributors. They provide a practical guide to righteous, moral, ethical, and godly living.
Ecclesiastes, from the Latin word for the leader of the assembly (*ecclesia*), presumably refers to Solomon, the traditional author.
Song of Solomon is a romantic poem or collection of poems for the marriage of Solomon. It is also called Song of Songs and Canticles. Traditionally read at Passover, it is a poetic portrayal of Solomon's ideal marriage of intimacy and bliss.
Major Prophets *Isaiah* lived in the eighth century BC and is the prophet most frequently quoted in the New Testament. His name means "Yahweh is salvation."
Jeremiah was a priest and prophet of Judah who ministered during Jerusalem's fall (626–586 BC). The meaning of his name is uncertain.
Lamentations records Jeremiah's laments over the destruction of Jerusalem, the temple, and the kingdom of Judah. To make matters worse, the prophets, priests, and kings would not listen to Jeremiah.

The Books of the Old Testament	
	Ezekiel prophesied among the exiles in Babylon (sixth century BC) while Jeremiah stayed in Jerusalem. His name means "God is strong" or "God makes strong."
	Daniel was a statesman and prophet who had been deported to Babylon in the late 600s BC. He is one of the Bible's outstanding examples of faithfulness. His name appropriately means "God is my judge."
Minor Prophets	*Hosea, Joel,* and *Amos* were prophets in the eighth century BC. Their names mean, respectively, "He (Yahweh) has helped" or "salvation" (as in Joshua and Jesus), "Yahweh is God," and "burdensome" or "burden bearer."
Minor Prophets	*Obadiah* was a sixth-century BC prophet who challenged Edom not to gloat over Jerusalem's fall. His name means "servant of Yahweh."
Minor Prophets	*Jonah* was a prophet in the eighth century BC. Ironically, his name means "dove"—quite a contrast with the prophet's prejudicial attitude and behavior.
Minor Prophets	*Micah* means "Who is like Yahweh (God)?" The book dates from the eighth century BC.
Minor Prophets	*Nahum* means "comfort."[2] Nahum prophesied against Assyria in the seventh century BC.
Minor Prophets	*Habakkuk* and *Zephaniah* were prophets in the seventh century BC, as Babylon was coming onto the world scene. Their names mean "embrace" and "Yahweh has treasured."
Minor Prophets	*Haggai* and *Zechariah* were prophets in the sixth century BC who encouraged the rebuilding of the temple after the Jews' return from exile. Their names mean "festal" and "Yahweh remembers," respectively.
Minor Prophets	*Malachi* was possibly named after a prophet in the fifth century BC. *Malachi* means "my angel" or "my messenger" (see Malachi 3:1).

Genre

The Hebrew Bible contains a single narrative, yet it isn't written like a novel. That is, it isn't a single genre, or type of literature. Within the pages of the Old Testament are multiple genres, such as poetry, history, and prophecy. The various books are therefore subject to various rules of interpretation. This means we need training to read the Bible. This book is designed to illuminate the major genres in the Bible and to help us learn to deal with them on their own terms.

Date and Chronology

The first testament was written roughly between 1000 and 400 BC. Consequently, it came together only gradually. The constituent documents were written in many countries, including Israel, Babylon (roughly modern Iraq), and Persia (roughly modern Iran). Some elements predate 1000 BC, and some final editing may have been done in the intertestamental period (the fourth century BC to the first century AD).

To the consternation of many readers, the Old Testament is only roughly chronological. There is a fair bit of jumping around, especially in the middle portions. But if we get the big picture ahead of time, we can read the Bible in any order, just as we can view our favorite movie over and over and begin wherever we please. If we already know the story, we won't be disoriented. Sometimes I read the whole Bible straight through; other times I jump around, though I always finish reading whatever book I'm studying at the time because each was written as a unit and is best understood when read that way.

Sources

The first testament has been communicated to us in human languages through the course of human history and quite freely utilizes the current culture's concepts, terms, motifs, stories, and writings. Just as a preacher might quote a popular song without approving of everything in the song, Bible writers quoted from other books that they considered useful but not inspired.

Chapter and Verse Numbers

When I began reading the Bible, I was taken aback by how short the chapters are—often just a paragraph or two. Yet a chapter is a heading.[3] Exodus 3:6 means the third chapter of Exodus, verse 6. The system takes a little getting used to, though in the end it will help you more efficiently navigate the 1189 chapters and approximately 31,000 verses of the Bible. The most efficient way to grow in our comprehension of Scripture is not to read verse by verse or chapter by chapter but rather book by book.

A Quick Review

The Bible is more of a library than a book. The first testament makes up three-quarters of the Bible and consists of 39 books and many literary genres. These books have incorporated at least two dozen extrabiblical sources. The Old Testament was written over a period of many centuries, in many countries, and by many authors in the ancient world. It is only roughly chronological, so some care must be exercised when reading straight through. As an aid to reading, chapters and verses are numbered, though these are not original. In the next chapter we meet the central character of the first testament. Of course, he is none other than the Lord God.

5

THE GOD OF THE OLD TESTAMENT

In the beginning, God...
GENESIS 1:1

God is the constant of Scripture, the infinite reference point, the foundation of being and creation and truth. Everything he created was good—very good—and he himself is essentially good. And yet many people feel that he is in some way inferior to the "nicer," more civilized, less judgmental "New Testament God." These people imply that the Old Testament God was as benighted as the sometimes savage characters that populate the Old Testament stories, and that somehow when Jesus came, God changed or improved, becoming "Christian." I'll respond to this sentiment by answering ten questions.

1. The Old Testament God seems unfair, unpredictable, capricious. Is he really just?

This was precisely Abraham's concern when he learned that Sodom and Gomorrah would be punished for their sin. (See Genesis 18:16-33. For a further explanation of why these cities deserved punishment, see Ezekiel 16:49.) He asked God, "Far be it from you to do such a thing—to kill the righteous with the wicked, treating the righteous and the wicked alike. Far be it from you! Will not the Judge of all the earth do right?" (Genesis 18:25). Abraham defended Sodom probably because he had family members living there, but even if that wasn't his motivation, this text demonstrates that our modern concerns are far from new.

In fact, perceived inconsistencies in the justice of God caused struggles for many figures in the Old Testament, including Jeremiah (Jeremiah 12), Asaph (Psalm 73), and Habakkuk (Habakkuk 1–2).

And why shouldn't Abraham the patriarch have been concerned about Sodom and Gomorrah's impending destruction? Abraham knew that if the Lord, the being who steers the universe, is fundamentally unjust, capricious, or immoral, then Abraham had much to fear (and so do we!). How would you feel if you were aboard a flight and learned that the pilot was a known terrorist or was inebriated?

Our peace of mind depends upon the knowledge that, in the end, good will be rewarded and evil requited. Only after Abraham expressed his concern and came to realize God's reasonableness did his fears subside. And so we perceive that his question is our question. The Lord assured Abraham, both through words and actions, that he is not only holy but also fair.

2. Does God show favoritism? Was no one on the planet saved before he chose the Jews?

Several Scriptures indicate that before the gospel was preached, the Lord in some sense let the nations go their own way (Acts 14:16; 17:30). We find a number of examples of persons who were apparently right with God even though they did not formally belong to the people of God, such as Melchizedek and Jethro (Genesis 14:18; Exodus 18:1-27). And yet nothing was unjust about God's selection of Abraham (father of the faithful), Jacob (his grandson and the father of the 12 patriarchs), and others in the line that led through David all the way to Christ.

After all, the Lord wasn't obligated to save anyone; he could have let us just go our way. The Old Testament makes it clear that the Jews were chosen not for their merit, but because of God's love (Deuteronomy 7:7-11; 9:4-6). The fact that in the old covenant God chose Israel, and that today he chooses those who accept the teaching of Israel's Messiah, should be recognized as signs of his grace. The same could be said of God's grace in the New Testament. We will have more to say on this topic in the next chapter as we explore what may be a surprising and inspiring theme.

3. Was Yahweh hot-tempered?

Not at all. God in the Old Testament is slow to anger, as many Scriptures affirm (Exodus 34:6; Numbers 14:18; Nehemiah 9:17; Psalm 86:15; 103:8; 145:8; Jonah 4:2; Nahum 1:3). To illustrate, in the time of Abraham, the sin of the Canaanites had "not yet reached its full measure" (Genesis 15:16). The passage says the Lord was willing to wait four generations. (I sometimes have difficulty waiting four *minutes* before becoming irritated.) Moreover, God is forgiving (Psalm 103:1-3; 130:1-8). We see in the Old Testament a distinct sequence of events when God passes judgment upon various peoples: He gives warnings through messengers; he provides an escape route, either through repentance or by literal fleeing; and usually, some of the residents respond in humility and are spared.

4. But still, didn't the Hebrew God play rough?

Life is rough. We cannot blame God for the negative consequences we bring upon ourselves through our own poor decisions. True, the consequences of sin were somewhat more physical under the old covenant, largely because Israel was a physical nation—unlike the church, which is not a political entity (it has no laws, army, physical borders, and so forth). In a physical nation, laws must be handled in a real-world way: Criminals must be restrained and brought to justice. So it was in the nation of Israel. But in a church setting (the church, not Israel, is "the people of God" in the New Testament), discipline for moral infractions is handled differently. Even so, note that in the New Testament, the Lord sometimes metes out rewards and punishments in a physical manner. For example, compare 2 Samuel 6:2-15 and Acts 5:1-11, or contemplate the physical imagery of the Apocalypse (Revelation 20:1-2).

5. Why isn't God as nice in the Old Testament as he is in the New Testament?

This question is similar to the previous one, except that it calls into question the character of God: What sort of deity ought he to be? In short, God is not *nice* in either the Old Testament or the New Testament. Actually, I think believers ought to take exception to that word.

Nowhere does it appear in the Bible, nor is it listed as one of God's attributes (for example, see Exodus 34:5-7, where God reveals his name). As the New Testament puts it, "Note then the kindness and the severity of God" (Romans 11:22 ESV). In neither testament is God described as nice in the sense of pleasant, moderate, inoffensive, compliant, or reluctant to rock the boat. "Compassionate and gracious, slow to anger, abounding in love and faithfulness"? Yes. Nice? No. (See Deuteronomy 4:31; Joel 2:13.) Consider these five points as well:

1. The Old Testament contains hardly a verse on hell (though we do find imagery pointing in that direction, as in Psalm 11:6; 140:10). For the doctrine of hell we must turn to the pages of the New Testament. And most references to the fiery place of final punishment are found on the lips of Jesus (such as Matthew 5:22; Mark 9:43-48).

2. The New Testament depicts God's wrath using imagery and terms that are just as strong as those we find in the Old Testament. For a few examples, see Matthew 24:45-51; Luke 13:1-9,22-30; Hebrews 12:14-29.

3. The most disturbing book in the Bible may be Revelation, where Jesus Christ is depicted not only as a Lamb but also as a Lion. The Lamb of God who takes away the sins of the world is led to the slaughter in the Gospels, and to be sure his love and self-sacrifice reappear in the Apocalypse (5:6), but notice that this is no harmless sheep. He is the Lion of the tribe of Judah (5:5). In the Gospels, do we not find numerous instances where Christ's behavior is unconventional and even offensive at times? Thus *nice* is not an appropriate epithet for a Christian. In fact, it could be taken as an insult, a testimony to how little the bearer of the name is following his Lord. In Luke 6:26, Jesus himself says, "Woe to you when everyone speaks well of you, for that is how their ancestors treated the false prophets."

4. Though God's love becomes most apparent through Jesus Christ, it is false to portray God as lacking in love in the Old Testament. Far more of the verses that describe the goodness and love of God are in the Old Testament than in the New. And because the Old Testament is the foundation for the New, that makes sense.

5. The Bible does not tell us to become nice people, as though the

goal were bland decency or conformity. The church was never meant to be an association of nice people, but an army on the move. Though we should not ignore the family imagery in Scripture, there is a reason the church is persecuted: Its message is disturbing, and those who proclaim this message must not compromise. In a world as dark and dysfunctional as ours, those who take the light will at times appear abnormal and even ungracious (though they aren't).

FAMOUS SAYINGS NOT IN THE BIBLE

God helps those who help themselves.

SIDNEY ALGERNON, C. 1666,
QUOTED BY BENJAMIN FRANKLIN, 1757

Cleanliness is next to godliness.

FRANCIS BACON, 1605, QUOTED BY JOHN WESLEY, 1791

This too shall pass.

ANONYMOUS PERSIAN POET, C. 1200

To thine own self be true.

SHAKESPEARE, HAMLET 1.3.78, C. 1600

Beauty is in the eye of the beholder.

MARGARET WOLF HUNGERFORD, 1878

---

6. It almost seems as if God is just waiting for us to trip up. Isn't that a bit sadistic?

Over and over, the Bible assures us that God wants to bless, not curse. Let me allow the Scripture to speak for itself.

> Therefore, you Israelites, I will judge each of you according to your own ways, declares the Sovereign LORD. Repent! Turn away from all your offenses; then sin will not be your downfall. Rid yourselves of all the offenses you have committed, and get a new heart and a new spirit. Why will you die, people of Israel? For I take no pleasure in the death of anyone, declares the Sovereign LORD. Repent and live! (Ezekiel 18:30-32).

Like a good parent, God is pulling for us. Yet he will not override our free will. When we are bent on self-destruction, his heart is filled with pain (Genesis 6:6; Luke 19:41-44).

7. Why was the Lord concerned only with outward behavior? The New Testament God looks at the heart.

Actually, God has always been concerned with the heart (1 Samuel 16:7). The Old Testament reflects this concern as much as the New Testament does. Here are three examples: Leviticus 19:17 instructed the Israelites not to hate one another in their hearts. In Deuteronomy 19:1-13, the Lord set apart cities of refuge, to which a person who had unintentionally killed another person could flee from avengers. Note that God was concerned with intention and not only action. Finally, in Psalm 19:14 we find these beautiful words: "May the words of my mouth and the meditation of my heart be pleasing in your sight, Lord, my Rock and my Redeemer." The Lord has always considered the inward self, the heart.

8. Wasn't the old covenant a covenant of works? No one could measure up, so weren't they always "in the doghouse"?

Being in the doghouse certainly doesn't feel good, but this is an unfair description of the way God treated the Israelites. As we have seen, he is quick to forgive, and his grace covers our sins.

I believe many preachers and theologians err when they speak of a covenant of works. In Eden, Adam was expected to obey—just as we are—but nowhere does the text speak of a salvation earned by good works. When James searches for two Old Testament examples of living faith, he cites Abraham and Rahab. Notice what James emphasizes— their obedience (James 2:8-26). In other words, works are an indispensable part of faith and are in no way opposed to grace. No one was ever saved under the old covenant apart from the grace of God, nor is anyone ever saved under the new covenant apart from works (James 2:26). This may offend some Christians' religious instincts (a Protestant overreaction, perhaps?), but the Bible has the last word. Both testaments agree.

9. Was the Lord just experimenting in the Old Testament? Why didn't ho got it right the first time?

This was no experiment. He was moving people along, bringing them from a state of idolatry, ignorance, inequity, and iniquity to a state of religious purity, enlightenment, justice, and holiness. The law accomplished that for which it was intended. Yet it was never meant to be permanent. Any fault with the first covenant was on Israel's part, not God's (Hebrews 8:7-13). The entire Old Testament points toward Christ and the new covenant, in which all people would have access to God through the Spirit (Ephesians 2:18). The old covenant laid the foundation for the new. As has been said, "The Old Testament is the New Testament concealed; the New Testament is the Old Testament revealed."

10. How could God approve of so many inhumane institutions? Why didn't he overthrow them instead of endorsing them?

As we have already noted, in the ancient world the treatment of citizens, women, children, enemies, and criminals fell far short of God's holy standard. Some change can take place overnight, but most change requires years, generations, or even centuries. Rather than devote the rest of this book to illustrating the point, let's undertake a single case study—slavery. Keep reading after the conclusion immediately below if you want to explore this further.

Conclusion

The Scriptures speak eloquently and consistently of one God (Deuteronomy 6:4; Ephesians 4:6). There is no "God of the Old Testament," for God does not and did not change (Malachi 3:6). His nature and character are the same in both testaments. He may have dealt with his people in different ways under one covenant than he does under another, but that does not mean there are two Gods in the Bible, one savage and one nice.

CASE STUDY: SLAVERY

The ancient world was full of injustice, prejudice, and barbarity. The old covenant helped people progress toward a society marked by justice, openness, and compassion. Yet such fundamental shifts require time—generations, if not centuries. For example, the ancient world allowed retaliation disproportionate to the offense, and punishments were especially draconian when one offended against a member of a higher social class. In contrast, the Law of Moses insisted that the punishment fit the crime and did not allow for a double standard—all were to be judged by the same law. And there is no evidence that "eye for an eye" was taken literally. In most cases, suits were settled through monetary compensation.

The apostle Paul describes the Old Testament Law as a guardian, tutor, schoolteacher, or pedagogue that led us to Christ (Galatians 3:24). The following short study will demonstrate the wisdom of God and the unfairness of those who try to use the Bible to discredit his justice.

Introduction

North American slavery had precedents in the Arab slave trade, and slavery throughout human history was hardly limited to Africa. In fact, slavery still exists. In Asia, girls are abducted or sold by their families to become sex slaves. In Africa, boys are captured and forced to become child soldiers.

American slavery endured for 400 years, with 40 million dying in the infamous "middle passage." Despite the American Civil War and the overturning of slavery, racism is still an ugly issue in the United States. Does the Bible support slavery—a thoroughly demeaning, dehumanizing institution? American slaveholders twisted the Scriptures to support their inhumane practices. Yet American slavery was very different from slavery in the ancient world. As we shall soon see, antebellum slavery provides only a false analogy.

Slavery in the Ancient World

In the ancient world, people generally became slaves because of poverty or war. Usually they were not kidnapped; they entered servitude through other channels. For example, some sold themselves in order to pay off debts. Slavery was not permanent; there was hope of eventual emancipation. Slaves possessed some legal rights, such as due process, property rights, and even the right to own their own servants. Slavery was not racially based. Only clothing (not skin color) indicated a person's status as a slave. Nor did slaves always occupy the lowest rung of society. Slavery wasn't even necessarily degrading—in some cases, it could be upgrading. Consider Joseph (Genesis 39:1-6). Slaves could lead normal family lives, and in the Roman Empire they sometimes even participated in the same clubs as their masters.

This is not to say that servitude was always desirable. Things were easiest for city slaves, less so for farm slaves, and hardest for those working in the mines or in prostitution. On the other hand, slaves did not serve only in menial positions. Some worked as civil servants, doctors, nurses, accountants, or writers. Famous ex-slaves in the ancient world include Felix (Acts 23–24), Aesop (fifth century BC), and Patrick (fifth century AD). Not all became free by paying off their debts; sometimes they were freed because labor was cheaper when the master wasn't also paying for a slave's room and board. Around the first century AD, slaves were so often emancipated that Augustus Caesar made a law that none could be freed before the age of 30. Obviously if this is what slavery looked like in the ancient world, it has far less in common with the North American variety than we ever imagined.

Slavery and the Old Testament

We should envision slavery in the Bible against the background of slavery in the ancient world, not against the ugly backdrop of American chattel slavery. In biblical times, the

Mosaic Law sought to regulate an inferior work arrangement, not idealize it. Slaves had dignity. God instituted stringent laws against kidnapping (Exodus 21:16), and where these were flouted, there was an outcry. Amos and other prophets spoke of the evil of human trafficking.

The Old Testament also established antiharm laws, and freedom was stipulated if a master permanently damaged his slave (Exodus 21:20,26). No other ancient law code held masters accountable for treatment of slaves. For example, Babylon's Code of Hammurabi permitted the master to slice off a disobedient slave's ear. Hittite laws required fines for people who sheltered runaways. The Code of Hammurabi demanded death for abetting runaways. In Babylon, returned runaways were branded and their ears slit. Slaves were just property.

In contrast, the Old Testament had an anti-return law: Israelites were commanded to shelter runaway slaves rather than send them back to their masters (Deuteronomy 23:15-16). In addition, many laws prevented the poor from undergoing such economic hardship that they became slaves. There were laws in favor of the poor, such as automatic debt cancellation in the Jubilee year (Leviticus 25). Hebrew slaves were to be freed after six years of service, though if they preferred, they could remain slaves permanently (Exodus 21:5-6).

Servitude existed because poverty existed (see Nehemiah 5). The Lord did not desire poverty or servitude (Deuteronomy 15:4,11). In short, Hebrew slavery was an oasis of liberty compared to typical slavery among the pagans.

In other ancient Near East law codes, regulations on slavery are addressed at the end of the codes, but in Exodus, they immediately follow the Ten Commandments. The Old Testament indicates a direct connection between righteousness before God and righteous dealings with our fellow man.

Foreign slaves did not enjoy the same privileges as Israelites who became slaves (Leviticus 25:42-46), but as we have seen, kidnapping was forbidden (Exodus 21:16). The biblical emphasis on compassion and the imperative to love the alien encouraged at least a modicum of dignity for foreign slaves. After all, Israel was to love the stranger in the land (Leviticus 19:33-34). Sometimes foreign servants were elevated (as in 1 Chronicles 2:34-35, here by marriage to an Israelite woman). They had inheritance rights. Since non-Israelites could not acquire land, perhaps foreigners had no option but to attach themselves to an Israelite family if they wanted a place to live or wanted to own land within Israel.

Slavery in the Roman Empire
and the New Testament

Slavery in Rome was different from slavery in ancient Israel. It has been estimated that perhaps one-third of the inhabitants of the Empire were slaves, and another third were freedmen. If this figure seems too high, consider that when the Czar freed the serfs in Russia (1861), one-third of the populace were toiling in an enslaved condition. Of course, the Romans were ruthless in putting down slave revolts (such as that under Spartacus), so we would be anachronistic to fault Paul and other early Christians for not stirring up rebellion.

What does the New Testament teach about slaves and masters?

1. Slaves should take the opportunity of freedom if possible. Otherwise, they should be content (1 Corinthians 7:21).

2. When the New Testament refers to groups of people, the powerless are mentioned first: wives before husbands, children before parents, slaves before masters. Masters did not have unlimited control over their servants (Ephesians 6:5-9; Colossians 3:22–4:1).

3. One's status in Christ did not depend on socioeconomic factors. In the early church, slaves often occupied positions of leadership (Galatians 3:28; Colossians 3:11).

4. The slave trade is mentioned as part of the commercial activities of Rome, the whore of Babylon (Revelation 18:13).

5. The slave trade is condemned (1 Timothy 1:10).

6. Nowhere are masters told to demand submission from their slaves. Rather, mutual respect is encouraged (1 Timothy 6:1-2).

7. True freedom has nothing to do with political rights, and real slavery is slavery to sin (John 8:31-32; Romans 6:17-18; 1 Corinthians 7:22).

It's not surprising that many slaves were attracted to the Christian faith. They would not have been drawn to it if they viewed Christianity as an instrument of suppression or the religion of abusive masters. For the same reason, minorities and women were also attracted to the fledgling faith. They were respected, welcomed, loved, honored. Stunningly, according to 1 Clement 55:2 (written about AD 96), some Christians sold themselves into slavery in order to free others.

Conclusions

Weighing all this evidence, well-informed readers are boggled that some people who are less acquainted with the Bible falsely accuse the word of God of injustice and barbarity. Here are a few closing considerations.

1. Hebrew slavery was more humane than slavery in the secular world. Recording the facts about slavery is not the same as approving them, and regulating slavery is not the same as approving it. The Scriptures attest to the cruelty of the ancient world without approving it. The laws for Hebrew slavery regulated a preexisting institution, one that was not going to disappear overnight. Consider the overall trajectory through history from chattel slavery, to Israelite treatment of foreign slaves, to Israelite treatment of Hebrew slaves, to eventual socioeconomic freedom in more modern times.

2. Throughout the course of biblical history, an ethic of dignity and respect was being cultivated. God's highest standard and will are revealed only in the New Testament.

3. Slavery in New Testament times was radically different from slavery in the more recent American experience.

4. People who have labored for emancipation, particularly in Britain and the United States in the 1800s, were deeply inspired by biblical principles. It was through Christian influence that slavery was eventually eliminated in most of the world. This change did not take place because of the influence of Hinduism, Islam, or any other major world religion. Christianity is not a cause or excuse for the injustice and brutality of slavery. Rather, the Spirit of Christ inspired the great emancipation movements.

5. Most criticisms of slavery in the Bible are based on caricatures of Christianity, ignorance of Hebraic law, and lack of exposure to the true message of the gospel.

6

GOD'S UNIVERSAL PURPOSE: ALL NATIONS

God our Savior...wants all people to be saved
and to come to a knowledge of the truth.

1 TIMOTHY 2:3-4

There is an old saying that goes, "How odd of God to choose the Jews." Certainly one could reason that the Jews were an odd choice. In fact, choosing one group out of many generally implies that the others are not chosen. If God is righteous, loving, and impartial, what is going on here?

If we carefully read through the Old Testament, we find that God never intended for the Jews to selfishly hoard his blessings or for the rest of the world to be excluded from them. In fact, Israel was called to be "a kingdom of priests" (Exodus 19:6; see also 1 Peter 2:9). The function of a priest is to bring God to the people and the people to God. When Israel failed at its mission to bring Yahweh to the world (Isaiah 26:18), the task then fell to the church (Matthew 21:43). Remember that through Jewish eyes the entire world consisted of only two kinds of people: Jews and Gentiles, us and them.

For the Jews, the idea that God had planned to bless the Gentiles from the very beginning was unanticipated and unacceptable. To address this lack of vision and love, God sent his prophets time and again to admonish the Jews that his love isn't parochial; it extends to all the world. He did not call the Jews in order to exclude Gentiles, but ultimately to include them. God's plan was that Jews and Gentiles alike would all have the opportunity to come to Yahweh. This all goes back to God's promises to Abraham, father of the faithful:

The LORD had said to Abram, "Go from your country, your people and your father's household to the land I will show you. I will make you into a great nation, and I will bless you; I will make your name great, and you will be a blessing. I will bless those who bless you, and whoever curses you I will curse; and all peoples on earth will be blessed through you" (Genesis 12:1-3).

God makes several promises to the great patriarch, the last of which is that the entire earth will be blessed through him. The promise is reiterated to his son and grandson, and the line of Abraham will eventually lead through David all the way to Jesus (Matthew 1:1-17). This thread of blessing can easily be traced through Scripture. Even in the book of Genesis we see partial blessings that come to outsiders, whose lives are affected for good by contact with the people of God.

The Theme Among the People of Israel

When Israel became a nation, after the Exodus from Egypt, it was not on the basis of the people's goodness. That is, the Lord's choice was not based on their merit. Their election by God was not because they were more numerous (Deuteronomy 7:7) or more righteous (Deuteronomy 9:5) than the other nations. Rather, Moses reminds the people that everything in the heavens and the earth belongs to God, and yet he selected them for no other reason but that he loved them. "The LORD set his affection on your ancestors and loved them, and he chose you, their descendants, above all the nations" (Deuteronomy 10:15).

It is true that God did for Israel what he did for no other nation (Psalm 147:19-20), and Jesus himself affirms that salvation is from the Jews (John 4:22). But we must look at the bigger picture and ask ourselves why God did this. He did it so that Israel would be a guiding light to the world, pointing them to God, and so that the nations would say, "Surely this great nation is a wise and understanding people" (Deuteronomy 4:6). He did it to keep his promise to Abraham: "All peoples on earth will be blessed through you" (Genesis 12:3).

Lest there be any doubt as to the Lord's inclusionary intentions, consider Psalm 117, the shortest chapter in the Bible. It begins, "Praise the LORD, all you nations." When Solomon, David's successor as king over the united kingdom of Israel, dedicated the temple, he prayed, "As for the foreigner who does not belong to your people Israel but has come from a distant land because of your name…when they come and pray toward this temple, then hear from heaven, your dwelling place. Do whatever the foreigner asks of you" (1 Kings 8:41-43). Israel's hymns and prayers referred to the day when the Gentiles would worship alongside the Jews (Isaiah 19:23). No disdain for outsiders here (Acts 10:28). No Pharisaic prayer: "I thank thee, God, that I was not born a Gentile, a slave, or a woman."[1]

God's people easily forget that they have been chosen for a purpose—to make known God's character to a watching world—so the Bible is full of frequent reminders. The prophets especially exhorted Israel back to a humble appreciation of her calling. In the eighth century BC, Amos preached a sobering message of love for the poor, the outcast, and the Gentile. "'Are not you Israelites the same to me as the Cushites?' declares the LORD. 'Did I not bring Israel up from Egypt, the Philistines from Caphtor and the Arameans from Kir?'" (Amos 9:7). What a concept: God was at work not only in Israel, but also in other lands. The Philistines (remember Goliath?) and the Arameans (perennial enemies of Israel) each also had their own exodus. Israel was unique (in being given the covenant and being called for service) and yet not unique (as though God had nothing to do with the rest of the planet).

Isaiah (who also lived in the eighth century) shared this theme.

> In that day you will say: "Give praise to the LORD, proclaim his name; make known among the nations what he has done, and proclaim that his name is exalted. Sing to the LORD, for he has done glorious things; let this be known to all the world" (Isaiah 12:4-5).

> The LORD says…"It is too small a thing for you to be my servant to restore the tribes of Jacob and bring back those of Israel I have kept. I will also make you a light for the

Gentiles, that my salvation may reach to the ends of the earth" (Isaiah 49:5-6).

It was always God's desire that the Gentiles—those who lived at "the ends of the earth" (far away from the land of Israel)—be saved. The second passage above applies not only to Isaiah but especially to the Messiah, Jesus Christ. Tying this all together, God is the light (Psalm 27:1; 1 John 1:5), and he has made a light for all people to be saved by sending his Son to be the light of the world (John 8:12) and by calling us to be a light to others (Matthew 5:14; Philippians 2:15). I especially like the next passage, also in Isaiah.

> And foreigners who bind themselves to the LORD to minister to him, to love the name of the LORD, and to be his servants, all who keep the Sabbath without desecrating it and who hold fast to my covenant—these I will bring to my holy mountain and give them joy in my house of prayer. Their burnt offerings and sacrifices will be accepted on my altar; for my house will be called a house of prayer for all nations (56:6-7).

Jesus quoted this passage when he expressed divine disapproval of the secularization of religion in his day (Matthew 21:13).

Yet my favorite Old Testament passage on this theme comes from the sixth-century BC prophet Zechariah: "This is what the LORD Almighty says: 'In those days ten people from all languages and nations will take firm hold of one Jew by the hem of his robe and say, "Let us go with you, because we have heard that God is with you"'" (8:23). What a beautiful vision. No one is excluded—all are welcome.

Let's consider one more Old Testament story before we trace this theme in the New Testament. The story of Jonah may be the most stinging rebuke to Jewish nationalism and refusal to love her neighbor. Israel had experienced the special presence of God. She had benefited from holy laws, divine guidance and protection, miracles, the covenant, the Scriptures, and an incredible heritage. And yet she kept it all to herself. This is not a story about a man being swallowed by a sea creature. It's an exposé of the ugliness in the heart of Jewish religious leaders of the day.

SEVEN FAMOUS BIBLE PASSAGES

In the beginning God created the heavens and the earth.

GENESIS 1:1

The LORD is my shepherd; I shall not want. He makes me lie down in green pastures. He leads me beside still waters...

PSALM 23 ESV

Those who hope in the LORD will renew their strength. They will soar on wings like eagles; they will run and not grow weary, they will walk and not be faint.

ISAIAH 40:31

In everything, do to others what you would have them do to you, for this sums up the Law and the Prophets.

MATTHEW 7:12

God so loved the world that he gave his one and only Son, that whoever believes in him shall not perish but have eternal life.

JOHN 3:16

Love is patient, love is kind. It does not envy, it does not boast, it is not proud...

1 CORINTHIANS 13:4-8

I can do all things through him who strengthens me.

PHILIPPIANS 4:13 ESV

Jonah was unwilling to take God's message to Nineveh (the capital of Assyria, a nearby and often hostile country), so he ran from the command of the Lord. Jonah wasn't afraid that the Assyrians would mistreat him or reject the message. Precisely the opposite! Jonah feared the hated Assyrians would embrace the gracious message of Yahweh, and he would rather die than give them that opportunity. Read the book of Jonah through in a sitting (it's only four short chapters), and you will easily see the point that eludes most readers.

The New Testament Emphasis

This grand theme of God's universal purpose continues in the books of the New Testament. Jesus emphasized it in his ministry, even making it the theme of his first sermon in his hometown of Nazareth—for which the townspeople tried to throw him off a cliff (Luke 4:14-30; see also Luke 10:25-37; John 4:9-10). Even if his preaching strategy did not immediately include the Gentiles (Matthew 10:5; 15:24), his long-term vision included all peoples (Matthew 28:19-20). The good news of the kingdom of God was not for the Jews only, but for all the world. The Bible tells us God "desires all people to be saved and to come to the knowledge of the truth" (1 Timothy 2:4 ESV).

Yet this was not easy for the Jewish people to grasp. Although they repeatedly came into close contact with the Gentiles through their experiences in exile, they retained a measure of aloofness from the nations. Such customs as circumcision, Sabbath observance, and kosher rules—all of which reinforced Jewish identity—also made it difficult for them to rethink their calling. This is the message of Acts 10–11. The narrative is sometimes referred to as the conversion of Cornelius (the Gentile who accepted the gospel), but in fact it presents the conversion of Peter—from hyper-Judaism to a more accepting, gracious attitude toward non-Jews. Would Jewish Christians accept their Gentile Christian brethren as equal partners (see Galatians 2:11-16)?

No wonder the most divisive issue in the first-century church was the Jew–Gentile controversy. Many letters addressed the matter, and eventually a council met to make a decision (Acts 15). In short, was it necessary for the Gentiles to become Jews before they could become Christians? Did they have to be circumcised before they were allowed to be baptized? God's answer was a resounding no.

Paul taught unity between Jews and Gentiles, and he breathed in the revitalizing air of this great biblical truth more than any of his contemporaries (Romans 2:17-24; Ephesians 2:11–3:13; Philippians 3:2-7; Titus 1:10-16). He may even have written the epistle to the Romans to ensure that the Jew–Gentile controversy did not divide the church. His basic argument is that if Abraham, the father of the faithful, was made right with God by faith *before* he was circumcised and before the Law was given (which would have included Sabbath and kosher regulations), then Gentiles need not become Jews before being welcomed into the community of faith.

Finally, as we saw in chapter 2, the New Testament ends with an all-inclusive and universal vision of believers from every nation and tribe, not just one (Revelation 7:9; 14:6). The good news is for all the world, not just Israel.

Conclusion: Challenges for People of Faith

The pieces of the Bible come together only within the frame of God's love for all people and his universal purpose, which is to be accomplished through his special people.

So what does this mean for us? Assuming we've traced the theme through Scripture and are convinced that the salvation of the world is indeed God's universal purpose, things can no longer be the same. Once we have comprehended the universal breadth of God's goodness and grace, we cannot help but emulate the same generosity and love toward outsiders.

If I am a Bible believer, am I willing to diligently study this important theme, reading everything the Law and Prophets have to say?

Is the church a place where we escape the world or a place where we are equipped to fulfill our mission to the world?

Do we love those who are different from us? Do we search for common ground, or do we mimic the world by dividing ourselves according to our dissimilarities? Do we seek out opportunities for our families to connect with people who are different from us in our schools, workplaces, and neighborhoods?

Is our openness reflected in our interest in international events? Do we pray for the entire world or only for our little corner of it?

Do racial prejudices keep us from reaching out to others? Are we willing to take to heart the Scriptures we have reviewed and apply them to our lives?

If we consider ourselves Christians, are we actively reaching out to those with whom we come in contact?

7

HISTORY AND GEOGRAPHY

From one man he made all the nations, that they should
inhabit the whole earth; and he marked out their appointed
times in history and the boundaries of their lands.

ACTS 17:26

Geography: An Aerial View

I took my first flight at age eight, traveling alone from New Jersey
to my hometown of Jacksonville, Florida. I still remember the exhil-
aration and longing to touch the clouds, which from the windows of
the propeller-driven plane looked like cotton. I couldn't wait to fly
again. Nevertheless, I had little desire to leave North America and see
the rest of the world. I thought to myself, "I can always buy a book or
see it on TV."

I'm so glad I didn't stay in the United States the rest of my life. At
20 I flew to Europe—was the Atlantic really that vast? Two years later
I moved to England, and seven years after that my British wife and I
relocated to Sweden. Twice we've lived in Australia, and we've lived all
over the eastern United States. I am highly blessed to have visited most
of the countries in the world. Today, 2000 flights later, I have a different appreciation for the planet than I had as a child. I have a feel for the
continents and oceans and the distances involved. I know the countries, their languages and capitals, and what they look like from the air.
The planet will never again look the same.

Developing an appreciation for the land of the Bible is relatively
easy because it occupies only a minuscule fraction of the world. Learn

how to locate Israel, Arabia, and Egypt in a Bible atlas. Become familiar with the seas and rivers, the mountains and towns. Pinpoint Jerusalem, Athens, Rome, and Babylon on ancient and modern maps. The more geography you learn, the more you'll enjoy reading the Bible. Place names will become less confusing, and you'll feel more at home. Learn how to draw a simple sketch of ancient Israel. The payoff is huge.

Why Israel?

In biblical times, the land of Israel lay in a highly strategic location on the trade route from Asia to Africa. Situated at the eastern end of the Mediterranean, it also had excellent access to sea routes. Jerusalem was small—a place people would be more likely to pass through than move to—so it was a great center from which ideas could spread (for example, between Egypt and Mesopotamia).

The geography also forced the people to depend on God. Water is a precious commodity, and the Holy Land depends on rainfall because it is situated near several desert regions. The land has historically been vulnerable to earthquakes, locust hordes, and invading armies. At the same time, it is "a land flowing with milk and honey." It's a beautiful but fragile land, tough yet vulnerable—an ideal stage for the drama of redemption.

Do your best to locate the following bodies of water, geographical regions, and political regions on the two maps that follow. You will come across them frequently as you read the Bible. Familiarizing yourself with these few features will go a long way in orienting you to the biblical world.

Bodies of Water

1. *Mediterranean Sea (Great Sea)*. The entire biblical drama unfolds in the vicinity of the Mediterranean, especially its eastern end.

2. *Sea of Galilee (Sea of Kinnereth, or Lake of Tiberias)*. Actually a freshwater lake, this serves today as the principal water supply for Israel and Syria.

3. *Jordan River*. This river collects the rainfall in the

mountainous north, flowing southward from the Sea of Galilee all the way to the Dead Sea.

4. *Dead Sea (or Salt Sea).* This is the deepest depression on the face on the earth, approximately 1400 feet below sea level at the surface.

Geographical Regions

1. *Coastal plain.* This is the fertile area near the Mediterranean coast.

2. *Hill country.* This refers to the elevated terrain between the coastal region and the Jordan Valley.

3. *Jordan Valley.* This valley runs north to south and is the eastern border for southern Israel.

4. *Trans-Jordan.* This refers to the land east of the Jordan River.

5. *Negev.* This southern desert is more rocky than sandy.

Political Regions

1. *Ammon.* A country east of Jordan populated by descendants of Lot.

2. *Moab.* A country east of Jordan and south of Ammon also populated by descendants of Lot.

3. *Edom.* A country east of the Jordan and south of the Dead Sea.

4. *Egypt.* The land from which the 12 tribes were delivered to freedom.

5. *Israel (the united kingdom).* This name is used in four senses in the Bible. First, it is the covenant name of the patriarch Jacob. Second, it is the name of the nation that was formed from his descendants under Moses' leadership at Sinai. Hundreds of years later, Saul, David,

and Solomon became kings of this nation. Third, it is the name of the northern kingdom after the split in 922. Last, it is sometimes used in the books of Chronicles as the name of Judah (the southern kingdom) because this constituted the remnant of the faithful Davidic remnant. The geographic area we call Israel was named Palestine by the Romans, after the Philistines.

6. *Israel (Ephraim)*. The northern kingdom, whose principal tribe was Ephraim.

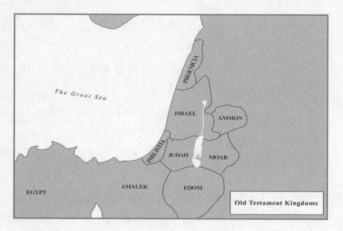

7. *Judah*. The southern kingdom, whose principal tribe was Judah. In New Testament times, the southern region was called Judea, which with Samaria and Galilee constituted three parts of Israel.

8. *Galilee*. The northern territory of New Testament Israel, hilly and green. It was cosmopolitan with Gentile influence.

9. *Samaria*. The territory between Judea and Galilee. The inhabitants were viewed as apostate Jews.

10. *Judea*. The southern territory, which included Jerusalem.

11. *Jerusalem*. The capital city, located in the center of Judea.

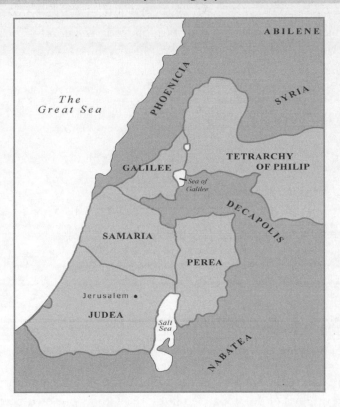

History: The Big Picture

As with geography, so with history. What may at first seem tedious turns out to be a key that opens the door to intriguing new worlds. As an undergraduate, I majored in history by default. Not that I disliked history, but I never really chose it as my intended major. I just had more credits in history than in anything else, so history it was. As I travel the world, I study maps and read some history so that I know something about the people I'm visiting. That combination of history and geography, along with on-site experience, has opened up the world for me. It has done the same for my Bible study.

The Flow of Old Testament History

We soon become disoriented when reading the Bible, both historically and theologically, unless we know the flow. I like to summarize the historical sequence by using the following 12 periods. Certainly there are other ways to divide biblical history, but this one works for me, and I think it will work for you too.

1. the primeval period
2. the patriarchal period
3. Egypt and the Exodus
4. the desert wanderings
5. the conquest and judges
6. the united kingdom
7. the divided kingdom
8. Israel's Assyrian exile
9. Judah's Babylonian exile
10. the Persian period
11. the Greek period
12. the Roman period

We are taught our national histories in school and remember the broad outlines of the story. Certainly we all know our own personal histories, and our closest friends know them too. If you're a follower of Christ, you are also able to tell the story of your journey in Christ (how your faith grew, when you finally became a Christian, and all that the Lord has been showing you since that day).

There's one more story I would like to challenge you to learn well enough to be able to tell it without notes (as Stephen did in Acts 7). It's the story of biblical history. This will probably be easier than you think. The following chapters will cover what happens in each period, so there's no need to explain it all now. Instead, please take a look at the annotated list below, which includes a few of the main events and characters of each period as well as the pertinent biblical books.

1. The Primeval Period

Context: Familiar stories from the ancient world are re-presented through the eyes of faith. The human predicament is put forth: On the run from God and determined to exercise personal autonomy, humans have become alienated from their creator.

Dates: undated

History: prehistoric

Characters: Adam, Eve, Cain, Noah

Literature: Genesis 1–11

2. The Patriarchal Period

Context: God chooses one man—Abraham—and promises to bless the entire world through his seed. The divine promise is continued through Abraham's son, grandson, and great grandsons—Isaac, Jacob, and Jacob's 12 sons—creating an important thread running through biblical history. The period ends with a famine that leads the family of Israel to seek refuge in Egypt.

Dates: Approximately 2000 BC till the Exodus (1446 or 1290 BC[1])

History: Abraham, the patriarchs, and the entry of the 12 tribes into Egypt

Characters: Abraham and Sarah; Isaac and Rebekah; Jacob, Rachel, and Leah; Joseph and his brothers

Literature: Genesis 12–50, Job

3. Egypt and the Exodus

Context: After several centuries pass, Israel becomes a threat to her Egyptian overlords. Reduced to abject slavery, Israel cries out in distress. God hears and sends Moses to deliver his people. Moses is to lead Israel into the Promised Land. Despite a series of plagues, the king (or Pharaoh) of Egypt is obstinate, and only after the plague on the firstborn does he release Israel. The night of their departure, they take part in the first Passover meal.

Dates: The traditional dates are 1876–1446 BC, but considering the archaeological and historical evidence, 1720–1290 BC is more likely.

History: The growth and enslavement of the people of Israel, the plagues on Egypt, the Passover, and the Exodus

Characters: Joseph, Jacob, Moses, Aaron, Miriam, Pharaoh

Literature: Genesis 46–50, Exodus 1–12

4. The Desert Wanderings

Context: The trip to the Promised Land should have taken only a few weeks, but the fledgling nation soon falls into ingratitude and idolatry. Most of her leaders compromise in their faith, and almost none of them—not even Moses—is permitted to cross the Jordan into the Promised Land (or Canaan, home of the Canaanite peoples). The only significant leaders who are allowed to enter some 40 years later are Joshua and Caleb. God gives the Law at Mount Sinai near the start of Israel's trek, and he gives it a second time right before the conquest of Canaan. The portable temple, or tabernacle, was constructed during this period.

Dates: The traditional dates are 1446–1406 BC, but 1290–1250 may be more accurate.

History: The Exodus under Moses' leadership, the giving of the Law (Torah), Israel's disobedience and wanderings, and the second giving of the law (Deuteronomy), and the spying out of the land

Characters: Moses, Aaron, Miriam, Joshua, Caleb, Jethro

Literature: Exodus 13–40, Leviticus, Numbers, Deuteronomy, Joshua

5. The Conquest and Judges

Context: Under Joshua, Moses' protégé and the new Israelite general, Israel takes much of the Promised Land in two campaigns. The southern campaign begins with the principal city of Jericho, and the northern campaign begins with the capital city of Hazor. Yet once again Israel slips into a vicious cycle of apostasy, divine punishment, cries for help, God's deliverance, and the people's ingratitude. The period of the judges, each of whom ruled only part of Israel and whose reigns often overlapped, is a time of moral and spiritual chaos and of theological anarchy, for God is not their true king. Instead, "everyone did what was right in his own eyes" (Judges 21:25 ESV).

Dates: Traditionally 1406–1050 BC, but more likely 1290–1050 BC

History: The crossing of the Jordan, the conquest and apportionment, and a succession of leaders (Judges) after Joshua's death

Characters: Joshua, Eli, Samuel, Ruth, Deborah, Gideon, Samson

Literature: Joshua 1–24, Judges, Ruth, 1 Samuel 1–8

6. The United Kingdom

Context: The last judge, Samuel, appoints the first king, Saul, who quickly turns aside from obeying the Lord. Saul's successor, David, is able to unite the kingdom, though it remains unified only until the death of his son Solomon. Under Solomon, a magnificent temple is constructed, finally replacing the tabernacle.

Dates: 1050–931 BC

History: The kingship of Saul, David, and Solomon; the consolidation of the empire; and the construction of the temple

Characters: Samuel, Saul, Jonathan, David, Joab, Bathsheba, Solomon

Literature: 1 Samuel 9–31, 2 Samuel, 1 Kings 1–11, 1 Chronicles 10–29, 2 Chronicles 1–36, some psalms, Proverbs, Ecclesiastes, Song of Songs (traditionally), and much more literature that is not in our Bibles (see 1 Kings 4:32)

7. The Divided Kingdom

Context: Despite his political wisdom, Solomon had ruled harshly. But in this he was outdone by his insecure and easily manipulated son Rehoboam. The kingdom divides in two. The tribes of Judah, Simeon, and Benjamin remain loyal to the Davidic dynasty and the religion of Judaism, forming the southern kingdom (Judah). The northern kingdom (Israel), however, led by Jeroboam, apostatizes. These tribes reject the priesthood established by Moses and Aaron, returning to worshipping golden calves and the gods of Canaan.

Dates: 931–722 BC

History: Israel divides, though kings of Judah (the southern kingdom)

continue the dynasty started with David; the people constantly seesaw in spiritual faithfulness; prophets challenge the people and their leaders.

Characters: Jeroboam, Rehoboam, Isaiah, Amos, Hosea, Ahab, Jezebel

Literature: 1 Kings 12–22, 2 Kings 1–17, 2 Chronicles 10–28, Isaiah, Hosea, Joel, Amos, Micah, Jonah

---

THE KINGS OF JUDAH AND ISRAEL

(Asterisks denote kings who were at least partially faithful to God.)

The Southern Kingdom (Judah)

Rehoboam	930–913	Jotham*	739–731
Abijah	913–910	Ahaz	731–715
Asa*	910–869	Hezekiah*	727–698
Jehoshaphat*	869–848	Manasseh	697–642
Jehoram	848–841	Amon	642–640
Ahaziah	841	Josiah*	640–609
Athaliah	841–835	Jehoahaz	609
Joash	835–796	Jehoiachim	609–598
Amaziah*	796–767	Jehoiachin	598–597
Azariah*	767–739	Zedekiah	597–587

The Northern Kingdom (Israel)

Jeroboam I	930–910	Jehoahaz	814–798
Nadab	910–909	Jehoash	798–782
Baasha	909–886	Jeroboam II	782–753
Elah	886–885	Zechariah	753–752
Zimri	885	Shallum	752
Omri	885–874	Menahem	752–742
Ahab	874–853	Pekahiah	742–740
Ahaziah	853–852	Pekah	740–732
Jehoram	852–841	Hoshea	732–722
Jehu	841–814		

---

8. Israel's Assyrian Exile

Context: Despite many prophetic warnings, the northern kingdom (Israel) does not repent and is taken into captivity by the Neo-Assyrian Empire. Much of the southern kingdom (Judah) is also taken, but the capital city, Jerusalem, narrowly escapes because of the faith of King Hezekiah.

Dates: 722–587 BC

History: Israel (the northern kingdom) is taken into Assyrian captivity (722 BC). Jerusalem (capital of Judah, the southern kingdom) is threatened (701 BC), but disaster is averted by Hezekiah's prayer. The Babylonians finally rout the Assyrians at Carchemish (605 BC).

Characters: Hezekiah, Manasseh, Josiah, Jeremiah

Literature: 2 Kings 18–24, 2 Chronicles 28–36, Jeremiah, Nahum, Zephaniah

9. Judah's Babylonian Exile

Context: Though Judah (the southern kingdom) had several righteous kings before the fall of Israel (the northern kingdom) in 722 BC, nearly all of Judah's next seven kings were wicked, and finally Jerusalem itself (the capital of Judah) falls to the Babylonians, who had recently taken Assyria's place as the dominant power in the region. The prophets decree that Judah's captivity (which took places in three waves) would last approximately 70 years. Israel longs for a return to the days of a king like David—a righteous Messiah who would come and deliver her.

Dates: 587–539 BC

History: Babylon takes Nineveh, the Assyrian capital (612 BC), defeats Egypt (605 BC) at Carchemish (Jeremiah 46:2), and deports the Judeans (605, 597, and 587 BC). Jerusalem is destroyed (587 BC).

Characters: Nebuchadnezzar, Daniel, Ezekiel

Literature: 2 Kings 25, Obadiah, 2 Chronicles 36, Daniel 1–5, Ezekiel, Habakkuk

10. The Persian Period

Context: When Persia comes to power, eclipsing Babylon (539 BC), the imperial policy of deportation and replacement of local rulers is reversed, and the Jews are allowed to return to their land. The Persians even subsidize the rebuilding of the temple. However, another world power is looming on the horizon.

Dates: 539–333 BC

History: Babylon falls (539 BC), the Jews are allowed to resettle in their homeland (reversing the Assyrian and Babylonian policy), the second temple is constructed (520–516 BC), work lies inactive after the foundation is laid (536–520 BC) but is revived under the preaching of Haggai and Zechariah (520 BC), Esther foils a plot to exterminate the Jews (480 BC), Ezra teaches the Law to those who have returned from exile (458 BC), and Nehemiah rebuilds the walls of Jerusalem (445 BC). Still, the kingdom is only a shadow of its former self.

Characters: Cyrus, Xerxes, Artaxerxes, Daniel, Esther, Ezra, Nehemiah

Literature: 2 Chronicles 36, Ezra-Nehemiah, Esther, 2 Chronicles, Daniel 6–11, Haggai, Zechariah, Malachi

11. The Greek Period (not recorded in Scripture)

Context: Alexander the Great, son of Philip of Macedon, is bent on conquest. Under his leadership as head of the Macedonian forces, the mighty Persian Empire is defeated. His dream is to *Hellenize* the world—to make it Greek in culture, customs, and language. By 333 BC he has taken the Holy Land from the Persians. After Alexander's death (possibly from malaria, transmitted by a mosquito bite), his successors to this part of the world are the Ptolemies (Egypt) and later the Seleucids (Syria). In the late second century, militant Jews rebel against the harsh program of Hellenization being prosecuted by Antiochus Epiphanes IV, and a revolution begins. Israel regains political autonomy for a century, from which time many of the familiar institutions of Judaism have their origin (synagogues, Hanukkah, Pharisees, and much more—see chapter 15). Dreams of a golden age for the people of God are simmering on the back burner. Rome is growing in power but is still too weak to challenge Greece.

Dates: 333–63 BC

History: Alexander the Great takes control of Syria (333 BC) and completely defeats Persia (331 BC). Hellenists try to force Greek culture on Jews. Pharisees and the synagogues are instituted. Judas Maccabaeus leads a revolt. Greek is now the majority language of Jews outside Palestine.

Characters: Alexander the Great, Antiochus Epiphanes IV, Judas Maccabaeus

Literature: Apocrypha (such as 1–2 Maccabees)

12. The Roman Period (not recorded in Scripture)

Context: The Greek Empire weakened, and Rome experienced a number of military successes in the second and first centuries BC, so leadership of the lands surrounding the Mediterranean changes yet again. In 63 BC, Pompey enters Jerusalem. From this point on—for many centuries—Rome will dominate political affairs in the land of Israel. The Jews are increasingly frustrated, and attempted coups and rebellions (especially in AD 66–73 and 132–135) characterize this period. Yet true freedom is not political; it is spiritual. When God himself visits his people in the person of Jesus Christ, he is recognized by only a few. Though the work of salvation is fulfilled in Jesus Christ's ministry, only a minority from among God's people accept him.

Dates: Begins in 63 BC

History: Rome eclipses Greece, and the empire is stabilized against enemies, bandits, and pirates. Communications are improved through roads, sea routes, and post. Koine Greek is used extensively in the Roman Empire.

Characters: Augustus Caesar, Herod the Great, Pontius Pilate, Annas and Caiaphas

Literature: 3–4 Maccabees (though no documents in the Old Testament or standard Apocrypha), the New Testament

In time you will acquire a feel for the order of the historical periods, just as a regular Bible reader develops an ability to turn to any book of the Bible, having developed a sense of what follows what. But rather than try to learn all the dates at once, begin with a few of the most important ones. In the list that follows you will find 25 index dates. Make yourself learn these, and in time you will be able to add other dates to the mental framework you are already constructing.

KEY DATES

2000 BC	Abraham
1720 BC	Jacob's family moves to Egypt
1290 BC	Exodus
1250 BC	conquest
1010 BC	David crowned
931 BC	kingdom divided
722 BC	fall of Israel (the northern kingdom)
700s–400s	prophets
701 BC	Hezekiah intercedes for Jerusalem
587 BC	fall of Judah and the destruction of Jerusalem
539 BC	fall of Babylon to Medo-Persia
400 BC	Old Testament is completed
167 BC	Maccabean revolt
63 BC	Romans take Syria from Greeks
6 BC	birth of Christ
26 AD	Pilate comes to Judea
27 AD	public ministry of Christ begins
30 AD	death and resurrection of Christ, start of the church of Christ
33 AD	conversion of Saul (Paul)
48 AD	Paul's first missionary journey
49 AD	Council of Jerusalem
60 AD	Paul released from prison, further missionary work

64 AD	Great Fire of Rome, Christians are blamed
70 AD	destruction of Jerusalem
95 AD	New Testament is completed

The Old Testament Narrative

The historical sections of the Old Testament are primarily narrative. True enough, the accounts are interspersed with poems, songs, genealogies, and royal annals, but the main genre is narrative. Under this there are several subgenres, including *epic narrative* (the patriarchs of Genesis), *heroic narrative* (David's mighty men in 2 Samuel), *tragic narrative* (the fall of Saul in 1–2 Samuel), and *primeval narrative* (Genesis 1–11).

The narrative of the Old Testament is not only the story of Israel but also the bigger story (or *metanarrative*) about how God works in the world. Here are a few keys to reading the narratives.

Don't read too much into the text or attempt to spiritualize it. Most narratives are straightforward. Allegories are rare in the Old Testament—and the New.

Look for common themes and words. The narratives are carefully edited literary masterpieces. Genesis, for example, is highly complex and textured. Recurring motifs reveal theological meaning. The writer and the Holy Spirit are trying to show us something.

Where possible, coordinate the narratives with other parts of the Old Testament that illuminate them or allow you to better understand them. For example, read Psalms along with the narratives of the life of David in 1–2 Samuel. Read the prophets along with the relevant historical sections of 1–2 Kings or 2 Chronicles. Read about the life of Solomon (1 Kings, 2 Chronicles) along with the wisdom literature associated with him (Proverbs, Ecclesiastes, and Song of Solomon).

Resist the temptation to moralize. Unless the moral of the story is given (as when Nathan explains his parable in 2 Samuel 12), let the text stand on its own. Of course, portions of the Law (Exodus through Deuteronomy) testify to the morality or immorality of the actions they describe. But more often than not, narrative writers record what they record to paint a picture. For example, we are not presented with the horrible account of Jephthah sacrificing his daughter (Judges 11:29–40) so that we may follow his example! The writer is showing how bad things were in Israel. Even the leaders—those who should have been relatively righteous—made terrible errors of judgment. In the same way, the final chapters of Judges (17–21) show us how lost Israel had become without God. The way is being paved for the monarchy (1 Samuel). There is little to emulate in these chapters.

Needless to say, the same principles apply for reading the narrative sections of the New Testament, which are found almost wholly in the four Gospels and Acts.

A Quick Review

Old Testament history (after the primeval period) covers nearly 2000 years. God was working in Israel's history, as he later did in the church, so it follows that without at least some understanding of what happened, we cannot comprehend the meaning of the text. Studying biblical history pays off.

As for the setting of the story, it all takes place around the eastern end of the Mediterranean. The Holy Land is surprisingly small—you can drive from the southern extremity of Israel to the north in a matter of hours—but we shouldn't underestimate its impact. Its crossroads location was perfect for acquisition and dissemination of ideas. Further, its vulnerability to both meteorological misfortune and foreign invasion influenced its inhabitants to turn to the Lord for guidance and protection. In short, because the grand story unfolds in time and space, wise readers will not shun history and geography, but rather make them dear friends.

RELIGIONS OF THE ANCIENT NEAR EAST

All who make idols are nothing,
and the things they treasure are worthless.

ISAIAH 44:9

In chapter 7 we conducted a broad sweep of biblical history. For centuries the Lord provided opportunity after opportunity for his people to connect with him—through creation, guidance, forgiveness, presence, deliverance, miracles, priests, prophets, and divine discipline. Yet despite the Lord's providential care and communication, the Israelites usually chose their own will over a relationship with God. They lived in the frustration that inevitably follows when we do not wholeheartedly embrace God's ways. God's laws were intended to protect his nation from the contamination of the surrounding pagan world and religions. Even though Israel was commissioned by God to eradicate the false religions of Canaan (Deuteronomy 7), the people were often attracted to them and repeatedly incorporated them into her worship. As a result, Israel lost its distinctiveness, its holiness. The temptation to *syncretism* (picking and choosing, or combining elements of various religions) is present in our day too. That means there is much we can learn from studying the idolatries of the ancient Near East.

Dozens of Divinities

Dozens of divinities are mentioned in the Old Testament. Egypt had numerous gods: *Amon* (Jeremiah 46:25), *Ra* or *Re, Maat, Ptah,*

Sakhmet, Nut, Isis, and many others. The gods of Assyria and Babylon also feature prominently in the biblical text, including *Nisroch* (2 Kings 19:37; Isaiah 37:38), *Rimmon* (2 Kings 5:18), *Nebo* (Isaiah 46:1), *Shamash* or *Molek* (2 Kings 23:10), and *Bel* or *Marduk* (Isaiah 46:1; Jeremiah 50:2; 51:44)—to say nothing of *Asshur, Enlil, Anu, Sin, [H]adad, Enki,* and *Ishtar.* The best-known Philistine divinity is *Dagon* (Judges 16:23; 1 Samuel 5:2-7; 1 Chronicles 10:10). In nearby Moab, *Chemosh* ruled (1 Kings 11:7; 2 Kings 23:13), while in Sidon *Ashtoreth* was ever popular (Judges 2:13; 10:6; 1 Samuel 7:3-4; 12:10; 31:10; 1 Kings 11:5; 2 Kings 23:13). Although Edom's chief god does not appear by name in the Bible, recent archaeological discoveries reveal that his name was *Qos.* In Ammon the main god was *Molek* (Leviticus 18:21; 20:1-5; 1 Kings 11:5-7; 2 Kings 23:10,13; Jeremiah 32:35; Zephaniah 1:5), who required that one's firstborn child "pass through the fire"—be offered as a burnt offering in the arms of the superheated statue of Molek.

Ample archaeological evidence (including idols, statues, and remains of temples) reveals that these deities were faithfully served not only by the Egyptians, Canaanites, and other pagans in the geographical vicinity of the Israel but also by the Israelites themselves. And no Israelite excavation has yielded more idols than Jerusalem!

Impersonal Gods

In the various systems of idolatry, whether Canaanite, Egyptian, or Babylonian, the gods were neither personal nor loving (Daniel 2:11). They had no desire to enter into intimate relationship with human beings. Rather, they depended on humans to make the proper sacrifices.

Mutual Manipulation

The essence of paganism is getting what one wants from the god or goddess by performing the right ritual. It all boils down to mechanics, not personal relationship, as in biblical religion. In a sense, one attempts to manipulate the deities—who in turn benefit in some way from the transaction. Thus paganism involves special formulas, spells, and rites. How one lives (morality and ethics) is irrelevant. Once people fulfill their religious duty, they are free to live as they want.

But before we look down our noses at paganism, does it not remind us of contemporary compromised Christianity? Sin throughout the week; confess and receive a blessing on the weekend. I see little difference between the two. But God calls us to something different. Nothing is to come before God. Our most vital relationship is with him, and to worship (or orient our lives around) anything else is idolatry.

Immorality

The gods of Canaan were not worthy of emulation. Like the gods of the ancient Greek, Roman, and Norse pantheons, they were governed by self-interest. They were capricious and vindictive. They lived for the same pleasures as pagan humans (Judges 9:13). They acted the same ways that human dictators behave, with all the markings of ego, intrigue, lust, rage, revenge, and self-interest. The notion of a deity being motivated by love to make a self-sacrifice, as in Christianity, was entirely alien. This is not surprising, considering that these other religions promoted self-interest before love for others.

Ritual, Not Righteousness

The rituals associated with idols, carried out either corporately by a priest or privately (Genesis 31:19; Judges 17:5; Isaiah 44:9-20), were thought to placate the gods and secure the benefits the worshipper desired. Yet right living had no part in worship—only right ritual. Biblical religion, however, insists that we are right with God only when we are right with each other (Amos 5:21-24; Micah 6:6-8; Romans 12:18; Hebrews 13:16; 1 John 4:7-20).

Nature Powers Personified

Pagan divinities were often nothing more than the powers of nature personified. Thunder, floods, storms, celestial bodies...all were viewed as divine. What a contrast to the Bible's perspective, where celestial and terrestrial bodies and events are part of the creation and thus inferior to their Creator. For instance, in Genesis 1:16, the sun and moon (worshipped in most ancient religions) are slightingly referred to as "the greater light" and "the lesser light." When Elijah, Yahweh's prophet, has the showdown on Carmel against the prophets of the fertility god Baal to determine who really controls the rain, Baal is exposed as the powerless imposter (1 Kings 18:16-39).

Polytheism

Pagan gods tended to be localized in their jurisdiction (1 Kings 20:23). There were national gods (2 Kings 17:29) and even city gods (Jeremiah 2:28; 11:13). This allowed room for many divinities, just as Hinduism acknowledges millions of gods. The ancients considered all deities equally real (2 Chronicles 32:19). That is, they gave allegiance to their own chief deity, but they did not deny the existence of the others. They did, however, view the gods of other peoples as inferior. Sometimes gods morphed when moving from one culture to another, as in Ekron's Baal-Zebub, or "lord of the flies" (2 Kings 1:2-6). In addition, there were household gods galore (Genesis 31:19). Of course, Judaism and Christianity are strictly monotheistic—they affirm the existence of only one God.

One Very Popular Pagan God: Baal

Most notorious—and ubiquitous—in the Old Testament was the multicultural, multiform Phoenician and Canaanite god Baal. *Ba'al* was a common word meaning "lord, husband, master."[1]

Baal was a fertility god. As the annual summer drought dried out the vegetation, he was thought to have died, as Mot, the god of death, triumphed. Then when winter rains brought verdure to the land, Baal was declared to have been reborn. This cycle repeated itself every year. Baal worshippers engaged in sexual acts to arouse Baal, who then brought rain to make Mother Earth (sometimes referred to as Asherah or Astarte) fertile. Many struggles were fought to eradicate Baal worship from the nation of Israel but with little lasting success (1 Kings 18:16-40; 2 Kings 10:18-28). His loose morals seem to have affected his worshippers, as in Numbers 25:1-5, where sexual promiscuity goes hand in hand with the Baal cult.

A Summary of the Characteristics of Polytheism

These are the major characteristics of the heathen divinities we meet in the Old Testament:

Ba'al with Raised Arm, fourteenth to twelfth century BC, found at Ras Shamra (ancient Ugarit). Used courtesy of the Louvre.

immoral or amoral (Numbers 25:1-5; 2 Corinthians 6:14-18)

impersonal (Daniel 2:11)

localized (1 Kings 20:23)

associated with fertility (1 Kings 14:22-24)

associated with the four seasons and weather

worshipped with occult practices (Deuteronomy 18:9-13)

worshipped with syncretism (2 Kings 17:29-34)

worshipped on high places (Numbers 33:52; Jeremiah 19:5)

New Testament Idolatry

In the Old Testament, people continually fell into idolatry, and people who lived in New Testament times were subject to the same danger (1 John 5:21). Of course, there were the literal gods adored in the Roman Empire—Greek and Roman gods such as Zeus, or Jupiter (Acts 14:8-18); Hermes, or Mercury (verse 12); Artemis, or Diana (Acts 19:23-41); and others not explicitly named in the New Testament.[2] These divinities offered such blessings as good health, clement weather, agricultural prosperity, wisdom, sexual prowess, safety through childbirth, and military success. In addition, several of the old Egyptian and other Eastern divinities were worshipped, especially Mithras, Cybele, Isis, and Serapis.

Modern Idolatry

What do people worship today? Modern idols may include the state (the military-industrial complex that guarantees a high standard

of living), the family (narrow concern for one's own progeny and posterity), and a host of other causes that prove to be ephemeral in the end.
After all, once we have passed through this world, all that remains is
our relationship with God. And so the biblical accounts of frequent
lapses into idolatry stand as a rebuke to all forms of idolatry, ancient
and modern. The wise person will periodically ask questions like these:
"Am I putting the Lord first, or has anything come before him? Have I
embraced an idol in my own life?"

A Quick Review

Pagan religions had a radical disconnect between religion and ethics. People could live any way they wanted as long as they went through
the motions of devotion to the gods. Without any expectation of holy
living, religion was reduced to mechanics. Worshippers could manipulate the deity, rather like a master manipulates his genie. There was
no sense of a personal relationship between gods and man. Herein lies
the most profound uniqueness of the Judeo-Christian view of God
and his connection to man—a difference that makes *all* the difference.

GENESIS: THE PRIMEVAL AND PATRIARCHAL PERIODS

Then the LORD God formed a man from the dust of
the ground and breathed into his nostrils the breath
of life, and the man became a living being.

GENESIS 2:7

Having scanned the religious landscape in which the biblical story unfolds, we are now prepared to begin exploring the text itself. Genesis is the introductory book of a 66-volume anthology called the Bible. The Bible is not short. Many people think a thousand pages sounds daunting, yet the same people manage to find hundreds of hours each year to read novels and magazines or to sit in front of television sets and computer screens. If we really understood that the infinite God has encapsulated his vital message in a book so compact and convenient, we would thank him and get busy reading!

Genesis is placed at the head of the biblical books for good reason, just as Revelation is perfectly positioned to close the canon of Scripture. The book that opens the Lord's written revelation to man must be approached with reverence. In Genesis the heart of God—his nature and his intentions for human beings—spills over onto the sacred pages. God is shown to be a God of order and supremacy as he conceives, creates from nothing (*ex nihilo*) by mere fiat, and then fills his creation. But he also displays his divine character through his limitless gift of grace to imperfect man.

The Primeval Period

The book of Genesis is a carefully constructed work. Though traditionally attributed to Moses—and it is certainly possible that he had a hand in its production—the book is anonymous and shows evidence of a number of earlier sources. At the simplest level it may be divided into two historical sections: the primeval period and the patriarchal period. According to the *Oxford Abridged Dictionary*, the term *primeval* means "pertaining to the first age of the world; primitive." The primeval period is undated, at least on one end. That is, Genesis 1:1 simply reads, "In the beginning." (The phrase is one word in Hebrew—*bereshith*). That there *was* a beginning is more important than *when* it took place. We simply don't know.

But Genesis is actually two beginnings. It is the beginning of God's story of creation, human disobedience, and divine redemption. But it is also the beginning book of the Pentateuch, or Torah, which is the story of God choosing and making a covenant with a people through whom he would bless all nations.

The primeval period lasts until after Babel (Genesis 11). History has preserved the memory of towers similar to the famous tower of Babel, and because the city of Ur, Abraham's first home (Genesis 11-12), has been excavated, we can roughly date the end of the primeval period to around 2000 BC.

The Patriarchal Period

A patriarch is a father and ruler of a family or tribe, so the term *patriarchal* refers to the era during which men—fathers and grandfathers especially—were heads of society. More specifically, the term can also refer to the era of Israel's patriarchs: Abraham, his son Isaac, his grandson Jacob, and his great-grandson Joseph, whose death is recorded at the end of Genesis. If you are a newcomer to the Bible, you might want to memorize that genealogical sequence.

Abraham lived around 2000 BC. When he visited Egypt, he would have seen the pyramids, which were already more than 500 years old! When Joseph brought his brothers and their families to Egypt, their part of the world was suffering a terrible famine. Through difficult circumstances, God brought the Israelites into Egypt, which was literally their salvation (Genesis 45:7; 50:20), though in time the name Egypt would be synonymous with enslavement—both symbolically and actually.

The Structure of Genesis	
The Primeval Period	The Patriarchal Period
Adam and Eve live in the garden	Abraham
Cain kills Abel in the field	Isaac (Abraham's son)
Noah and his family are saved from the flood	Jacob (Isaac's son)
People build a tower at Babel	Joseph (Jacob's son)

Their Questions, Our Questions:
A Closer Look at the Primeval Period

During the last 40 years I have read hundreds of books and articles about Genesis, sometimes to prepare myself to answer other people's questions but more often to answer my own. My fascination with the subject matter of Genesis, which began during my high school years, partially prepared me for conversion to Christ as a college student. As an eager freshman with fire in my eyes, a yearning in my heart, and time on my hands, I grabbed and read everything I could find that might address the things that intrigued me: cosmology, biology, evolutionary science, and so on.

Today as a lecturer (still eager, though with less time on my hands), I speak endlessly on these matters (so it seems), take questions from the floor, and handle a large load of correspondence from inquirers the world over. Many of these questions are concerned with the early chapters of Genesis. Yet we should ask ourselves whether such modern questions—How old is the earth? Was Darwin right? What was the scope of Noah's flood?—are central to biblical theology. That is, these may be *our* concerns, but were they *theirs* (the ancient Hebrews')? The ancient Jews cared about which was the true God, why believing in Yahweh was better than believing in Baal or Molek, whether their crops would come in and their livestock survive, and whether they could count on Yahweh through the hard times that are the stuff of life.

How Literal Is Genesis 1?

People often ask how literally we are to understand the cosmogony (creation story) of Genesis 1. Usually they don't realize that the Bible contains more than one description of creation, and if these accounts are pressed literally, the details diverge. How familiar are you with the various pictures of creation in the Scriptures?

Genesis itself has two accounts: the majestic and poetic version (1:1–2:4), and the more human-centered and relational details of the sixth day (2:5-25). But there are other descriptions in the Bible. In Job the heavens are supported above the earth by pillars (Job 9:6; 26:11). In Psalm 104:2-5 the heavens are stretched out like a tent or canopy, heaven is supported by beams, and the earth rests on foundations. In the magnificent Isaiah 40:12-22 the canopy is a sort of umbrella over the circle (disc) of the earth. In Proverbs 8:23-31 and 9:1-6 creation takes place through the agency of a craftsman, Wisdom—who in Colossians 1:15-17 is identified with Jesus Christ. Which of the above accounts is true? *They all are.* Are we helped or are we hindered when we strain to read the details literally? Is Scripture diminished or is it enhanced by the presence of multiple accounts?

Perspectives on the Two Creation Accounts

One may legitimately ask why Genesis contains two creation accounts. Modern readers often try to harmonize the accounts in every detail, not realizing that the accounts are deliberately written in a way that emphasizes different aspects of the story. Are liberal theologians correct when they say the two stories contradict? Why don't the details neatly mesh together? What can we conclude from the text?

Keep in mind that the focus of Genesis is man, not the creation. It is helpful to have dual perspectives, each highlighting different things. Genesis 1 gives us a panorama, and then chapter 2 zooms in on man and his relationship with God. The focus narrows further as Genesis recounts the life of Abraham, then his descendants through Isaac, then Isaac's descendants through Jacob.

Some Bible critics find a discrepancy in the two stories. Genesis 1 has the animals being created before man, but Genesis 2:19 reports the animals being created after man. Several translations take the verb of verse 19 as a pluperfect (as in the NIV "had formed"), solving the apparent chronological problem. Yet we may feel as though we are imposing our own chronology on the text.

Genesis 1 shows man's special place in the creation, and Genesis 2 shows man's special relationship with God. A difference in emphasis does not mean contradiction. The two accounts should be read as complementary rather than intersecting. Each is true in its own way. We need to allow the text to speak to us, straining to hear what God is telling us about himself and our place in his world.

Ancient Stories and Motifs in Genesis

One of the most interesting features of Genesis is the way the writer(s) of Genesis retooled a series of themes and stories that were long familiar in the ancient Near East and used them to make important points about God. This is certainly not to imply that the stories aren't true, for God's truth is conveyed through each one.

The retooled stories were adapted principally from the mythology of Sumeria and Babylon, though there are also points of contact with Egypt and the other surrounding nations. This does not mean that the biblical writers naively accepted mythology. On the contrary, everything the biblical writers did with these ancient traditions suggests the opposite—the stories have been demythologized; the truth about God has now been told. The process is so interesting and well documented that entire books have been produced on the subject. Here we'll have to make do with a brief sketch of what the brilliant writer(s) of Genesis accomplished.

Ancient Near Eastern Myths	The Primeval Narrative of Genesis
A dragon is slain. The upper half becomes heaven, the lower half becomes Earth.	God deliberately creates heaven and Earth.
The primordial waters of chaos are menacing and must be tamed.	The waters present no threat; they too are part of God's good creation.

Ancient Near Eastern Myths	The Primeval Narrative of Genesis
The sun, moon, and stars are deities.	The celestial bodies are part of the created order; they are not divine.
Giants are the offspring of angels and men.	Nephilim are destroyed in the flood and later defeated in Canaan (Genesis 6:4; Numbers 13:33).
The flood is sent to silence noisy humans.	The flood is sent to purge the earth of sin and to give creation a clean start.
Ages are idealized as thousands of years.	Ages are idealized as hundreds of years.
Some 30 ziggurats have been discovered in the Near East—centers of astronomy, astrology, and idolatry. The Babylonian writing Enuma Elish finishes with the construction of a tall tower to Marduk.	The Tower of Babel fails to reach heaven. Human hubris is thwarted as God intervenes to protect man from himself.

A New Epoch: The Patriarchal Period

As we leave the primeval period for the patriarchal, we enter an entirely new epoch. Whereas Genesis 1–11 was a "tract for the times," a radical rewriting of a familiar Near Eastern story, the same is not true of Genesis 12–50. There is no sign of previous stories being adapted, nor are the remaining chapters of Genesis quite so intentional in their subverting traditional pagan themes. And yet, of course, there are multiple points of contact with pagan culture throughout all of Genesis.

Generational Schema

The simple primeval–patriarchal division of Genesis is not necessarily the only way to approach Genesis. There is another way to analyze the book, explicit in the original Hebrew text itself. Genesis is a story of beginnings, and the Hebrew word for *generations* appears conspicuously in ten locations. Generations are about people, relationships, influence. Notice that Abraham and Joseph are absent from the *generations* formula, another indication that the schema of Genesis is stylized. (In the same way, Matthew's genealogy of Jesus is arranged in three sets of 14, skipping several names in order to follow the formula.) These are the ten generations:

> the heavens and the earth (Genesis 2:4)
> Adam and his descendants (5:1)
> Noah (6:9)
> Ham, Shem, and Japheth (10:1)
> Shem (11:10)
> Terah (11:27)
> Ishmael (25:12)
> Isaac (25:19)
> Esau (36:1)
> Jacob (37:2)

The "ten" motif also shows up in the ten generations from Adam to Noah (chapter 5) and the ten generations from Noah to Abram (chapter 11). The author of Genesis is tracing the "chosen seed of Israel's race"—that is, the generations of the chosen people, the Jews—genealogically from the first man on down. Life is not random, nor does it meander like some dreamy stream. It is directional, fraught with meaning and purpose. To discover our origin is to discover our destiny.[1]

Concentric Circles

In characteristically biblical fashion, Genesis is structured in concentric circles that tighten until the spotlight is very narrow indeed. We move from mankind in general, to the line of Seth (through the line of his descendant Noah), to one man, Abraham. After Abraham, the man of faith, the circles widen once again to Isaac and Jacob, then to the tribes of Israel (who are his descendants) and ultimately, thanks to Jesus Christ, to the entire world.

Major Characters

Abraham, Jacob, and Joseph dominate the remaining chapters of Genesis. (Isaac, the son of Abraham and father of Jacob, is a relatively minor character.) All three are men of faith, though they differ widely from one another. Abraham, called to follow God in his old age, does not waver through unbelief. Jacob, his grandson, is sure God wants to bless him but cannot resist relying on his own devices to guarantee those blessings. Joseph's life is one of the clearest displays of divine providence in the entire Bible. He was sold into slavery by his own brothers, but as a result he was graciously able to save his entire family—and the line that would one day lead to the birth of the Messiah—by bringing them to his new home, Egypt.

Patience

Abraham has to wait 25 years before his promised son is born. Jacob runs in fear for his life to the land of Haran, not reuniting with his brother Esau until after his wrestling match with God 20 years later. And Joseph too suffers for some 20 years before God lifts him up and places him in a position where his life becomes a blessing for the entire world. Often in the Bible, men and women of faith have to wait for God's promises to be fulfilled. This waiting period often runs into decades, not merely months or years. One more example: Consider that Jesus Christ is at the point of understanding his identity by age 12 (Luke 2), but he has to wait 20 more years before launching his public ministry. This underscores a prominent feature of the Bible—its realism. We often must wait for the good things of life, and there is no hurrying God, who is never early or late, but always on time. God cares for us, but he isn't a machine (pull the lever, receive the blessing). With respect to the Lord's will, our lives may pass in decades, not years, and we are called to patiently wait.

The Triple Promise

Genesis 12:1-7 is a key text for understanding the book—indeed, for understanding the entire Bible. Here the Lord makes the triple promise to Abram: a land promise, a nation promise, and a spiritual promise. The fulfillment of these three promises in Scripture constitutes an important framework for discerning biblical history. According to Joshua 21:43-45, the land promise was fulfilled more than 3000 years ago. The nation promise, too, was fulfilled (Exodus 19:6; Deuteronomy 4:34; 26:5). And yet the spiritual promise—that through Abram's seed the entire world would be blessed—was not fully realized until Jesus Christ. We too are children of Abraham if we live by faith (Galatians 3:7). Keep the triple promise in mind as you study Genesis, and it will open up new insights on the entire book.

Jacob's 12 Sons (the 12 Tribes of Israel)	
by Leah...	Reuben, Simeon, Levi, Judah
by Rachel's servant, Bilhah...	Dan, Naphtali
by Leah's servant, Zilpah...	Gad, Asher
by Leah...	Issachar, Zebulun
by Rachel...	Joseph, Benjamin
There are two anomalies in the 12-tribe division of the Promised Land. As the priests of Israel, Levi had no tribal territory. Yet Joseph's sons, Manasseh and Ephraim, became two tribes. Thus the total number of tribes is 12.	

Twelve Themes

As we have already noted, when we study the period in which Genesis was written, we must understand that ancient readers were little interested in modern scientific questions. Rather, they were concerned about theology, and particularly the truth about the one holy God, Yahweh. In fact, the 50 chapters of Genesis present the creation in hardly more than 50 verses. The focus rapidly narrows from the heavens and the earth to the creation of mankind in the first family, and then it continues to narrow along the genealogy that ultimately leads (in the next testament) to the birth of the Savior of the world. Truly Genesis is a book of origins, not a work of cosmology or biology. As Galileo put it, "The Holy Spirit intended to teach us in the Bible how to go to heaven, not how the heavens go."

In Genesis, the Lord spells out how life works—not the incredibly complex mechanisms of microbiology, but meaningful life on this planet as God intended it. The themes of Genesis are the themes of the

Bible. Many of these themes are assumed, or taken for granted, later in the Bible. With this in mind, let's take a peek at a dozen major biblical themes introduced in Genesis.

1. God. He is the Creator, and human beings are favored above all other creatures. We were made uniquely spiritual in all of creation (1:27; 2:7; 4:26; 5:1). God does not beg for our service, nor does he require worship out of some sense of insecurity. His blessings toward us do not flow from any need on his part but rather from the wellspring of his kindness and initiative. None of the pagan gods are so eagerly desirous of personal relationships with humanity. God is a God of order, his creation is good, and he is consistently rational and good. The Lord is not whimsical, sadistic, or erratic. In order to please him, we must submit to the order he has established. The world teaches that we are not uniquely special, but God tells us otherwise. These divine attributes stand in stark contrast to the weak deities of the pagan religions of the day.

2. Worship. We are to worship only one God. The other deities are false gods. Worship is for our benefit, not his.

3. Sin and guilt. Morality is objectively real (not just a matter of opinion), and sin is at the root of our problems. A number of moral failings are recounted in Genesis, including bigamy (4:19), revenge (4:24), violence (6:11), drunkenness (9:21), sexual perversion (9:22-27), incest (19:33-35), and deceit (12:10-20; 20:13). Sin fills the heart of God with grief and pain (Genesis 6:6).

4. Sacrifice. True religion is based on true sacrifice. God requires sacrifice of us, just as he too sacrifices, giving his best and never holding back. Moreover, God cannot be manipulated by sacrifice. We don't control God, for he is sovereign over all creation.

5. Grace. God is always willing to give us a fresh start. This is one of the strongest themes in Genesis. Grace is extended to the first couple after their rebellion. They do not die immediately, nor are they heartlessly expelled. The Lord ensures that they will be able to cope with their new rugged environment. Similar scenarios are repeated four more times in Genesis. After the murder of Abel, God spares Cain, giving him a fresh start. In the great deluge, God spares Noah and his family. At Babel, God again protects man from himself. And grace is extended through God's call of Abram, as the patriarch is called out of idolatry to a relationship with God. Out of God's strength, his grace meets our need in our weakness.

6. Providence. God provides for his creation, anticipating needs generations in advance. His providence is especially visible in the descendants of Abraham. We can trace the generational theme from the seed of Eve through Abraham, Isaac, Jacob, Judah…all the way to the Messiah.

7. Selection. In Genesis, God selects individuals, families, and peoples. Yet this selection often works against the grain of society: Younger children are favored over the firstborn, women over men, foreigners over natives, lowborn over highborn, and so on.

8. Marriage and family. God affirms marriage and family. The ancient Canaanites and other peoples resorted to prostitution, surrogate childbirth, and fertility cults. According to Genesis, these will not do. When it comes to building family, God expects faithfulness. If we do things God's way, these relationships bring great blessing.

9. Work. Man is created to work, not to be lazy. The institution of work was present in the condition of paradise (Genesis 2:15). It predates the Fall.

10. Justice. Crime must be requited with punishment. Or conversely, as Gilbert and Sullivan put it, "Let the punishment fit the crime." A sense of justice runs deep and strong in the Old Testament (Genesis 4:10-12; 6:6-8; 9:24-27; 18:16-23…).

11. Covenant. God longs for friendship with man, but this can happen only on certain terms in a covenant relationship. God makes some promises without condition (Genesis 3:15; 9:8-17; 15:9-21) and others that are contingent on man's obedience to a condition (Genesis 2:16-17; 17:7-14). Yet this is hardly a relationship among equals. God is virtually 100 percent the benefactor, and we are 100 percent the beneficiaries.

12. Faith. Righteousness is appropriated through faith (15:6). We can do nothing to earn right standing in God's sight, yet we receive his favor only through walking in faith. In other words, an obedient lifestyle is integral to being right with God.

A Quick Review

Genesis is the gateway to the Bible. The Creator has spoken; our job is to listen and to respond. The Bible is his word, and Genesis is the introduction. Just as watching the first ten minutes of a movie may be essential for understanding the plot, so reading all of Genesis is integral to grasping the rest of Scripture. Like the straight-edged pieces of a jigsaw puzzle that make up its frame, Genesis frames our exploration of the entire Bible. And the story starts where it ends—but you'll have to see the whole story to get there.

Here all the major biblical themes are introduced. Here we encounter the "kindness and sternness" of God (Romans 11:22). He means business (Adam was expelled, the flood came, and so on), and yet he delights in showing compassion. He rewards the faithful and shows his grace over and over again—to Adam, to Cain, to Noah and his family, to the people at Babel, and to Abraham and his descendants. Perhaps above all, in this book we realize that God created us in love and for a reason.

10

EXODUS AND THE LAW

Then we cried out to the LORD, the God of our ancestors,
and the LORD heard our voice and saw our misery, toil and
oppression. So the LORD brought us out of Egypt with a
mighty hand and an outstretched arm, with great terror and
with signs and wonders. He brought us to this place and
gave us this land, a land flowing with milk and honey.

DEUTERONOMY 26:7-9

In this chapter we will survey the second to fifth books of the Old Testament, in which Israel becomes a nation and receives God's Law. The setting begins with the Exodus from Egypt, continues throughout the wilderness wanderings, and ends on the border of the Promised Land of Canaan. Most scholars locate the events of these four books in the thirteenth century BC.

In the second part of this chapter we'll take a peek at the legal section of the Pentateuch. Remember what you learned from Genesis about the character of God and his dealings with people. The Law makes most sense once we know the character of the Lawgiver.

The Scenic Route

After the Exodus, the fledgling nation could have made it to Canaan in a matter of weeks, but because of their sin, they wandered for 40 years until the generation of the Exodus had died. A sampling of Israel's perennial failings are mentioned in 1 Corinthians 10:1-13.

1 Corinthians 10	Old Testament Passage
idolatry (verse 7)	the golden calf (Exodus 32)

1 Corinthians 10	Old Testament Passage
sexual immorality (verse 8)	Phinehas stops the plague (Numbers 25)
testing God (verse 9)	the bronze snake (Numbers 21:4-9)
grumbling (verse 10)	Korah, Dathan, and Abiram (Numbers 16)

Such a story is unlikely to have been made up. If it weren't true, a more glorious past could easily have been constructed. Nevertheless, there are moments of glory in these four Old Testament books, most notably in the historical and spiritual events of the Exodus, the construction and dedication of the tabernacle, and Moses' faithfulness. Several centuries later, Israel's high points would include David's reign, the construction and dedication of the temple, and significant victories over Israel's enemies. Jews rightly look back at Exodus and 2 Samuel the way Christians look at the Gospels and Acts. We will now review some of the salient features of these four books of the desert period: Exodus, Leviticus, Numbers, and Deuteronomy. The Exodus is the central redemptive event of the Old Testament, so we will linger longer in our overview of that book.

EXODUS

Exodus is the Latin form of the Greek word *exodos* ("departure"). It refers to Israel's dramatic departure from Egypt after 430 years of slavery (Exodus 12:40-41).

Moses

The hero of Exodus is Moses. His life falls into three 40-year periods: (1) growing up and being well educated in Egypt, (2) building a family in Midian and learning how to survive in the rugged wilderness of the Sinai Peninsula, and (3) returning to Egypt and leading the people out. In Jewish thought, 120 was considered the age of spiritual perfection.[1] Moses was assisted in his leadership by his older siblings, Aaron and Miriam.

Like everyone, Moses struggled with sin. In his anger at the people's continued grumbling, he strayed from God's spoken directions to him and was therefore denied permission to enter the Promised Land (Numbers 20:8-12; 27:12-14). Nor was he above making excuses, as we read in Exodus 3–4. Still, he was not driven by ego or ambition. Of all the Old Testament heroes, none embodied a more humble heart (Numbers 12:3). Moses was remembered as a powerful leader, lawgiver, and wonder-worker.

The book of Deuteronomy proclaimed that a second Moses would come and that those who ignored him would do so at the peril of their salvation (Deuteronomy 18:15-19). Jesus Christ—powerful leader, miracle worker, and revealer of God's word—fits the prophecy perfectly, and the similarities in many of the events during their lives make the connection hard to ignore. The early (Jewish) Christians clearly recognized this fulfillment of Old Testament prophecy and preached that Christ was Moses' rightful successor (Acts 3:22-26).

The Nation

Jacob's sons had gone to Egypt (to escape famine) as a company of barely 70 persons, but in their providential isolation in the northeast section of the Nile Delta region (the land of Goshen), their population eventually grew to about 600,000 men (Genesis 47:27; Exodus 12:37). The increase in the Hebrew population became a threat to Egyptian political stability, and in time the people of God were enslaved. Yet they were not properly a nation until they left Egypt and received the Law at Sinai. And *that* was not going to happen until Pharaoh changed his mind and released them. Yet this monarch was so stubborn that only a series of progressively more serious plagues moved him to accede to Moses' repeated requests.

Plagues

After the ten plagues against Egypt (Exodus 7–12), Pharaoh finally let the people go. The Bible says that the plagues were delivered in judgment on the Egyptian gods (Numbers 33:4). You may not be aware of how humiliating these plagues would have been to worshippers of the Egyptian pantheon, and there is a clear polemic element in the account, so clarifying the connections will be worthwhile.

1. Plague of blood. The Nile turned to blood, and so the first plague was a slap in the face to the Egyptian god Khnum, creator of water and life; to Hapi, god of the Nile; and to Osiris, whose bloodstream was a great river and source of life for all the land. This plague would have subjected the Egyptian economy to considerable strain.

2. Plague of frogs. The second plague was an insult to Heket (Heqt), wife of the creator of the world and goddess of childbirth. She was represented as a frog.

3. Plague of lice. Geb, god of the earth, is the likely target of the third plague, as the dust of the ground is turned into lice (or gnats) that cover man and livestock alike.

4. Plague of flies. The next plague suggests the importance of Khepri, who had the head of a fly. This deity was connected with creation, rebirth, and the movement of the sun. Three of the plagues (the third, fourth, and sixth) had implications for the Egyptian priesthood, which valued smooth (shaved) skin for one to enter the presence of the supposedly divine Pharaoh.

5. Plague on livestock. Hathor, mother and sky goddess, took the form of a cow, and Apis, who symbolized fertility, took the form of a bull, so plague five underscored their powerlessness.

6. Plague of boils. Handfuls of soot were taken from the furnace to cause the sixth plague. Certainly this was redolent of the furnaces manned by Hebrew slaves. The soot caused boils, which Isis, god of nature, magic, and medicine, was powerless to avert. Similarly, Thoth, also god of medicine, was shown to be a charlatan. The stigma of the boils covered Pharaoh's sorcerers, who were unable to protect themselves, much less the Egyptian people.

7. Plague of hail. The devastating plague of hail, which included severe lightning and thunder, made Nut, goddess of the sky, look bad. This was obviously no conjurer's trick, but the work of the true God.

8. Plague of locusts. Plague number eight was aimed at Seth, who manifested himself in wind and storm; Nepri, the god of grain; and Ermutet, goddess of childbirth and crops.

9. Plague of darkness. Darkness, with its association with judgment, hopelessness, and death, was the penultimate plague. This terrible plague cast aspersions on the integrity and reality of the solar deities Ra (Re), Aten, Atum, and Horus, who were associated with the sun.

10. Plague on the firstborn. The final plague took the lives of the firstborn, including the son of Pharaoh, and was thus a declaration of judgment against Osiris, patron deity of Pharaoh and judge of the dead; Apis and Heket (fertility); Min, god of procreation; Isis, goddess of fertility; Selket, guardian of life; Meskhenet, goddess of childbirth; Hathor, one of the seven deities that attended births; and perhaps most of all Renenutet, the cobra-goddess who was the special guardian of Pharaoh.

Pharaoh was considered to be the son of Ra, so the personal nature of this plague was highly discrediting.[2] Those whose doorframes were smeared with lamb's blood were spared as the destroying angel "passed over" them—on the evening of first Passover.

Thoth. © 2010 Steven G. Johnson. Used by permission through Creative Commons.

The egregious failure of the magicians (traditionally named Jannes and Jambres—see 2 Timothy 3:8) exposed as frauds three more Egyptian divinities. First, how could the bloodthirsty Sakhmet retain credibility as god of war and protector of Pharaohs after the loss of firstborn men throughout the Egyptian army and of Pharaoh's own son? Second, how could the Egyptian and Nubian god of wealth and incense, Dedwen, allow the Lord to make the Egyptians give the Hebrew slaves all they asked for in flocks, herds, clothing, silver, and gold (Exodus 12:32-36)?

But for me personally, the most amusing of all the Egyptian gods is Thoth, god of wisdom. Thoth is regularly depicted as a baboon. As the apostle Paul would later muse, "Where is the wise person? Where is the teacher of the law? Where is the philosopher of this age? Has not God made foolish the wisdom of the world?" (1 Corinthians 1:20).

Passover

The commemorative meal was instituted on the eve of the Exodus (Exodus 12) and was to be celebrated by all future generations of Jews. As you read through the Old Testament, make note of the times that the nation of Israel did and did not obey God's command to annually celebrate the Passover. You will find that it is always tied to the nation's corporate faith and spirituality. The Passover was probably never celebrated during the 40 years of desert wandering because the males were uncircumcised and therefore ceremonially unclean (Joshua 5:5-7). Even more telling, the Israelites consumed no bread or wine in the desert (Deuteronomy 29:6). The result was the sifting of the unfaithful (1 Corinthians 10:5).[3] Understanding the significance of the Passover will lead to a deeper and richer understanding of Jesus' Last Supper and the disciples' partaking of communion.

The Passover was to be eaten in haste, in memory of the hasty dinner before the Israelites fled Egypt. The Egyptian army unsuccessfully pursued the fleeing Hebrews and perished in the water of the Sea of Reeds (considered at that time to be part of the Red Sea). Yet despite Israel's liberation, the people soon fell to complaining. They clearly had not internalized the Spirit of God.

Redemptive Parallels	
Old Testament Judaism	New Testament Christianity
redemption from Egyptian slavery	redemption from slavery to sin
blood of the Paschal Lamb	blood of the Lamb of God
waters of the Red Sea	waters of baptism
commemorative Passover meal	commemorative Lord's Supper

Law

While the people encamped at the foot of Sinai (Horeb), Moses ascended the mountain to receive the Law (*Torah*, which can be rendered *law* or *instruction*). Yahweh inscribed the Ten Commandments (Decalogue, from the Greek for "ten words") on two duplicate tablets—one for Israel and one for himself. These formed the nucleus of the Law and were later augmented to a much fuller code (roughly Exodus 20 to Deuteronomy 30). Prominent features of the Law include animal sacrifice, the Sabbath, circumcision, and the three mandatory annual feasts (Exodus 23:14; Deuteronomy 16:16). Exodus also gives elaborate instructions for the construction of the tabernacle (a portable tent for worship and sacrifice) and its paraphernalia, such as the ark of the covenant.

The tabernacle and the ark.

There are sacrificial laws (e.g. Leviticus 1–7), rules for the priesthood (Exodus 28–29; 39; Leviticus 8–9; 21–22), directions for the construction of the tabernacle (Exodus 25–38; 40), dietary and hygienic laws (especially Leviticus 11–15), and various moral and ethical rules (such as Leviticus 18–20). Later rabbis counted 613 laws—248 positive commands and 365 prohibitions—though the exact numbers are disputable.

The five books of Moses are also called the Pentateuch, from the Greek word for "five rolls." Strictly speaking, Genesis does not contain much legal material, but it does lay out many of the principles underlying the hundreds of laws in Exodus–Deuteronomy, so it has traditionally been recognized as the first book of the Law.

For many readers first approaching these books, all the regulations can be tedious. Therefore it is helpful to get an overview before working one's way more slowly through these biblical chapters.

How to Read the Law

The keys to reading and interpreting the Law are different from those for reading other literary genres (such as narratives, poetry, and wisdom writings). Here are some things to keep in mind.

1. The Law is the word of God for us just as it was for the Jews of old. All of the books of the Law are the word of God. We should study them, reflect on them, and do our best to understand them.

The high priest.

2. And yet the Old Testament laws are not *our* laws. Christians aren't necessarily obligated to keep them. The Israelites were required to keep them, but we are not.

3. There is one exception: We must follow the laws that are repeated in the New Testament. For example, the New Testament upholds most of the Ten Commandments (Exodus 20; Deuteronomy 5), the greatest commandment (Deuteronomy 6:4-5), and the command to love our neighbor (Leviticus 19:18).

4. At the very least, the Law should be seen as an expression of God's holiness.

5. Jesus predicted that the temple order would be dismantled and voided (Matthew 24:2), as did the epistle to the Hebrews (chapter 8). In other words, those laws pertaining to sacrifices and cultic rituals were temporary. This was even prophesied in the Old Testament itself (Jeremiah 31:31-34).

6. The focus of the Law is the heart, not outward behavior. Leviticus 19:17-18—to cite just one passage—makes this crystal clear. No

one was saved in the Old Testament by keeping the Law. The old covenant, like the new, was a covenant of grace.

FEASTS AND HOLY DAYS OF JUDAISM

Monthly
Rosh Hodesh ("head of the month")
English name: New Moon
Significance: celebration of a new month

Autumn
Rosh Hashanah (Leviticus 23:23-25, "head of the year")
English name: Feast of Trumpets
Significance: Israel's New Year's Day

Yom Kippur (Leviticus 16:8,10,26; 23:27-32; Numbers 29:7-11)
English name: Day of Atonement
Significance: celebrates God's grace and forgiveness

Sukkot (Exodus 23:16-17; 34:22; Leviticus 23:33-43;
    Deuteronomy 16:13-15; 31:9-13)
English name: Feast of Tabernacles or Booths
Significance: celebrates the Exodus

Winter
Hanukkah (John 10:22)
English name: Feast of Lights or Dedication
Significance: celebrates the dedication of the temple in 165 BC

Purim (Esther)
English name: Festival of Lots
Significance: celebrates Israel's deliverance from the Persians

Spring
Pesach (Exodus 12)
English name: Passover
Significance: celebrates deliverance from the tenth plague

Hag Hamatzah
English name: Unleavened Bread
Significance: celebrates the Exodus

Shavu'ot (Exodus 23:16; 34:22; Leviticus 23:15; Numbers 28:26)
English name: Pentecost, Whitsunday, or Feast of Weeks or
    Firstfruits or Harvest
Significance: celebrates the reception of Torah at Sinai

Summer
Tisha b'Av
English name: Ninth of Av
Significance: commemorates the day the temple fell to the
    Babylonians in 587 BC. This is traditionally also recognized
    as the day the temple fell to the Romans in AD 70.

Four Things the Lord Gave Israel

If a lot of this is new material to you, focus on the following four items. These are the most significant gifts the Lord gave to Israel.

Freedom (Exodus 12–14). The Israelites were liberated from slavery, led out of the land of oppression and idolatry and into a bright future. The Exodus has inspired many a freedom fighter to take up arms against his oppressors. Notice, however, that the Israelites never fought until they crossed the Jordan River, and even then, they were successful only when God commanded them to do so. The Lord alone led them out of Egypt and slavery and into the Promised Land.

Law (Exodus 20). God revealed his heart and his ways to Israel by means of the Law given through Moses. At first this may seem to be a paradox. Isn't freedom antithetical to law? Yet it is not. Absolute freedom does not exist—even God isn't free to contradict his own nature. To have freedom, we need guidance. A locomotive isn't free to move away from the rails that guide its course and prevent it from derailing. In the same way, we need laws, and we need to obey them if we are to be truly free (John 8:31-32).

Mission (Exodus 19). Israel was called to be a kingdom of priests and a holy nation—just like its New Testament counterpart, the church (1 Peter 2:9-10). Through the Israelites' obedience to God's Law, they were to demonstrate to the watching world the wisdom, goodness, and love of the one true God.

God's name (Exodus 3:13-15; 34:6-7). Yahweh reveals his name to Israel. His name is not a word—much less a word that must be pronounced correctly. God's name is his nature, which includes compassion, grace, justice, wrath, and love. We cannot understand God if we don't understand his nature. The mission of the man or woman of God is to reveal this name to the world (John 17:11), to spread the knowledge of the true God. This takes place not only with words but also with a credible witness to those words—a life lived in conformity with God's Law and with his heart of compassion and love for others.

LEVITICUS

Israel's religious observances are led by Levites, descendants of the patriarch Levi—hence the name Leviticus. Numerous sacrificial laws are legislated, as well as other laws related to the fasts, feasts, and faithful obedience of Israel.

NUMBERS

Numbers is so named because of the two military censuses in the book. Here we also learn that though led by pillars of cloud and fire, Israel still needed human assistance in her journey (Numbers 10:11,31). We may be led by the Spirit of God, but that doesn't mean it's "just us and the Lord." In humility we need to be willing to stop and ask for directions. Obstacles to spiritual victory in Numbers include challenges to the authority of Moses and Aaron, intertribal misunderstandings, and idolatry.

DEUTERONOMY

Here the Law is given for a second time because the Exodus generation has died out. The title comes from the Greek words *deuteros* ("second") and *nomos* ("law"). Besides the reiteration and amplification of the Law, the people are prepared for the transition from Moses' leadership to Joshua's. Above all, Deuteronomy urges that loving God means obeying him (similar to Jesus' emphatic words in John 14). Israel is exhorted to choose life (Deuteronomy 30:19).[4] The book ends with the death of Moses.

The Torah and the New Testament

It is clear that the Law, or Torah, tells us much about God's nature—his goodness, wisdom, providence, justice, and so forth. It is equally clear that not all aspects of the Law apply to our day. After all, the Jerusalem temple is no longer standing, the sacrifices are no longer offered, most Jews live outside Israel, and if the Christians are right, the Messiah has already come. How could a government implement the political and social legislation of the Mosaic Law (as we see in such passages as Exodus 21–22) now that church and state are separate, the opposite of the situation in ancient Israel? Therefore, which parts of the Old Testament "apply" today? That is a central question of Old Testament interpretation.

We will therefore conclude this chapter with a brief look at the ways in which the two testaments differ. This short study highlights the connections and differences between Judaism and Christianity, throwing light on the structure of God's revelation and the entire Bible. We begin with a cursory discussion of the Sabbath.

The Sabbath

Many in the religious world today insist that Christians observe the Sabbath. Most interpret this to mean that on Sundays, Christians should have a day of rest. But what does the Bible say? To begin with, the Sabbath is the seventh day of the week, not the first. And Saturdays aren't the only Sabbath days according to the Old Testament. Sabbatical and Jubilee years (Leviticus 25) count too, and thus in a 50-year span, a Jew who followed the letter of the Law would have observed more than 5000 Sabbath days, compared to only 2600 for the modern "Sabbath keeper." Moreover, on the Sabbath, the people of God had to stay at home (Exodus 16:29). No sports, no visiting friends, and (strictly speaking) no attending church services. Nor may any cooking be done—all food must be prepared in advance (Exodus 16:23-29). All work is prohibited. Finally, the Old Testament teaches that failure to observe the Sabbath is punishable by *death*! (See Numbers 15:32-35.) Who really observes the Sabbath today? No one, strictly speaking. Obviously, some parts of the old covenant have not carried over into the new (including sacrificing lambs and pigeons). Are we bound by the Sabbath? Or other holy days ("holi-days")? Is there a priesthood today, a clergy-laity system? Is the church building really the "house of God"? In short, exactly what *is* the relationship between the old and new covenants?

Sabbath and the Early Church

The early church (as seen in Acts) used Sabbaths for evangelistic purposes, knowing that they would find Jews in the synagogues. The main meeting day for Christians was Sunday, not Saturday (Acts 20:7). Sunday as a day of rest finds its way into Christianity only after two centuries. Early second-century writers interpret Sabbath as a Jewish legal requirement no longer required for Christians.[5] The early Christians did not view themselves as bound by any Sabbath observance. Only centuries later was Sunday mandated as a "Christian Sabbath."

Double Standards

Clearly, if some days are holy, the others must be unholy. In practice this means that people try harder to please God on the special (or holy) days than at other times. This reminds us of the man who gets drunk every Friday, rationalizing that he will be given a clean bill of health as long as he takes Mass on Saturday. Two standards of commitment thus emerge. Yet faith is meant to be a daily lifestyle (Luke 9:23; Romans 12:1), not a weekly observance. *All* time is holy. In fact, the transformation goes beyond time. The Old Testament distinction between holy and unholy has been invalidated or transformed, so all days and times are now holy, all space is holy, all things are holy, all people are holy.

Holy Time

As we have seen, we are no longer bound by Sabbath observance (as in the fourth commandment—Exodus 20:8-11). This is made explicit in Colossians 2:16. Attempts to be justified by observing special days, seasons, and such are misguided (Galatians 4:8-11). It is true that the early church often met on Sundays (Acts 20:7; Revelation 1:10), partly in commemoration of Christ's resurrection (Matthew 28:1), which took place on a Sunday, but Sunday is nowhere called a Sabbath. The lesson for us is that *all* time is holy. It is not a sin to observe a special day (Romans 14:6), but it is a sin to coerce others to do so.

Holy Space

As with time, so with space. God cannot be confined to "holy" space (John 4:24; Acts 7:48-49). The Old Testament subdivided space, physically restricting access to God (Hebrews 9:1-8), but the New Testament does not limit access to God in this way (Matthew 27:51; Ephesians 2:18). We worship God wherever we are; our everyday lives express our worship (Romans 12:1). Although the church is called God's household (Ephesians 2:19), a church *building* is no more holy than any other building. The lesson for us is that we should strive to do our best for God wherever we are. We do not absorb holiness from the place where we worship; we are to approach God "in spirit and in truth" (John 4:24).

Holy People

Similarly, there are no saints (holy people) in the traditional sense of the word. All Christians are holy, or saints (Ephesians 1:1). Nor is there any special priesthood today except that of Jesus himself (Hebrews 7:23-28). All disciples form a royal priesthood (1 Peter 2:9), yet no one needs to go through another person in order to reach God, and no one needs to present a sacrifice, because Christ has been sacrificed once for all. There is only one mediator between God and man, and that is Jesus Christ (1 Timothy 2:5). No one can be saved by the merit of another person—except that of Christ—regardless of how righteous that other person is (Ezekiel 14:14; Jeremiah 15:1; 18:20). Thus praying to the saints is misguided.

Preachers and teachers do not represent a spiritual elite. In that sense, there is no divide between clergy and laity (Matthew 23:9). All Christians are to be equally committed. Christians do have different gifts and functions, but all disciples are expected to obey all the commands all the time. All disciples are called to full-time ministry, regardless of how they earn their living. The lesson for us is that nothing could be further from the spirit of Jesus Christ than a double standard of commitment.

Holy Cow!

And there are many other changes from the Old Testament to the New. We no longer have holy foods (Mark 7:19; 1 Timothy 4:3; Hebrews 13:9) or holy altars (Hebrews 7:27; 13:10). New Testament worship does not include holy vestments (Exodus 28:2), holy water (Numbers 5:17), or holy incense (Exodus 25:6). Of course, worshipping images and icons is ruled out by both testaments (Exodus 20:4, 1 John 5:21). Nevertheless, humans have venerated holy medals, relics, languages, formulae, crosses, and much more. The importing of Old Testament categories (holy and unholy, sacred and profane) into the New Testament simply will not do.

Two Covenants

Hebrews 9:15-17 shows that the new covenant (or will, or testament) superseded the old covenant. Two wills cannot be in effect at the same time, and neither can two testaments. The heart of the Law carries over into the New Testament (Matthew 22:37-40; Galatians 5:14), but the Law and its specific commandments were nailed to the cross and invalidated (Colossians 2:13-14). Thus Christians are not bound to observe the regulations of the Old Testament. But we are bound to love and show compassion as Jesus did.

> An expert in the law tested [Jesus] with this question: "Teacher, which is the greatest commandment in the Law?"
>
> Jesus replied: "'Love the Lord your God with all your heart and with all your soul and with all your mind.' This is the first and greatest commandment. And the second is like it: 'Love your neighbor as yourself.' All the Law and the Prophets hang on these two commandments" (Matthew 22:35-40).

From Shadows to Light

Colossians 2:17 teaches that the Law was only a shadow of reality, which is found in Christ. Yes, there are many parallels between Old Testament shadows and New Testament realities, but the two covenants are distinct. Today the Old Testament is obsolete (Hebrews 8:13). Let's leave the shadows of the old covenant and come into the light. That's where real freedom is.

A Quick Review

Because of moral and spiritual compromise, the Israelites were doomed to wander in the desert. After the glorious triumph of the Exodus, what should have taken only 40 days actually took 40 years. This makes for an interesting backlight to Jesus' own successful 40 days of testing in the desert 50 generations later. The Israelites failed to enter the Promised Land in Exodus, but they received four magnificent things: God's redemption, his Law, his mission, and his name.

In Leviticus, through the sacrificial system and other regulations associated with the priesthood, Israel was called to be holy. Viewed another way, whereas in Exodus God's purpose is to get his people out of Egypt, in Leviticus it is to get Egypt out of his people. Numbers highlights several obstacles: challenges to Moses' leadership, intertribal tensions, and multiple temptations to sin. Last, in Deuteronomy, which was written for the generation that finally entered the Promised Land, the Law is given a second time, updated for the conditions of settled existence in Canaan. In the next chapter we will study Israel's entry into Canaan, their conquest of the land, and the ensuing period of spiritual anarchy.

THE CONQUEST, CONFEDERATION, AND MONARCHY

Now fear the LORD and serve him with all faithfulness. Throw away
the gods your ancestors worshiped beyond the Euphrates River
and in Egypt, and serve the LORD. But if serving the LORD seems
undesirable to you, then choose for yourselves this day whom
you will serve, whether the gods your ancestors served beyond
the Euphrates, or the gods of the Amorites, in whose land you are
living. But as for me and my household, we will serve the LORD.

JOSHUA 24:14-15

The Exodus generation, with the exception of Joshua and Caleb,
failed to make it into Canaan. Instead, their children inherited the
Promised Land. We read about the conquest in the book of Joshua.
This is followed by the period of the judges (rulers), recounted in Judges,
Ruth, and 1 Samuel 1–8. The monarchy emerges from this time of spiritual chaos. The united kingdom, however, does not last long (1 Samuel
9–1 Kings 11), and after the death of Solomon, the kingdom is divided
in two (1 Kings 12; 2 Chronicles 36). Because of persistent sin, especially in the lives of the leaders, the Israelites are exiled—the northern kingdom (Israel) under the Assyrians in 722 BC and the southern
kingdom (Judah) under the Babylonians in 587 BC. In chapters 9 and
10 we looked at the first five books of the Old Testament; this chapter
will lead us through the next nine books. The time frame is from about
1250 to 587 BC.

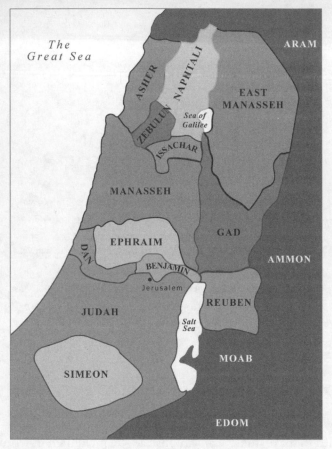

The twelve tribes of Israel.

Conquest

Joshua, who was appointed Moses' successor (Numbers 27:15-23) and called to be a man of great courage (Joshua 1:6-9,18), wages two military campaigns against Canaan. The first begins after the Israelites cross the Jordan from the east. The first city to fall is Jericho. This southern campaign is followed by the northern campaign, beginning with the capital of the northern Canaanite federation, Hazor. The second half of Joshua relates the mammoth task of apportioning the land to the tribes, followed by a call to Israel to spiritual faithfulness. Let me now address several misunderstandings about the conquest.

1. Only three cities were totally destroyed (Jericho, Ai, and Hazor), which is consistent with archaeological evidence (burning in the destruction levels). Thus Joshua's warfare was no scorched-earth campaign.

2. The Canaanites were driven out more than they were exterminated. With plenty of advance warning, they were evacuated from the land.

3. Many Canaanites intermarried with the Israelites. The biblical and archaeological evidence supports the thesis that they were absorbed more than displaced or destroyed. Their spiritual standards were low (as we saw in chapter 8), so such interblending obviously portends trouble for Israel.

4. The casualties of battles were nearly exclusively soldiers, not civilians.

5. Descriptions of the battles may read as if the campaign was one massive blitzkrieg, but the end of Joshua and the beginning of Judges make clear that the job is far from finished. The conquest was only a partial success.

THE JUDGES AND THEIR TRIBAL ORIGINS

Othniel (Judah)	Jephthah (Gilead)
Ehud (Benjamin)	Ibzan (Bethlehem, but not the city of David)
Shamgar (?)	
Deborah (Ephraim)	Elon (Zebulun)
Gideon (Manasseh)	Abdon (Ephraim)
Tola (Issachar)	Samson (Dan)
Jair (Gilead)	Samuel (Ephraim)

Confederation

Following the death of Joshua, a series of judges (better translated as *rulers*) led Israel. The tribes were only loosely allied—a situation somewhat resembling the United States during the years it was governed by the Articles of Confederation, before its Constitution and the emergence of a strong central government.

Twelve of these rulers are mentioned in the book of Judges. Samuel, who does not appear until the book that bears his name, will later serve as a pivotal figure. He was the last of the judges and appointed the first king, Saul. The book of Ruth, the eighth book of the Old Testament, fits into this time period. Again, let us clear up some of the misconceptions about this period of Israel's history.

1. The tribes were politically disjointed but ethnically and culturally connected.

2. No single judge (with the possible exception of Samuel, who came later) ruled over all of Israel. The judges' influence normally extended only a short distance beyond their own tribe.

3. The judges' periods of leadership must have overlapped. Judges 11:26, 1 Kings 6:1, and other passages make it clear that their reigns cannot simply be laid end-to-end.

4. Unlike the kings, who would come later, the judges were charismatic leaders and often exhibited miraculous powers.

5. This period was spiritually and politically turbulent. The nation was caught in a death loop of apostasy, divine punishment (usually through the oppression of enemies), desperation and repentance, and finally deliverance—only for the cycle to repeat (Judges 2:10-19).

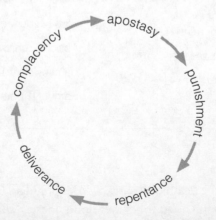

The point Judges is making is that in the absence of a king, the people wander in a state of spiritual chaos. And yet the point of the book is not so much that Israel needs a human king (read 1 Samuel 8) as that they need *God* to be their king—and he clearly isn't. This vital theological lesson is repeated in Judges 17:6; 18:1; 19:1; 21:25.

Monarchy

Samuel appoints Saul to be king over Israel (around 1050 BC), but the country isn't fully united until the time of David and his son Solomon. The chapters pertaining to the united kingdom are 1 Samuel 9–1 Kings 10. This is a time of relative peace (despite problems with Philistines). Yet it lasted barely a century, and the nation split in 931 BC.

Saul, David, and Solomon, the first three kings, are the best known of all. Not to say there aren't other memorable monarchs. Among the rulers of Judah, the colorful Jehoshaphat, Hezekiah, Manasseh, and Josiah are well known. Among the rulers of Israel, who could forget Ahab and Jezebel, or Jehu? Yet overall, the kingdoms' experiment with the kingship was a failure, for the kingdom of God will not be ushered in through politics or government. Even in our day we must take care not to place our hope in institutions that can never bring us to God or meet our deepest needs. In fact, the Lord allowed Samuel to anoint Saul the first king of Israel only reluctantly.

> So all the elders of Israel gathered together and came to Samuel at Ramah. They said to him, "…Appoint a king to lead us, such as all the other nations have."…This displeased Samuel; so he prayed to the LORD. And the LORD told him: "Listen to all that the people are saying to you; it is not you they have rejected, but they have rejected me as their king. As they have done from the day I brought them up out of Egypt until this day, forsaking me and serving other gods, so they are doing to you" (1 Samuel 8:4-8).

Three Kings

Saul, of the tribe of Benjamin, reigned as the first of the kings of

Israel from about 1050 to about 1010 BC. He initially showed signs of promise, but his propensity to rationalization and jealousy quickly disqualified him as king. His son Jonathan was killed in battle, so his dynasty came to an end. As 1 Chronicles 10:13-14 put it, Saul died because of unfaithfulness to the Lord.

David, from the tribe of Judah, was his successor (1010–970 BC). Under his leadership, Israel took Jerusalem from the Jebusites. He reigned 7½ years in Hebron and 33 more in Jerusalem. His glaring weaknesses included adultery with Bathsheba and the murder of her husband, Uriah; reliance on the flesh in the census he ordered (2 Samuel 24; 1 Chronicles 21); and a detached parenting style that allowed his family to run amok (2 Samuel 12–24). And yet more than any other king, David was renowned for his capacity for repentance (2 Samuel 12; Psalm 51). He was an inspiring leader (2 Samuel 23) and a courageous man (1 Samuel 17). He wrote many fervent psalms and is most remembered for his spirituality as a man after God's own heart (Acts 13:22). His dynasty was perpetuated through his son Solomon and lasted 400 years.

The expected Messiah, one of whose epithets was Son of David, was to come from the tribe of Judah, the lineage of David, and the town of David, Bethlehem (Genesis 49:10; Ezekiel 34:23; Micah 5:2). Jesus Christ perfectly fulfilled these expectations.

Under Solomon (970–931 BC), the borders of the kingdom reached their maximum geographical extent. He had an encyclopedic knowledge (1 Kings 4:29-34), was a skilled administrator (1 Kings 3; 2 Chronicles 1), forged good diplomatic relationships with surrounding nations, and built the temple, which replaced the portable tabernacle. He is also credited with the writing of much of the Old Testament wisdom literature: a bit of Psalms, much of Proverbs, Ecclesiastes, and Song of Solomon. On the negative side, his leadership style could be oppressive (1 Kings 12:4), and he was guilty of serious spiritual compromise (1 Kings 11:1-8; be sure to compare this with Deuteronomy 17:14-20). Immediately after his death the kingdom ruptured, with only the southern kingdom (called Judah and comprised of the tribes of Judah, Benjamin, and part of Levi) remaining faithful to the Law of Moses.

Two Kingdoms

Solomon's son Rehoboam was insecure and overly aggressive as a young leader (1 Kings 12). Unfortunately this led to the secession of the northern tribes, who retained the name Israel, while the southern part of the united kingdom was called Judah.[1] The roots of north–south antipathy were deep, dating back to hostility among the sons of Jacob (Genesis 37). It was mirrored in the strife concerning the trans-Jordan tribes (Joshua 22) and intertribal struggles in the period of the Judges (Judges 8–9; 12; 17–21), and it was exacerbated when Judah and some Israelites turned against Saul during his reign (1 Samuel 22; 30; 1 Chronicles 10–11). Even after Saul's death, Ishbosheth ruled over the ten northern tribes, while David ruled over Judah at Hebron (2 Samuel 2). All Israel eventually came under the reign of David and Solomon but only for 73 years.

The period of the two kingdoms lasted from 931 until the northern kingdom fell to Assyria in 722 BC, after which the southern kingdom stood alone until the final Babylonian assault of 587 BC. The fall of Jerusalem and the destruction of Solomon's temple at the hand of the Babylonians were tragically paralleled by the fall of Jerusalem and destruction of Herod's temple at the hand of the Romans in AD 70. Tradition has it that both temples fell on the same day of the year.

Let us return to the north–south split. Rehoboam's rival, Jeroboam I, ignoring the prophetic words that challenged his independent move, essentially started his own religion. He watered down religious requirements for priests and worshippers alike (1 Kings 12). Rather than risk the northern tribes reverting to Jerusalem, he established conveniently located shrines at Dan and Bethel (in violation of God's command in Deuteronomy 12) and set up golden calves as worship objects (redolent of Aaron's folly in Exodus 32). Jeroboam removed the legitimate Levitical priests (ignoring the directives in Numbers 18) and instituted a rival festival to the Feast of Tabernacles (described in Leviticus 23). The expectations for membership were low, and sin was winked at. The goal was to preserve the status quo.

Through Israel's entire decline into spiritual malaise, the prophets persistently warned God's people of the dangers of idolatry and of the

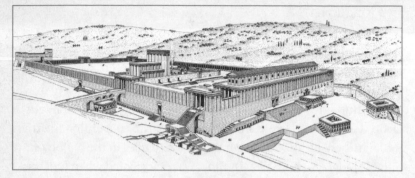

The temple mount.

judgment certain to come. Yet the words of Amos, Micah, Hosea, Isaiah, Jeremiah, Habakkuk, Zephaniah, and others were ignored. The southern kingdom was somewhat responsive to the voice of the prophets in the lead-up to the Assyrian siege of Jerusalem in 701 BC. After that, Judah too gradually slid into spiritual decline. (Scan the list of the kings of Judah and Israel on page 72 for a visual grasp of the declining faithfulness of the southern kings.) Overall, it would be fair to say that Judah was *frequently* unfaithful and Israel was *consistently* unfaithful. Keep in mind that these comments in the Bible are not anti-Semitic. These criticisms stem from Jewish critics of their own people.

In keeping with the threat of captivity in the books of the Law (issued in such passages as Leviticus 26 and Deuteronomy 28), God used Assyria and Babylon to chasten his people (Isaiah 10). This effectively constituted the end of Israel's political sovereignty, although beginning in the second century BC, after the Maccabean revolt, Israel enjoyed approximately one century of political autonomy before the Romans put an end to that.

A Quick Review

Israel's conquest of the Promised Land was only a partial success. Instead of taking it as their possession, Israel intermarried with the local peoples and stooped to their low spiritual standards. Out of the chaotic period of the judges emerged the monarchy, patterned on the political plan of the pagan nations. Yet the Lord's way was divine theocracy, not human autocracy. Neither morality nor spirituality could be leg-islated, and after Solomon's reign, the kingdom fractured. The north-ern kingdom slid precipitously into compromise and was taken into exile by the Assyrians two centuries later. The southern kingdom held on to God for another century and a half before being led into cap-tivity by the Babylonians. Understanding how their spiritual compro-mise impacted their history is essential for making sense of the history of the Old Testament.

Why did things go so badly? The voice of the prophets, who called the people back to the Law, was usually ignored. People preferred a more reassuring voice, as we will see in the next chapter.

12

PROPHETS FALSE AND TRUE

The lion has roared—who will not fear?
The Sovereign LORD has spoken—who can but prophesy?

AMOS 3:8

I f the Israelites had lived by the Law of the Lord, they would have fulfilled their mission to be a light to the nations. They would have enjoyed a deep and rich relationship with her God. And they could have avoided centuries of heartache, dislocation, and alienation. Yet the Lord does not force us to follow him; we always have a choice (Deuteronomy 30:11-20; Joshua 24:14-15). That does not mean, however, that he won't send us reminders of what is right and true. The prophets were spokesmen for God (Exodus 7:1; Deuteronomy 18:14-22; 1 Samuel 3:19-21; Amos 3:7). Through them, God spoke the message he wanted people to hear; they never "spun" their revelations from God. From the ninth century BC to the fifth, the Lord reminded Israel of his holy Law through the prophets. The Law of Moses was being neglected. A holy God cannot ignore such negligence.

Voices of Dissent

The refrains of the prophets were several. The following themes appear in many of the prophetic books, and most prophets proclaimed all of them.

- Do not compromise with pagan idolatry.
- Resist the allure of the world.

- Turn back to the Law of God.

- Faith and ethics are inseparable.

- Take care of the underprivileged.

- There is hope for the repentant but doom for the impenitent.

Doom and Hope

Indeed, the prophets brought messages of doom and messages of hope. For those who preferred a more lax approach to faith, these radicals were "unbearable extremists," as Rabbi Abraham Heschel describes them in his classic work *The Prophets*. This trenchant section is aptly called "The Blast from Heaven."

> To a person endowed with prophetic sight, everyone else appears blind; to a person whose ear perceives God's voice, everyone else appears deaf. No one is just; no knowing is strong enough, no trust complete enough. The prophet hates the approximate; he shuns the middle of the road. Man must live on the summit to avoid the abyss. There is nothing to hold on to except God. Carried away by the challenge, the demand to straighten out man's ways, the prophet is strange, one-sided, an unbearable extremist...
>
> The prophet disdains those for whom God's presence is comfort and security; to him it is a challenge, an incessant demand. God is compassion, but not compromise; justice, though not inclemency. The prophet's predictions can always be proved wrong by a change in man's conduct, but never the certainty that God is full of compassion.
>
> The prophet's word is a scream in the night. While the world is at ease and asleep, the prophet feels the blast from heaven.[1]

Heschel is right. Yet not all the prophets of the Old Testament so faithfully represented the holy God. In fact, the majority who called themselves prophets were nothing of the kind; they implicitly rejected the word of God, replacing it with their own oracles of comfort. For example, in 1 Kings 18 the fearless Elijah challenges the 850 prophets of Baal and Asherah. In 1 Kings 22, the audacious Micaiah confronts the 400 mendacious prophets of Ahab. The true prophet has always been outnumbered by the false, even as those following the Way (Acts 9:2) have always been outnumbered by faith's fair-weather friends—those merely claiming to follow (Titus 1:16).

After looking more closely at the true prophets, we will also examine the message of the false ones. The prophetic books make up at least 30 percent of the Old Testament, so the insights we glean will serve us well as we continue to explore God's word.

Prophet	Approximate dates BC	References
Moses	1290–1250	Deuteronomy 18:17; 34:10
Elijah	870–850	1 Kings 17:1– 2 Kings 2:18
Elisha	855–800	1 Kings 19:16-21; 2 Kings 2:1–9:3; 13:14-21
Jonah	785–745	2 Kings 14:25; Jonah
Hosea	785–745	Hosea
Amos	760–750	Amos
Isaiah	740–700	2 Kings 19–20; Isaiah
Micah	735–710	Jeremiah 26:18; Micah
Nahum	686–612	Nahum
Zephaniah	640–622	Zephaniah
Jeremiah	626–586	2 Chronicles 36:12; Jeremiah
Habakkuk	612–605	Habakkuk
Daniel	605–530	Daniel
Ezekiel	593–573	Ezekiel

Prophet	Approximate dates BC	References
Obadiah	586	Obadiah
Joel	586 (?)	Joel
Haggai	522–515	Haggai
Zechariah	522–515	Zechariah
Malachi	435	Malachi

Canonical and Noncanonical Prophets

Canonical prophets are those after whom books in the canon of Scripture are named. The main noncanonical prophets were Moses (thirteenth century BC), Elijah and Elisha (ninth century), to say nothing of Deborah, Huldah, and other prophetesses. They were dynamic characters, daring to speak truth and work miracles. (Other prophets were not charismatically endowed.) Elijah and Elisha are not known as writing prophets, though one letter of Elijah has survived (2 Chronicles 21:12-15). Lesser known noncanonical prophets include Ahijah, Azariah, Eliezer, Gad, Hanani, Iddo, Jehu, Micaiah, Nathan, and Obed.

The major canonical prophets are Isaiah (740–700 BC), Jeremiah (626–586 BC), and Ezekiel (593–573 BC). In the Christian Bible, Daniel (605–530 BC) is also reckoned among the prophets, though in the Hebrew Bible he is not included among the prophets at all. Most prophesied before the two exiles, though the ministries of some reached past the Babylonian captivity, including Jeremiah, Habakkuk, Ezekiel, Obadiah, and Daniel.

Prosperity Theology

Most of the prophets spoke in the 300-year window from the 700s to the 400s BC, a time of rapid socioeconomic change. Amos, Hosea, Micah, and Isaiah, for example, challenged the Israelites in the eighth century. The 760s and 750s were boom years. International trade was strong, neighboring nations were too weak or distracted to constitute any significant threat to the prosperity of Israel, and the borders were restored to the limits of 931 BC (the end of the reign of Solomon). Yet while the leisured upper class lived a decadent lifestyle (Amos 2:8; 4:1; 6:1), the poor were oppressed. God seemed to be smiling on the aristocracy. The people misinterpreted their situation: "God is good. Life is good. Doesn't prosperity mean the Lord is with us?"

The prophets knew better. The rich were smugly ignoring God's laws regarding the treatment and care for the poor (Deuteronomy 15:4-8,11; Leviticus 25). Through the prophets, God let them know that judgment would follow. In contrast to pagan religion, where faith and ethics were separated, biblical religion always insists on righteousness (Micah 6:8; James 2:14-26; 1 John 3:16-18). Those who do not actively love their fellow man are deceiving themselves. The Lord is not on their side. What a crucial lesson for our own day, when so many churches tout a popular prosperity theology: "Put Jesus first, and God will bless you financially."

The Nature of Prophecy

The prophets' messages generally pertained to their present situation (as they were primarily heralds of truth) or to the immediate future, not the distant future. ("Repent now, or next year your nation will be invaded.") There was no guesswork in prophecy; their messages needed to be completely accurate, under penalty of death (Deuteronomy 18:20). God gave his people a clear way to know whether a prophet was anointed by him. If he was a true prophet, his prophecies came true (Deuteronomy 18:21-22). Last, as Rabbi Heschel noted, there was always room for God's intervention (Jeremiah 18:7-10; Jonah 3:10). God is merciful, and he longs for the repentance of his lost sons and daughters (Ezekiel 18:32; Luke 15:11-32).

Sometimes God spoke his message directly to the prophets (1 Samuel 3:19-21), but more often their oracles were based on visions mediated by dreams (Numbers 12:6). Joseph and Daniel even had the ability to interpret dreams.

Last, their oracles were delivered not only to Judah and Israel but also to a number of nearby nations. Obadiah preached to Edom, Jonah and Nahum to Assyria, Daniel and Ezekiel to Babylon.

Creativity

The prophets' teaching methods were interesting, catchy, memorable. Not that they attempted to entertain—only to grab people's attention. Then they plunged the knife of truth into the heart and twisted. The only acceptable outcome was repentance. Their message was never novel, but their methods were certainly varied.

allegories (Ezekiel 16)

apocalyptic imagery (Isaiah 24–27)

everyday illustrations (Isaiah 45:9)

lessons from history (Nahum 3:8)

letters (2 Chronicles 21:12)

metaphors (Ezekiel 31:3)

parables (2 Samuel 12:1-10)

parody (Isaiah 44:12)

proverbs (Ezekiel 18:2)

puns (Jeremiah 1:12)

sarcasm (1 Kings 18:27)

symbolic actions (Hosea 1:2)

symbolic names (Isaiah 7:3,14)

visual aids (Ezekiel 4:1)

Such a panoply underscores God's concern for us—that he communicates his message in multiple ways—whereas we sometimes tend to put God in a box, thinking we know it all, flattening the text as though the entire Bible were literal prose. We need to leave room for alternative modes of expression, variations in style, and even for the element of surprise. Such diversity within God's revelation underscores the importance of literary sensitivity—of cultivating more reflective ways of reading the text. In other words, we should open our minds to the way the Bible *is* as opposed to the way we supposed it would be.

Dress and Pay

The prophets led colorful lives in more ways than one. Many wore strikingly distinctive dress—a hairy garment (2 Kings 1:8; Zechariah 13:4; Matthew 3:4). They were paid for their work with persecution (Amos 7:12; Zechariah 13:5-6; Matthew 5:12; 23:37; Luke 6:22-23; Acts 7:52). The false prophets too wore the prophet's garb, belonged to professional prophetic guilds, and received compensation. Yet they were not persecuted (Luke 6:26). Why is that?

The Message of the Popular (False) Prophets

How did the false prophets modify the message of God so as not to cause offense—to retain their popularity with the world?

- They soft-pedaled sin (Lamentations 2:14), proffering a comforting platform of "peace, peace" (Jeremiah 6:14).

- Sexual sin was not only tolerated but celebrated (Numbers 25:1-18).

- They lived lives of self-indulgence (Isaiah 56:10-12; 2 Peter 2:1-22).

- Participation in the temple activities was deemed sufficient despite significant failings in morality and justice (Jeremiah 7:4).

- Worship of other gods was permitted and even encouraged (Jeremiah 44:17-18). Some false prophets claimed to represent Yahweh, but their eclecticism incorporated elements of idolatry.

- A premium was placed on political correctness. False hope was derived from strength in numbers (1 Kings 22:13).

- They interpreted prosperity as a sign of divine favor (Zechariah 11:5). As long as the establishment was flourishing financially, they aligned themselves with and supported the status quo.

- Religious acts were believed to manipulate God (1 Kings 18:16-29).

- They appealed strongly to the subjective (Jeremiah 23:25), downplaying the word of God.

- They gave voice to "lying spirits," perhaps even Satan, rather than God or his angels (1 Kings 22:22).

- They opposed the true prophets as extremists who demanded too much commitment (Numbers 16).

Many of these popular prophets were charismatics: They impressed others through their claimed miraculous abilities and direct access to the will of God. Although they claimed to speak from God, their messages originated in their own minds. Their dreams were delusions, merely psychological, diluting the commitment of the people by imparting false hope. To some extent they expected the Lord to speak to them, yet in their minds God's word and their word were hopelessly confused (Jeremiah 23:9-40). The Bible warns us of any spiritual experience that contradicts the word of God, even if it appears to be genuine (Deuteronomy 13:1-5; 2 Thessalonians 2:9-11), so we should never follow a path that leads us away from the Lord, despite the agent's impressive credentials (Galatians 1:7-8; 2 Corinthians 11:3-15; Colossians 2:18-19).

By now two things should be clear: why the masses favored the false prophets over the true, and why human religions worldwide, even in our own day, tend to follow popular trends rather than overturn them.

The Cessation of Prophecy

The voice of prophecy was apparently stilled sometime after the 400s BC. This is the consistent view of the Jewish writers from the time of Malachi till the end of the first century AD.[2]

Renewal of Prophecy Under John

The voice of prophecy was renewed in the person of John the Baptist (late AD 20s), who prepared the way for the coming of the Messiah. It is important to note that John the Baptist was not the same person as the apostle John. The Baptist's appearance is prophesied in the Old Testament (Isaiah 40:3; Malachi 3:1) and recorded in all four Gospels and Acts.[3]

Many scholars agree that he was a Nazirite (Numbers 6; Luke 1:15), as were Samson and Samuel. His message: We need to get right with our fellow man if we are to get right with God. His was a ministry of reconciliation (Malachi 4:5-6; Luke 3:11-14). He also accustomed people to immersion for forgiveness of sins and explained that baptism under Christ would confer the long-awaited Holy Spirit. He humbly directed his disciples to follow Jesus (John 1:6-8,15,19-35).

Prophecy was also vibrantly present in the church of New Testament times (Acts 2:17-18; 11:27-30; 21:10-11; Ephesians 3:5; 4:11). Today, however, the foundation of the apostles and the New Testament prophets has been laid (Ephesians 2:20). One can argue about whether the voice of the prophet is still present in the church of the twenty-first century, but no one can deny that the world desperately needs prophetic preaching and teaching. To this all true believers can and should commit themselves.

Reading the Prophets

The prophets called the people of God back to the Law of God. They did not generate new doctrines or give new commands. Everything points back to the Torah. Keep this in mind as you read through the major prophets (Isaiah–Ezekiel) and the minor prophets (Hosea–Malachi). All of these men prophesied in the 700s to 400s BC, a three-century window when the people of God were slipping spiritually. Here are three keys for benefiting from their messages.

1. Read Deuteronomy 28 and Leviticus 26, which include rewards for following the covenant and penalties for violating it. Much of the language of the prophets refers to promises related to Moses and the Law.

2. The prophets' writings tend to be arranged topically, not chronologically. Material dealing with similar themes tends to be grouped together. Chronological indicators occasionally appear, but many of the prophetic oracles contain no indicator pointing to the original time and circumstances of the oracle. Notice the scheme and focus on the theme. Don't obsess over the chronologically erratic.

3. Where possible, envision yourself acting prophetically—sharing

with your friends about God, speaking up at work about discrimination or a breach of company policy, or reminding your family about the righteous standards of God.

A Quick Review

The prophets strove to call the people back to the Law of Moses but with only limited success. The Jews preferred rather to listen to the more comforting, less challenging words of the false prophets. This perspective helps us to make sense of the flow of Old Testament history, which featured a constant alternation between commitment and compromise.

Believers in Christ must not imagine themselves beyond succumbing to similar temptations. The apostles foretold a day when the community would be overrun by false teachers (Acts 20:29-30; 2 Timothy 4:3-4; 2 Peter 3:1-3; 1 John 4:1; Jude 4). Jesus Christ explained that the popular prophets would reject the narrow way of his teachings, offering instead a more palatable and dazzling way of faith. They would stray from the word of God (Matthew 7:13-23). As with the ancient Jews, so with us—there are consequences to hardening our hearts to the word of God (Ephesians 4:17-19).

Finally, all believers are called to speak out prophetically. Indeed, unless we are resisting the Holy Spirit, we cannot help but do so (Acts 4:20; Romans 1:16-17; 1 Corinthians 9:16).

THE EXILE AND RETURN

When the LORD restored the fortunes of Zion,
we were like those who dreamed.
Our mouths were filled with laughter,
our tongues with songs of joy.

PSALM 126:1-2

This chapter covers the exilic and postexilic events that occurred from the late 700s to the late 400s BC. These events can be generally summarized like this:

- Assyria takes the northern kingdom into exile (732–539 BC)
- Babylon takes the southern kingdom into exile (605–539 BC)
- the fall of Jerusalem (587 BC)
- life in exile
- the Jews' return (539 BC)
- life after the return

This is our last chapter on Old Testament history, yet really it's a chapter on God's goodness and grace. You may recall that in earlier chapters (7, 9–11) we examined the historical flow from creation to the fall of Jerusalem in 587 BC. In chapter 11, we left the southern kingdom of Judah facing their Babylonian attackers. A period of some 70 years will elapse between the first deportation in 605 BC and the resettlement under the Persian Cyrus the Great in 538. In chapter 12 we suggested that much of Jewish history makes best sense when interpreted in connection with the people's obedience to the Law of Moses—depending on whether they accepted or stifled the prophetic voice. As we will see in this chapter, divine discipline is followed by divine grace.

Assyria Takes the Northern Kingdom into Exile

In the eighth century BC, Assyria was increasing in military strength. Meanwhile, the northern kingdom of Israel not only engaged in many transgressions of idolatry and oppression but also put its trust in political alliances rather than in Yahweh. The capital city of Samaria fell first. Then, ten years later, all of the ten northern tribes were led away into captivity. At this time the Assyrians even captured many of the towns in the southern kingdom of Judah, but Jerusalem held firm. It was not Judah's time. In short, Israel was exiled because of sin. Here are six historical facts about the captivity.

1. Samaria fell in 732 BC.

2. The entire northern kingdom fell in 722. The Jews did not return from captivity until 539, so Israel's captivity lasted more than a century and a half.

3. Such powerful prophets as Amos, Joel, Hosea, Isaiah, and Micah tried to avert the destruction through their preaching, but their message fell on deaf ears.

4. Second Kings 17 details the enormous degree of syncretism (blending of religious traditions) at this time. It also explains the origin of the Samaritans, a mixed race born of foreigners the Assyrians forcibly settled in the land.

5. In 701 BC the Assyrian army besieged Jerusalem, but through his humble faith, King Hezekiah averted catastrophe.

6. After Assyria took the northern kingdom into exile, we can speak of "the ten lost tribes" (the other two, Judah and Benjamin, were in the southern kingdom). They were lost to history—not by destruction or dislocation, but through intermarriage with the Gentiles. This is not to say they ceased to exist, but that the purity of their genealogical

pedigree was compromised. They were no longer identifiable as genetically pure members of their ancestral tribes.

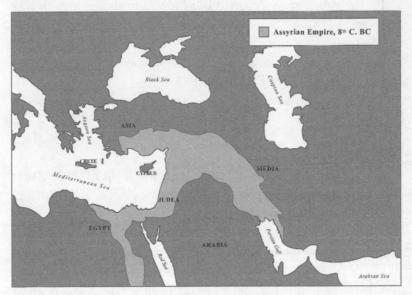

The Assyrian Empire.

Babylon Takes the Southern Kingdom into Exile

The two southern tribes comprising Judah eventually followed in the footsteps of their northern neighbors, sliding into apostasy. Though the Lord sent prophets, they were heeded less and less. And the popular prophets of the day failed to bring revival to the nation. Lamentations 2:14 is telling: "The visions of your prophets were false and worthless; they did not expose your sin to ward off your captivity. The prophecies they gave you were false and misleading." Here are six of the salient facts.

1. Babylon took Nineveh, the Assyrian capital, in 612 BC. As Assyria continued to weaken, the Egyptians grew stronger (609–605 BC). In 609 Judah's King Josiah was killed at Megiddo by Pharaoh Neco (2 Kings 23:29). Then the Egyptians were defeated by the rising nation of the Babylonians at Carchemish in 605 BC (Jeremiah 46:2).

2. The Lord sent Isaiah, Zephaniah, Jeremiah, and Habakkuk, but they were largely ignored.

3. The Babylonians deported the Judeans in three waves in 605, 597, and 587 BC.

4. Jerusalem, along with its beautiful temple, was destroyed in 587.

5. In Babylon the Judean captives presumably joined a handful of survivors from the northern kingdom (Israel).

6. The captivity (reckoned from 605 to 539 BC) spanned seven decades, as prophesied in Jeremiah 25:9-12 and Daniel 9:1-3.

The Fall of Jerusalem

The unbelievable finally happened: Jerusalem fell (2 Kings 25). After a siege of a year and a half, the city fell in the summer of 587 BC. Siege conditions were horrific. The prophet Jeremiah predicted the destruction that would follow if Judah ignored the voice of Yahweh. The book of Lamentations, traditionally attributed to Jeremiah, expresses the shock, devastation, and hopelessness of the remnant. But Jeremiah also shares a glimmer of hope for God's people. Thus the two books can be viewed in this way: Jeremiah is the "before," and Lamentations is the "after." To better envision the stress and horror of times of siege (including loss of morale, crisis of faith, starvation, and even cannibalism), read Lamentations 1:1-9,11-12,20-21; 2:11-13; 4:3-10.[1] This was a "dress rehearsal" for the even more tragic and permanent fall of Jerusalem at the end of the First Jewish War in AD 70.

The alliance of the kingdoms of Media and Persia eclipsed Babylon in 539. Soon after, the Persian king decreed a return to Israel for all the Jews who wanted to go back.

Although one would naturally think the Jews would have plunged into a dark age during this period, they actually made great advances in faith, theology, and spiritual maturity. Here is a summary of the key dates in this period:

605—first Babylonian deportation

597—second wave of deportation

587—Jerusalem falls

539—Persia takes power from Babylon

538—the Jews are permitted to return

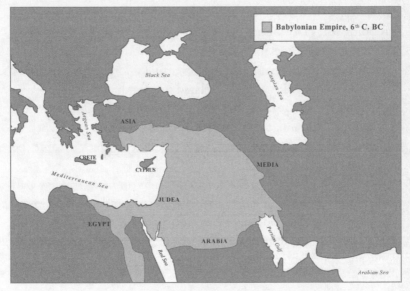

The Babylonian Empire.

Life in Exile

Life in exile threw the Jewish community of faith into crisis. How could the Jews exist as a nation of God apart from their promised land? Where was the God of justice? And yet the deportation had been explicitly predicted in the Law and the Prophets. Just as Adam and Eve were expelled on account of their sin, so the Jews had been forcibly removed. The Jews may have been thrown off guard, but this was no surprise to the Lord.

What was life like in Babylon? What changed? Consider the following new realities.

Feelings of sadness. See Psalms 126; 137. The people were separated from their homeland, temple (now in ruins), and in many cases, friends and families.

Politics. Without political autonomy, the exile was a virtual return to the days of Egypt. Foreigners were once again giving the orders. After centuries of mounting frustration, especially once the Greeks came to power (in the fourth century BC) and attempted to force pagan culture on the Jews, there was a violent protest. Tensions erupted in the Maccabean revolt (in the second century BC). This led to a short season of autonomy (the Hasmonean period) that ended when the Roman general Pompey took Israel in 63 BC.

Language. The Jews in captivity eventually forgot how to speak Hebrew and adopted Aramaic, a related tongue that had become the international language of the day. Many chapters of the Old Testament were written in Aramaic, especially in Ezra and Daniel. In Egypt and other locations where the Jews had been scattered, Greek became the mother tongue.

Theology. With time to reflect, and through contact with new Babylonian and Zoroastrian ideas, the Jews were stimulated to develop many doctrines that had only been embryonic in the Hebrew Scriptures, including the resurrection; angels, demons, and Satan; numerology; and apocalyptic thought.

Organization. In the absence of temple worship and other traditional religious structures, this is most likely the time when synagogues were first formed. Synagogues are not places of sacrifice, but rather places where small groups gather to study and discuss the Torah.

Scriptures. The Jews took stock of their sacred writings. Some of the earlier books (such as those of the Pentateuch) went through their final editions, and others were penned for the first time (including Esther, Ezra–Nehemiah, and Chronicles).

The Jews' Return

The return from exile had been promised in the Law (Deuteronomy 30:1-5) as well as in the Prophets (Jeremiah 29). This fulfilled the "70 years" prophecy of Jeremiah (25:1-14; 29:10; Daniel 9:2). The 70 years can be calculated from 605 to 538 BC if construed as an approximation. The Lord had never intended to punish his unfaithful people permanently; after the Fall came an opportunity of grace. How did God bring his people back to Israel?

Once the Persians overcame Babylon, the fortunes of the Jews changed. Persia reversed several of the more restrictive policies of the Assyrians and Babylonians. Rather than executing national leaders, deporting the population, and settling conquered territory with outsiders, the Persians preferred to rule through local leadership. They even subsidized the religions of those they conquered.

Remnants of both kingdoms of Israel were given the option to return home to their land by royal decree in 539 BC. The imperial edict is recorded not only in 2 Chronicles 36:22-23 and Ezra 1:1-4 but also on the famous Cyrus Cylinder, currently housed in the British Museum. The prophet Isaiah goes so far as to call Cyrus, the Persian king, the Lord's "anointed" (the same Hebrew word that can be translated *messiah*), specially chosen to rebuild Jerusalem and set the exiles free (Isaiah 45:1,13). Yet it is clear that many did not want to return, and even among those who made the difficult transition back to the land of the patriarchs, some did not necessarily want to live in Jerusalem (Nehemiah 11:1). To this day, Jews who live outside of the Holy Land are called the *Diaspora* (Greek for *dispersion*).

Eventually, however, the Persians were overthrown by Alexander the Great in 331 BC, during the intertestamental period, which we will visit in the next chapter. The Greeks were not so accommodating of the Jewish religion.

MODERN ISRAEL

The Balfour Declaration of 1917 and the eventual reestablishment of the modern state of Israel in 1948 are not direct fulfillments of the prophesied return to the land. They are 2454 years too late. Israel *did* return to her land after the decree of the king of Persia in 539–538 BC. Moreover, most orthodox rabbis reject twentieth-century political events as in any way fulfilling prophecy. By and large, secular Jews (mainly agnostics and atheists) reformed the modern state of Israel. This is not to say that the Lord may not have special plans for Israel or for any other nation—but this is difficult to prove from Scripture. Thus those who see current Middle Eastern events in the Scriptures, or who predict doomsday in connection with events in the Arab world, are on shaky ground.

Life After the Return

The exiles who returned to the land found it rough going. The Persian period included many physical, political, and spiritual obstacles to rebuilding the nation. This is what they accomplished in the late 500s and the 400s BC.

- The temple was rebuilt. Work started in 536 BC but soon came to a halt. This was revived in 520 BC, and the second temple was finally completed in 516–515 BC thanks to the encouraging preaching of Haggai and Zechariah, two of the minor prophets (Ezra 5:1-2,16; 6:15).

- Genocide was averted through the courage of Esther in 480 BC.

- The Law and the joy of communal Scripture study were restored under the teaching priest, Ezra, in 458 BC. Read about it in Nehemiah 8.

- The walls of Jerusalem were rebuilt under the bold leadership of Nehemiah and with significant constructive community action in 445 BC. Study Nehemiah 1–6.

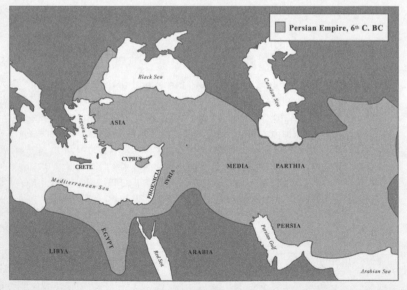

The Persian Empire.

- Pure worship was demanded by a prophet in 435 BC. Read the sermon in the short book of Malachi.

- A number of Old Testament books were written: Ezra–Nehemiah (originally a single work), Esther, Haggai, Zechariah, Malachi, and 1–2 Chronicles. Thus the last Old Testament books were completed in the 400s BC.

Lessons for Us

We may not live in Babylon in the sixth century BC, but the message to the Jewish exiles, recorded in the final books of the Old Testament, is as relevant for us as it was for them. We are discouraged, our walls have been demolished, we lack security, and God's word does not occupy the place it should in our lives. The inspiring books of Ezra, Nehemiah, and Esther will pick us up and point us in the right direction. They inspire us to earnestly seek and embrace God's purpose and plan for our lives.

Or we may be wandering in a dark place as a result of our failure to heed the principles of God's word. Remember that with divine punishment comes divine grace. God is not against us; as our loving Father, he's pulling for us. Our restoration may take some time—even decades—but the Lord's ultimate purpose is that we once again enjoy strength, welfare, and joy in him. Read Hebrews 12 to see how this works. God is good, and we need not abandon hope.

THE TEMPLES

Two temples were erected in the Bible: Solomon's temple in the tenth century BC (1 Kings 6) and the second temple (Ezra 6:15), which was later radically rebuilt by Herod the Great, starting in 20 BC (John 2:20).

Two more temples were built in Egypt in intertestamental times. The first was constructed on the largest island in the Nile, Elephantine, in about 500 BC and destroyed in 410 BC. The other was built at Leontopolis in about 300 BC and destroyed in 73 AD.

The Samaritans built a temple atop Mount Gerizim, which was

destroyed in 129 BC. This helps us make sense of the interchange between Jesus and the Samaritan woman in John 4:20-21.

The temple of Ezekiel 40–48 contains many symbolic flourishes. The details do not provide a workable blueprint for construction, and the geography of the Holy Land is stylized, not realistic. Nevertheless, some Jews and Christians expect another temple to be built in Jerusalem in connection with the return of the Messiah.

Jesus unequivocally stated that the true temple was his body and that it was to be raised on the third day (John 2:19-22).

The church is the temple (1 Corinthians 3:16-17)—the locus of God's glory and the means by which he spreads the knowledge of the gospel into the world. Consequently, there is no need for a future temple.[2] This is connected with the heavenly temple (Revelation 11:19; 21:22). The book of Revelation seems to be saying that Ezekiel's vision is fulfilled in the glorified church.

World Powers in the Bible		
Assyria	722–609 BC	defeated Israel and most of the cities of Judah and repopulated the land
Egypt	609–605 BC	interlude
Babylon	605–539 BC	defeated Judah and took most of the people to Babylon
Persia	539–333 BC	permitted the Jews to return to their homes
Greece	333–167 BC	came to power through Alexander the Great of Macedon
Hasmonean	167–63 BC	a brief period of Jewish independence
Rome	63 BC...	in command through the entire New Testament period

A Quick Review

As a result of sin, God's people were exiled by Assyria and Babylon. Yet in his mercy, the Lord gave them a fresh start. The story of Adam and Eve took on a special significance at this time. Like the Jews, they too were removed from their land (Genesis 3:23). And yet not all was lost; there was grace and a new beginning. The Jews' new beginning was even described as "new heavens and a new earth" (Isaiah 65:17). God's work through his "messiah" Cyrus, affording a fresh start to his (relatively small) people Israel, foreshadowed his saving work through *the* Messiah, Jesus Christ, giving a new beginning—potentially, at least—to all the earth.

The Lord's action in Israel's history reflects his loving discipline and grace. He is never soft on sin, but he does offer grace to help us in our time of need (Hebrews 4:16). This theme runs through every book of the Bible and is a healthy corrective to wrong views of God as ungracious, capricious, vindictive, or unjust.

Despite the Persian restoration, Israel was never again the proud and independent nation it was during the time of David and Solomon, and the sense of captivity continued into early New Testament times (Luke 1:67-79). True peace and security could never come by political means because the kingdom of God is within (Luke 17:21; John 18:36).

14

THE WRITINGS

The fear of the LORD is the beginning of knowledge,
but fools despise wisdom and instruction.

PROVERBS 1:7

So far, most of the chapters in this book have covered the narrative portions of the Old Testament, though chapter 12 explored the prophets. We recognize that narrative is a broad literary genre, as is prophecy, and we must take care to interpret Bible stories according to the rules of their genre. In this chapter we will focus only on two more broad genres: psalms and wisdom literature.

Many of the psalms and proverbs were penned during the exile, though many others go back much further, even to the time of the united kingdom. Both genres are common in the Writings, the third division of the Hebrew Bible (which includes some history as well). Without "getting" the genres, we won't see how the grand themes of the Bible dovetail. Yet with a basic feel for the genres—which is within reach through a careful reading of this book—it all comes together.

It may help to think of the ancient Jewish writings as an archery target with four circles. The bull's-eye is the Torah. The Prophets, which form the second section, point God's people back to the Law. The next circle, the Writings, constitutes the third division of the Hebrew Bible, as we saw in chapter 2. The Writings are by and large reflections on God, the word of God, the ways of God, and human experience in the light of God. (Don't worry for now about the fourth circle, as we'll come to that in the next chapter.)

Poetry

The Psalms are 100 percent poetry, and so is most of the wisdom literature. In fact, about 30 percent of the Hebrew Bible is poetry. This means we'd better become comfortable reading Hebrew poetry, or we will cut ourselves off from a large part of God's revelation to man.

English poetry often rhymes, but Hebrew poetry hardly ever rhymes. Wordplays are common, as well as alliteration and a plethora of similes. "Thought rhyme" is a better description of the poetic sections of the Old Testament. Simply put, the initial line is amplified somehow in the following line. The lines are parallel—usually two lines, though occasionally there are more—so analysts speak of parallelism as the hallmark of Hebrew poetry. The three basic types of parallelism are *synonymous* (a restatement of the idea in different words), *antithetical* (a statement of the opposite idea), and *synthetic* (a second idea that builds on the first). Here are a few examples.

Synonymous	Listen, my son, to your father's instruction and do not forsake your mother's teaching (Proverbs 1:8).
Antithetical	The wicked are overthrown and are no more, but the house of the righteous stands firm (Proverbs 12:7).
Synthetic	I run in the path of your commands for you have broadened my understanding (Psalm 119:32).

The rules for interpreting poetry are not the same as those for interpreting prose. Poetic license permits hyperbole (overstatement for effect), metaphor (saying something is something else when it really isn't), and other figures of speech that, if taken literally, land us in nonsense or contradiction. For example, I would question the wisdom of using Psalm 51:5 as a proof text for original sin. In poetry, feelings may be stated as facts, and in any case poems are not the most promising texts to mine for biblical doctrine. They reflect the state of mind of the worshipper or sage—thus serving as vehicles of revelation—but not necessarily the mind of God. This will become especially clear when we examine the wisdom literature.

Last, to maximize your appreciation of Hebrew poetry—unless you have time to learn Hebrew—be sure to read the Bible in several versions, not just one, because it is difficult for any single version to capture the color, texture, and nuance of the original Semitic poetry.

Psalms

A psalm is a prayer or hymn that was originally sung to a plucked instrument. (In ancient Greek, *psallo* meant pluck, as with a lyre or harp.) There are 150 in all, arranged in five books, mirroring the five-fold division of the Law (beginning with Psalms 1; 42; 73; 90; and 107). Psalms 117 and 119 are the shortest and longest chapters of the Bible, respectively. The Psalter (all the psalms as a collection) was like a prayer book and hymnal for ancient Jews and early Christians.

There are many types, or subgenres, of psalms: praise psalms, historical psalms, imprecatory psalms (prayers against one's enemies, something common in the Old Testament but forbidden in the New Testament), sin psalms, the Psalms of Ascent (chanted while pilgrims went up the steep ascent to Jerusalem), messianic psalms, and laments (sometimes called psalms of disorientation—something at the heart of the human condition).

Some psalms are acrostics. That is, each line or stanza begins with the next letter of the Hebrew alphabet. Psalm 119 is the longest acrostic in the Bible. Each stanza is eight verses long and begins with the next letter (*alef, beth, gimel, daleth*...). The Hebrew alphabet has 22 consonants (vowels are not included), so this psalm has 176 verses. Acrostics strike the reader or listener not only verbally but also visually, not only by their thoughts but also by their sounds.

All of the psalms are poems, so make sure you are not reading them as prose. For insights into the human condition and our longing for truth, justice, meaning, and God, they are a wonderful place to visit. Reading them to glean eternal truths, God's laws, and his will for our lives is somewhat less useful.

Psalms capture the full range of emotions. They teach us to pray openly and genuinely. Honest, colorful, and laden with authentic emotion, they offer models of genuine prayer and theological reflection so integral to the spiritual health of people who are set on following the Lord. Psalms is the most quoted book in New Testament (and in the Dead Sea Scrolls).

Wisdom Literature

The wisdom literature includes Job, Proverbs, Ecclesiastes, Song of Solomon, several psalms (such as 1 and 19), and a number of other assorted passages in both testaments. Like the Psalms, this genre contains several subgenres. Most ancient cultures had extensive collections of wisdom literature. Much of the wisdom literature of the Egyptians and Babylonians, for example, has survived to our day. The Old Testament writers were choosing to communicate in a medium well known in the ancient world.

Wisdom literature often offers observations about life. These observations may capture general truths, but they seldom present absolute rules. For example, if a proverb said that a greedy man will end up poor and in rags, this does not mean there are no exceptions. (Some greedy men actually end up being quite rich, right?)

The books of Job and Ecclesiastes must be read with extra discernment because each book contains lessons in wrong theology. The book of Job refutes the ideas that all suffering is a result of sin and prosperity is a result of virtue. Job and his counselors had been taught that God is more involved in human life than he really is, and only at the end of the book, when the Lord speaks from the whirlwind, do we learn that much of what has been said in chapters 3–37 (especially the words of Job's counselors) is incorrect. Obviously, taking a verse out of context can easily result in misrepresenting God.

In a way, Ecclesiastes is the inverse of Job. Here the jaded writer ("the Teacher," or assembly leader) feels the absence of God. Although he concludes that obedience to God's ways is true wisdom, his world features little of the wonder and majesty of, say, the Psalms or Job. God is hardly involved at all, leaving us to ourselves. The negative example of the Teacher's theology is hardly to be emulated, but it does show us where we end up when we seek pleasure or even wisdom as an end in itself.

The Song of Solomon, often classified with the wisdom literature, is unrestrained in its depiction of sexual love between a man and his wife. Here is a vital lesson for our age: Sexual fidelity between a man and his wife—heterosexual monogamy—is a wonderful thing. Sadly, in his later years Solomon appears to have forgotten this lesson (1 Kings 11:1-10).

Proverbs, the best-known part of the wisdom literature, contains dozens of general truths. They are not necessarily absolutes. For example, in English we say not only "Look before you leap" but also "He who hesitates is lost." Both these adages contain wisdom: the need for caution and the need for action. Taken together, they present a more rounded picture of the truth. Separately, they can be used to justify excessive conservatism or impulsiveness.

Proverbs 16:3 does not teach we will always get what we want—the Lord does not spoil us. But there is wisdom in presenting our requests and plans before him. Proverbs 22:6 is not meant to say that anything a child does wrong is actually the parents' fault or that good parenting never produces rebels. These are general truths. Like facets of a gem, the general truths of Proverbs should be taken all together.

A Quick Review

The Writings, the third part of the Hebrew canon, contain many documents in the broad genres of wisdom literature and psalms. The first brings us to weigh certain insights, the second, certain feelings. Both reveal how men and women of all generations have struggled with faith, trying to understand God and to make sense of the world. We must not read these genres as we would straight narrative, for they contain little narrative. Each biblical literary genre is to be interpreted according to the rules of that genre.

In the next chapter, we will consider the intertestamental period. Though this era, roughly 400 BC till the time of Christ, is not part of Old Testament history proper, familiarity with it enriches one's grasp of the Bible and should not be omitted by any serious student of the Scriptures. Please don't skip over it.

THE INTERTESTAMENTAL PERIOD

There were others who were tortured, refusing to be released
so that they might gain an even better resurrection.
HEBREWS 11:35 (REFERRING TO 2 MACCABEES 7:7)

I f we were to halt our review of biblical history with the last chapter, we would be bewildered as soon as we entered the world of the New Testament. On exiting Persian-dominated, fifth-century BC Israel and jumping right into the four Gospels, we are bombarded by much that is novel or unprecedented. The Persians have long left—now the Romans are in charge. Why then is most of the world speaking Greek instead of Latin? The Jews still have their temple, but what are synagogues, and where did they come from? Who are the Pharisees, Sadducees, and scribes? Why are the zealots so radical? Why are the high priests now appointed annually? After all, the Torah stipulated a lifelong appointment. Since when has there been a Sanhedrin? Crucifixion, demonic possession, taxes to Caesar...will someone please tell me what's going on?

If we're going to understand, we need to be filled in. Would a student go from algebra to calculus without trigonometry? Or from learning the alphabet straight into working as a proofreader without learning grammar? Maybe the analogies are overdone, but don't skip this chapter, because the intertestamental material does many things for us.

- It connects the testaments.
- It provides the backdrop for many New Testament beliefs and institutions.

- It contains the origins of several misguided doctrines in postapostolic times.

- It preserves a time-honored part of Christian tradition.

- It is interesting in its own right.

This chapter will explore the intertestamental period, starting with the history, moving to the developments within Jewish doctrine and denominations, and finally examining the writings known as the Apocrypha.

The Transition from Persian to Greek Rule

The Persians controlled the land of Israel from the fall of Babylon in 539 BC until the troops of Alexander the Great prevailed. The official date of the transition is 331, but by 333 the Greeks (Macedonians) already controlled the Holy Land. Upon Alexander's death, and because he did not leave a son, his generals divided up the kingdom. In time the Seleucids acquired the land of Israel. After a century and a half, Antiochus Epiphanes IV launched a rigorous campaign of hellenization (the imposing of Greek culture). This modernization program included...

- classical Greek education

- participation in Hellenic sports (including nude athletics, which was offensive to Jewish morals)

- theater (with all the profanity of pagan drama) and other cultural events

- the prohibition of circumcision under pain of death

- forcible consumption of nonkosher foods, such as pork

- the offering of swine flesh on the altar

- the extensive use of the Greek language, which lasted for centuries into Roman times even though the official language of the Romans was Latin

Some Jews capitulated to this secularization of their society, but others resisted. The Maccabean revolt, led by Judas Maccabaeus (Judah the Hammer), was a violent revolution that successfully overthrew the Greek overlords. In 165 BC the temple was purified and rededicated. In commemoration of the rededication of the temple, the Festival of Lights (Hanukkah) was instituted. The tumultuous events leading up to the revolution were prophesied in Daniel 11, but because all the books of the Hebrew Bible were already written before this rededication, the only Scripture referring to Hanukkah is found in John 10:22. One of the best-known Jewish holidays is found only in the Christian Scriptures!

Following the revolution, Judea was semiautonomous until 110 BC, when it became fully independent. It was led by the Hasmonean dynasty (descendants of the brother of Judah the Hammer). Ruling were several kings and even one queen, Alexandra. This ended with the rise of Rome.

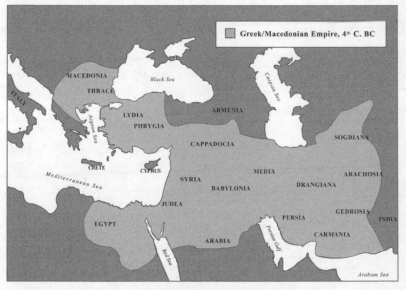

The Greek Empire.

Enter the Romans

In the second century BC the Greek Empire was weakening, and Rome was in the ascendancy. In the first century BC, Rome ruled the

Mediterranean lands, and General Pompey conquered Judea in 63 BC. The region was administered directly or indirectly by the Romans through the family of the puppet king Herod the Great (73–4 BC), who had ingratiated himself to Augustus Caesar. Herod was half Edomite (Idumean), half Roman. In addition, Roman prefects (governors), such as Pontius Pilate, ruled from Caesarea Maritima on the Mediterranean coast of Judea.[1] Thus the region was ruled simultaneously by Romans and Jews, though all answered to Rome.

The Roman Empire was far larger in military power and geographical extent than the Greek empire, and peace was kept in the many provinces and territories by armies (Roman legionaries and—much greater in number—non-Roman auxiliary troops). The Romans maintained control by means of effective governance and laws, a crackdown on bandits and pirates, patrol of the roads and seas, a criminal justice system that included crucifixion, taxation, and of course the army. This was the world of the New Testament.[2]

The Temple

The second temple was completed in about 515 BC. In 20–19 BC Herod the Great inaugurated such an extensive construction program that the temple was thereafter often called Herod's temple. He built up the temple mount to an area of 35 acres (about 14 hectares) and replaced the stones of the temple with white marble blocks. The final product was so stunning that the Babylonian Talmud states, "He who

Herod's temple.

has not seen the Temple of Herod has never seen a beautiful building."[3]
Whereas the smallish structure that replaced Solomon's original temple was unimpressive (Haggai 2:3), Jesus' disciples found this edifice unspeakably impressive (Mark 13:1; Luke 21:5).

The high priesthood was a lifetime appointment in the Law (Numbers 35:28,32). But in the time of Antiochus Ephiphanes IV, high priests were appointed by the (pagan) overlords and replaced at whim. Synagogues (which probably originated in the exile—see chapter 13) became so common that we can assume that Jewish life centered there, not in the Jerusalem temple.

Religious Sects

Division characterized Judaism from its inception—intertribal jealousy, war between the house of Saul and the house of David, animosity between north and south, and so on. In intertestamental times, the alienation increased. A number of competing schools of thought emerged, and the tensions among them are apparent not only in the New Testament but also in the extrabiblical Jewish writings, the Dead Sea Scrolls, and the writings of the eminent Jewish historian Flavius Josephus (37–100 AD). We'll take a quick glance at these sects now and flesh them out in chapter 17. This list roughly follows the order of their appearance.

- Scribes preserved the Scriptures and answered legal questions. They stood in the tradition of Ezra (Ezra 7:6,10).

- Pharisees emerged to call the people back to follow the Bible and to resist assimilation to pagan culture (an enormous temptation, especially after the exile).

- Samaritans modified the ancestral faith of the Jews and incurred their wrath. Descended from the northern tribes and other peoples mentioned in 2 Kings 17:24, they were geographically and culturally distinct from the Jews.

- Sadducees were wealthy priests who collaborated with the Romans. Descended from Zadok, the high priest under Solomon (1 Kings 4:4; Ezekiel 40:46), they were perennial rivals of the Pharisees.

- Zealots were radically political and embraced terrorism as a means to oust the Romans. They continued in the spirit of Judah the Hammer and were at the other end of the spectrum from the Sadducees.

- Herodians were a political party supportive of Herod the Great (73-4 BC) and his descendants who ruled after him.

- Essenes were radically apolitical. They gave up on the corrupt temple system and withdrew into the desert. Some lived near the Dead Sea, and others lived in the vicinity of Jerusalem.

All these groups are on the scene when the curtain rises on the New Testament, and none of them appears in the Old Testament. The intertestamental period also saw the origin of the Sanhedrin (the court of 71 judges who led the Jewish people in matters of faith), which figures so prominently in the trial of Jesus (Luke 22:66). The Sanhedrin was composed of Pharisees and Sadducees and was recognized by the Romans as the ultimate authority in matters of Jewish religion. The Sanhedrin died out in the fifth century AD.

The Hebrew Bible Is Completed

During intertestamental times, the Old Testament books were circulated broadly and grouped in their traditional threefold arrangement: Law, Prophets, and Writings (Luke 24:44). In Hebrew, the acronym *Tanakh* (*TaNaKh*) is used to refer to the Scriptures. *T* stands for *Torah,* or law; *N* stands for *Nevi'im,* or prophets; and *Kh* stands for *Khetuvim,* or writings. The last book to be written was likely 1–2 Chronicles (in about 400 BC), although the majority of critical scholars assign this distinction to Daniel (written in either 530 or 165 BC). Regardless of the dating, the entire Old Testament was finished generations before the birth of Christ.

Apocryphal Books

A number of other ancient Jewish writings were copied and transmitted along with *Tanakh*, at least until sometime in the early Christian era. These are the Apocrypha. An *apocryphon* is literally a hidden thing, and thus the Apocrypha are the hidden things—now brought to light. Unlike the genuine Old Testament writings, they were not written in Hebrew. They were included in the Greek translation of the Hebrew Scriptures (the Septuagint, or LXX, which was completed in the third to second century BC) and were extremely familiar to the early Christians. Today, the Apocrypha are not accepted as Scripture by the Jews and most Protestants, but Catholic and Orthodox Christians include them in their Bibles.

At the beginning of chapter 14, we imagined the Hebrew Scriptures as a target. The bull's-eye is the Law. The Prophets are the next circle, followed by the Writings. The Apocrypha are the fourth and final circle—not as valuable as the Law, Prophets, and Writings yet still useful even if they lie outside the pale of Scripture.

Some contain valuable historical information, while others are of little value as sources.

Their theology is inferior because they include notions that are not found in the Old Testament, and some are at variance with teachings of the Bible. These include the doctrines of purgatory (Wisdom 3:1-7), almsgiving for forgiveness (Tobit 12:9), sex for procreation only (Tobit 7:18,22 in the Vulgate), and prayers to or for the dead (Tobit 12:12-15; 2 Maccabees 12:39-45; 15:14).

I checked every extrabiblical reference to the Apocrypha in the first three centuries of Christianity. Only a few citations are from the first half of the second century. A huge number are from the second half of that century, and the third century sees even more references. The number continues to increase in the fourth century, when writers routinely quote apocryphal works as Scripture. Their inclusion in the Latin Bible (the Vulgate) in the late fourth century did not happen without some protest. To sum up, the belief that the Old Testament Apocrypha are inspired evolved over time.[4]

Why Study the Apocrypha?

Familiarity with the Apocrypha (and the entire intertestamental period) is a bonus for Bible readers for several reasons.

- It helps to clarify the origins of later doctrines not found in the Bible.
- In contrasting so much with the genuine books of Scripture, the Apocrypha highlight the differences between the authentic and the inauthentic.
- They form part of Jewish heritage and culture.
- The New Testament alludes to them many times.

The Apocrypha	
(Books in italics appear in standard Roman Catholic Bibles. The others appear in Orthodox Bibles.)	
Title	Number of chapters
1 Esdras	9
2 Esdras	16
Tobit	14
Judith	16
Additions to Esther	6 (Esther 11–16); the LXX contains 2 (Esther 10–11)
Wisdom of Solomon	19
Sirach (Ecclesiasticus)	51
Baruch	5
Letter of Jeremiah	1 (Baruch 6)
Song of the Three	1 (between Daniel 3:23 and 3:24)
Susanna 1	(Daniel 13)
Bel and the Dragon	1 (Daniel 14 in Latin; added to Daniel 12 in Greek)
Prayer of Manasseh	1
1 Maccabees	16

The Apocrypha	
2 Maccabees	15
3 Maccabees	7
4 Maccabees	18
Additions to Psalms	1 (Psalm 151)

Allusions to the Apocrypha in the New Testament	
There may be no indisputably direct quotations from the Apocrypha in the New Testament, but there are a good many allusions. Here is a sampling.	
Wisdom of Solomon	2:15-16 in Matthew 27:43
	7:26 in Hebrews 1:3
	9:13 in Romans 11:34
	9:15 in 2 Corinthians 5:1-4
	13:5-8; 14:24-27 in Romans 1:20-29
	12:12-20; 15:7 in Romans 9:20-23
Tobit	4:7 in Luke 14:13
	4:15 in Luke 6:31
Sirach (Ecclesiasticus)	5:11 in James 1:19
	7:14 in Matthew 6:7
	15:11-12 in James 1:13
	35:9 in 2 Corinthians 9:7
Other	1 Maccabees 4:59 in John 10:22
	2 Maccabees 6:18–7:42 in Hebrews 11:34-35

In the original edition of the King James Version, which included the Apocrypha, the canonical books had 113 cross-references to the Apocrypha. What are we to make of New Testament allusions to the Apocrypha? There are numerous citations in Scripture of pagan writers. All seem to serve by way of illustration. Paul, for example, occasionally quotes Plato, but that does not mean Paul believed Plato was inspired by God. Thus the New Testament writers (the apostles of Jesus and their immediate disciples) did not necessarily consider the Apocrypha to be inspired Scripture.

Interesting Apocryphal Teachings	
Tobit	"For almsgiving delivers from death, and it will purge away every sin" (12:9).
	The practice of offering food to the dead is apparently supported in 4:17.
	In 6:6-8 we find that demons are repulsed by the offensive odor of fish organs.
Judith	In 1:1-6 the Babylonian king Nebuchadnezzar appears after the exile.
	In 16:17 we read (for the first time anywhere) about a hell of infinite conscious torment. "Woe to the nations that rise up against my people! The Lord will take vengeance on them in the day of judgment—fire and worms he will give to their flesh—they shall weep in pain forever."[5]
Sirach (Ecclesiasticus)	Unlike Luke 6:27-31, Sirach 12:4-7 teaches that we shouldn't give to the unrighteous.
	"He who loves his son will whip him often" (30:1).
	"Yoke and thong will bow the neck, and for a wicked servant there are racks and tortures" (33:26).
	"Stick to the advice your own heart gives you" (37:13). This contradicts Proverbs 14:12.
	Anti-Edomite and anti-Samaritan prejudice appear in 50:25-26: "With two nations my soul is vexed and the third is no nation: Those who live on Mount Seir and the Philistines and the foolish people that dwell in Shechem."
1 Maccabees	Written in the second century BC, this book is extremely valuable for filling in the gaps in our understanding of Israel's long history and second-century history in general.
	Facing the Hellenistic challenge—the pressure to eat pork, embrace idolatry, violate the Sabbath, become "uncircumcised," and so on—the faithful admirably resist. "But many in Israel stood firm and were resolved in their hearts not to eat unclean food. They chose to die rather than to be defiled by food or to profane the holy covenant; and they did die" (1:62-63).

	Interesting Apocryphal Teachings
2 Maccabees	In 12:43-45 we find approval of prayer and sacrifices for the dead, and 15:11-16 supports intercessory prayer for the dead.
2 Maccabees	"So I too will here end my story. If it is well told and to the point that is what I myself desired; if it is poorly done and mediocre that was the best I could do" (15:37-38). The Apocrypha contain no "Thus says the Lord." That does not prove it is uninspired, but it does call into question its authenticity, especially in comparison with the confidence in which the genuine biblical books were offered.
2 Esdras	This book was omitted by the Roman church because 7:36 and the verses following explicitly deny the efficacy of prayers for the dead. (On the other hand, 2 Maccabees 12:43-45 affirms the value of prayers for the dead.) Similarly, 7:105 allows no intercession for the wicked on the day of judgment.
2 Esdras	First-century messianic expectations are demonstrated in 7:28. Chapters 13–14 equate the Messiah with the Son of God.

How Should We View the Apocrypha?

How should you view these writings? Many of us have "helps" in the back pages of our Bibles: tables of weights and measures, maps, and reference notes. This material is useful but not inspired. In the same way that we may grow fond of the extra material at the end of our Bibles, so the early church grew fond of the extra material in their books. This does not mean that it is inspired Scripture. But it is extremely valuable all the same.[6]

A Quick Review

The New Testament world is quite different from the Old Testament world. Familiarity with the intertestamental period enables us to make a smooth transition between the two.

During a space of several centuries, a number of significant developments took place: The world power changed from Persia to Greece to Rome, the Old Testament was canonized, the extra books of the Apocrypha were written, the temple was refurbished, various sects rose up within Judaism, religious life became more centered in synagogues than in Jerusalem, and frustration with this world led to piqued anticipation of the kingdom of God to come in the next world.

Part 3

THE SECOND TESTAMENT

16

NEW TESTAMENT, SAME GOD

In the beginning was the Word, and the Word was with God,
and the Word was God...The Word became flesh and made his
dwelling among us. We have seen his glory, the glory of the one
and only Son, who came from the Father, full of grace and truth.

JOHN 1:1,14

The second testament makes up the final fourth of Scripture. It consists of 27 books that in turn have incorporated excerpts from more than a dozen extrabiblical sources. The 260 chapter numbers, like the verse numbers, are not original, though they help us navigate the text. The New Testament was written over the span of five decades, and the documents were produced all over the Roman Empire. Most of the letters were published before the Gospels, though in its final form the New Testament places the Gospels first, probably because they tell the story of Jesus Christ, and the rest of the New Testament is based on his life and teaching.

Many people see Christ as so extensively redefining God that they cannot help seeing a new version of God in the New Testament. We will address this error in the second half of this chapter. For now, let's explore why there are two testaments.

Why Two Testaments?

Why did God have to update his word—give us a "new" testament? Why come to Earth to deliver revised instructions when he could have gotten it right the first time? Here's the short answer: This was his plan, and in his providence he anticipated that a new covenant would be necessary. But hold on for a moment.

The biblical story unfolds in an amazing plan of fulfillment as God's promises to the patriarchs are inherited by the people of Israel and then by the church of Christ. The Law showed us God's love, wisdom, power, justice, mercy, grace, and most importantly, our need for him in a sinful world. Yet the Law and its prescribed sacrifices could never completely deliver us from our sin—they were never intended to. For that, only the new covenant could do. Note that the Greek *diatheke* means both "testament" and "covenant." The writer of Hebrews pursues the important connection between covenant and testament in Hebrews 8:6-13; 9:15-17 and elsewhere.

There are major differences between the old and new covenants. Under the Torah the people of God sacrificed animals. Not so now; Jesus himself is the Lamb of God (Leviticus 1:10-13; John 1:29; 1 Corinthians 5:7). The change itself was predicted in Jeremiah 31:31-34 and other passages. Under the Law, polygamy was tolerated (though never commended), divorce was easier, oaths were taken, war was permitted, and of course Sabbath days and years were central. Under the new covenant, much has changed. Matthew 5:21-48 stresses this in striking terms.

Just as there is a transition from the old to the new covenant, numerous biblical doctrines that appear embryonically in the Hebrew Scriptures are well developed by the time of the Greek New Testament. The doctrine of Satan was partially worked out in the Old Testament but completed in the New. The person and role of the Messiah become clearer in the later books of the Old Testament and are revealed and explained in the New. God's personal presence progresses from the Garden of Eden to the tabernacle to the temple to the church to the heavenly city symbolically depicted in Revelation.

The Law was a sort of schoolteacher (Romans 15:4; Galatians 3:24), and so these are examples of progressive revelation—earlier lessons supplemented and augmented by later ones. A good teacher does not get too far ahead of the students (Mark 4:33). In the same way, God revealed his will in the pages of Scripture gradually.

Many readers who supposedly discover a new view of God in the pages of the New Testament fail to make the important distinction between the testaments. The old plan was a blueprint for a nation-state, or really for a church-state, a theocracy along political lines. The new plan is not a political system. Through the course of church history, whenever the two testaments have been unthinkingly combined, the results have been tragic. For example, when sixteenth-century reformer John Calvin administered the city of Geneva by a combination of Christ's new teaching and the old provisions of the Law of Moses, contradiction resulted. Morality was legislated, and heretics were executed. This hybrid was never envisioned by Christ.

Hebrews 9:15-17 shows that the new covenant superseded the old covenant. Just as two wills or testaments cannot be in effect at the same time, neither can two covenants. Although the heart of the Law carries over into the New Testament (see Matthew 22:37-40; Galatians 5:14), the Law and its specific commandments were in some sense nailed to the cross, both fulfilled and made obsolete by Christ (Matthew 5:17; Ephesians 2:14-16; Colossians 2:13-14; Hebrews 8:13). Thus Christians are not bound to observe the regulations of the Old Testament.

As Bible readers we must take great care to distinguish the testaments. Both tell us much about God, but only the second tells us how to live. Unless principles in the Old Testament reappear in the New, we are not under obligation to follow them. Indeed, we do so at our peril.

Time Perspectives

As we read the New Testament, we should be aware of three perspectives of salvation.

1. The Gospels point forward. They describe the last days of Old Testament Judaism as the kingdom of God is beginning to break in. Technically speaking, there are no Christians in the Gospels (John 7:39; Romans 8:9)—the church has not yet begun. All the references to Christian conversion are future (Matthew 28:19; Mark 16:16; John 3:5).

2. The letters and Revelation point backward. That is, they look back on and assume Christian conversion. References to becoming followers of Christ all have time referents in the past (Galatians 3:26-27;

Ephesians 4:20-21; Colossians 2:11-15). These documents were not written to tell believers how to become saved. If anything, they were written to instruct them how to stay saved.

3. Only in Acts, where people first become Christians, do we see conversion in the present tense. This is the only part of the New Testament in which we actually see men and women having their sins forgiven *and* receiving the Spirit. Acts 2:37-41 is the first such passage, though there are many more.

THE APOSTOLICITY OF
THE NEW TESTAMENT DOCUMENTS

Apostles wrote most of the books of the New Testament. This list shows that all the others were written by people closely associated with apostles.

- Mark was a companion of the apostle Peter.

- Luke (who also wrote Acts) was a companion of the apostle Paul.

- Hebrews was written by another associate of the apostle Paul.

- James was the brother of Jesus Christ and was called an apostle in Galatians 1:19.

- Jude was another brother of Jesus Christ.

BOOK NAMES OF THE NEW TESTAMENT

- Matthew, Mark, Luke, and John are named after their traditional authors.

- The Acts of the Apostles would more accurately be named The Continuing Acts of Jesus Through His Church (Especially Peter and Paul) by the Power of the Spirit. But that wouldn't fit on the contents page.

- Romans to 2 Thessalonians are Paul's letters to churches, arranged longest to shortest.

- First Timothy to Philemon are Paul's letters to individuals, arranged longest to shortest.

- Hebrews is apparently written to Jewish (Hebrew) Christians. The author is unknown.

- James is named after the author (a brother of Jesus Christ, not the apostle James).

- First Peter to Jude are letters written by the apostles Peter and John and by Jude, a brother of Jesus Christ.

- The Revelation of Jesus Christ (also called The Apocalypse) is titled after the Greek word *apocalypsis* ("unveiling"). In this book the veil is pulled back, and we take an inspired peek behind the scenes at true spiritual reality. The contents were revealed to the apostle John on the island of Patmos. The traditional view is that he wrote down his revelation while living in Ephesus in the late first century AD.

The Same God?

So there are two testaments but only one God. As we saw in chapter 5, the Scriptures affirm that God does not change (Malachi 3:6; Hebrews 1:12; 13:8). Both testaments reveal a God of judgment and a God of grace. He is no less holy in the New Testament than in the Old Testament (compare Leviticus 11:44 and Revelation 15:4), nor is he less forgiving in the Old Testament than in the New Testament (compare Psalm 116 and Luke 15:11-32.)

Moreover, the Old Testament was the Bible of the early church. We may forget that the first New Testament document was not penned until the church was nearly 20 years old. Repeatedly the New Testament avers that the Old Testament is good and that it has much to teach us about theology—the study of God and all that his being implies (Matthew 5:17; Romans 15:4; 1 Corinthians 10:11; 2 Timothy 3:16-17). Furthermore, in calling him "the Lord Jesus Christ," the New Testament writers equated Jesus Christ with the Lord God of the Old Testament (Psalm 110; Acts 2:29-36).

Furthermore, the New Testament tells us that to truly understand the God of Scripture (the God of the Old Testament), we need only look at Christ (John 1:1,14,18; 10:30; 14:9; 20:28). When we see Jesus, we see God in all his fullness (Colossians 2:9). Theologians speak of the *incarnation,* the physical embodiment of something that was not physical. God became man in Jesus Christ, the Son of God. The incarnation puts a human face on God, making the abstract concrete and the unknowable relatable.

If this is still hard to get a handle on, let me offer some inferior analogies. (Of course, no analogy captures the poignancy and power of Scripture.) Have you read Jane Austen's *Pride and Prejudice?* Darcy, who at first seems a disagreeable fellow, becomes more and more admirable. Elizabeth, who to some degree had misjudged him, comes to admire and deeply love him, even though he was essentially the same person. To use a more modern illustration, the Darth Vader of the earlier Star Wars films turns out to be Luke Skywalker's father—to everyone's surprise. Once we understand his motives and how he came to go over to the dark side, we even feel a certain pity for him. Our feelings about the character may change, but he is the same person. Here's one last picture—my marriage. When my wife and I were getting to know each other (from 1983 to 1985), we became great friends. As fellow believers, we had much in common despite the ocean that separated us culturally. Once we were married, the intimacy of our relationship took a quantum leap. I know her so much better now than then—yet she is the same person. (Of course, unlike God, we have both changed, but no analogy is perfect.)

In a similar way, the God of the Old Testament is the God of the New Testament. He has not changed—but we have. In maturing, learning from Israel's history, and coming to trust our Creator, we begin to see him in a new light.

A Quick Review

We have uncovered two major truths. First, we must take great care to distinguish the two testaments. We should not neglect the Old Testament—it is the word of God as much as the New Testament—but we must continually keep in mind the sequence of the covenants. Careless blending of passages from the two testaments has led to a number of strange doctrines. Second, we meet the same God in both testaments. We certainly learn about him in the Old Testament. Don't ignore the first three quarters of the Bible! Distinguishing between God in the Old Testament and God in the New Testament is a serious error based on false contrasts.

The word of God is dynamic, both in its development and in its impact on our lives, and it comes to us in two consecutive phases, or covenants. Yet the God of the Bible is one, and he "does not change like shifting shadows" (James 1:17).

And now, to the books of the New Testament.

Famous Foreign Words and Phrases in the Bible			
Word	Language	Meaning	Sample location
abbá	Aramaic	father, or papa	Mark 14:36
hosanna	Hebrew, Aramaic	save	Matthew 21:9
hallelujah	Hebrew	Praise the Lord!	Revelation 19:1
marana tha	Aramaic	Come, Lord!	1 Corinthians 16:22
amen	Hebrew	truly, let it stand	Psalm 89:52
ecce homo	Latin	behold the man	John 19:5
Yahweh	Hebrew	the Lord (I am)	Exodus 3:14

HISTORY AND GEOGRAPHY

In the fifteenth year of the reign of Tiberius Caesar—when Pontius
Pilate was governor of Judea, Herod tetrarch of Galilee, his brother
Philip tetrarch of Iturea and Traconitis, and Lysanias tetrarch of
Abilene—during the high-priesthood of Annas and Caiaphas, the
word of God came to John son of Zechariah in the wilderness.

LUKE 3:1-2

Were you bored in your high school history classes? As I mentioned earlier, history was only mildly interesting for me at first. That may be because I'm a math and science sort of guy. As a first-year student entering Duke University, I decided to prop up my math and science education with lots of humanities and social sciences. I wanted to become a well-rounded renaissance man. I studied European history, Roman history, history of science, Chinese history, and so on. Three years later, I had a degree in history—somewhat to my surprise. It was by default more than by design.

Eventually I took classes in Old Testament history, New Testament history, and church history. I spent a month in the British Museum studying the ancient Egyptians and Assyrians. I took ten years of classical language study. I studied the histories of all the major world religions, especially Buddhism, Hinduism, and Islam. I studied archaeology, which brings the ancient world to light. I especially wanted to know the historical background of each book of the Bible—where it fits in the bigger scheme of things. I still read history; I'm hooked. Since many parts of both testaments are opaque unless the reader has a little background knowledge, I hope you'll join me in the quest to grasp the main outlines of history. In this chapter we're especially interested in learning how history and geography illuminate the New Testament.

The Roman Empire

The geography of the Bible is basically the geography of the eastern Mediterranean world. Old Testament world history centers on the great civilizations of Egypt, Assyria, Babylon, and Persia. Greece is the major power during intertestamental times, and the story of the New Testament unfolds in the Roman Empire.

Events in the Gospels take place almost exclusively in Palestine, a small plot of land at the extreme east end of the Mediterranean. Things begin to open up with the book of Acts, especially after the persecution of chapter 8 (Acts 8:1; 11:19). Then the journeys of Paul, "the apostle to the Gentiles" (Romans 11:13; Galatians 2:8), take us to Syria, Cyprus, Greece, Italy, and many other lands. (More on this in chapter 21.)

God's word comes to us in a true story unfolding in time and space. The existence of 80 persons named in the Bible has been confirmed by extrabiblical sources, and likenesses of nearly 20 people (mostly kings and queens) have survived. Nearly 30 people named in the New Testament are known from other records. Luke, the author of Luke and Acts (one-quarter of the New Testament) was an exact and careful writer, as the verses at the beginning of this chapter demonstrate. He had a deep concern for history and used the correct terminology for a number of political figures. His geographical accuracy is equally impressive. He mentions 32 countries, 54 cities, and 9 islands—a total of 95 place names. He commits no errors. These are all real persons, real places. The characteristic vagueness of legend and fairy tale is wholly absent ("Once upon a time, in a land far away, lived a very good king...")

Moreover, archaeologists have unearthed hundreds of artifacts that illuminate biblical life and times, a number of which have refuted skeptical critics. These finds confirm or illustrate statements in both the Old Testament and the New Testament. I have personally seen abundant evidence in various excavations in Israel, Lebanon, Jordan, Turkey, Greece, Egypt, and Italy, and I have seen artifacts relocated to European and North American cities.[1]

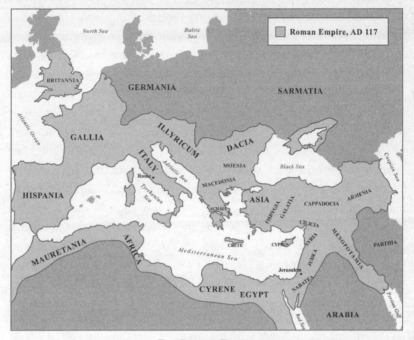

The Roman Empire.

The Spectrum of Judaism

To understand the religious world in which Christ and his early followers moved, we need to appreciate the thinking of the various groups on the Jewish religious spectrum. The sects of first-century Judaism were introduced in chapter 15 because most have their roots in the intertestamental period. Now we will explore these groups in greater detail because each one casts light on the New Testament. We will explore seven sects.

Pharisees

The Pharisees, the most important of the sects, were separatists. The name is derived from a Hebrew word that means "separate." They were not advocating separation from the mainstream of society—unlike the Essenes, whom we will meet in a moment—but separation from worldliness. To protect believers from compromise and sin, the

Pharisees created extra rules as a fence around the Law so that people wouldn't even come close to violating it. For example, to ensure no one ignored the tithing law (Leviticus 27:30), they required tithing even from one's garden herbs (Matthew 23:23). The Law forbade boiling a young goat in its mother's milk (Exodus 23:19), so the rabbis declared that meat and dairy could not be consumed in a single meal. In about AD 400, the Talmud even required separate plates for meat and dairy.

The motive behind these additional rules was commendable, but they went beyond what was written, ironically breaking the very Law they were intended to keep (Deuteronomy 4:2). As a partial justification, the Pharisees claimed there were *two* Torahs—the scriptural Law given by God at Sinai as well as an oral law also given at Sinai *and* divinely expanded through the ongoing discussions of the rabbis. Jesus was highly critical of the Pharisees, especially when their rules contradicted the spirit of the Law (for example, see Mark 7:1-13).

The Pharisees were proud of their religious society and considered their interpretations of God, his word, and his Law as the only valid ones. They were, therefore, also known as *hasidim* ("pious ones"). This self-proclaimed assurance, of course, led them to bitter disputes with other groups. The first was with the Sadducees, who combined the priesthood and the throne of the Jews under one of their own, Simon Maccabeus, older brother of Judas Maccabaeus, in about 143 BC. Other disagreements took place with John the Baptist (Matthew 3:7-10; Luke 7:28-30) and Jesus (Matthew 5:20; 12:1-14; 21:23-27; 23:1-39), who challenged their teachings and religious practices.

The Pharisees' fundamental doctrines included belief in a spiritual life, including the immortality of the soul, which would be rewarded for good works on Earth while the wicked would be banished to the underworld. They promoted a strict adherence to both the written and oral Judaic laws and believed that although God has foreknowledge of human destiny, man has free will to act.

This is not to say that their religion was necessarily harsh. For example, the "eye for an eye" kind of laws were not applied literally. Instead, they required monetary compensation, except in the case of murder.

Yet in creating a structure of legalism, they placed a heavy burden on the people (Matthew 23:4).[2]

Not all Pharisees were opposed to Christianity. Nicodemus was open to Jesus' teaching (John 3:1-21; 7:50-51) and generally supportive of him and his ministry (John 19:39). In the Sanhedrin, Gamaliel suggested the possibility of the Christian movement actually being from God (Acts 5:27,34-39). Saul of Tarsus was a Pharisee who encountered Jesus on the road to Damascus (Acts 9:1-19), and he later became known as Paul, the apostle to the Gentiles (Acts 13:9; Galatians 2:7-8). Even as late as AD 49, many Christians still self-identified as Pharisees (Acts 15:5; see also Acts 21:20).

The approximately 6000 Pharisees during the time of Jesus were immensely popular among the people, in part because they stood in opposition to the aristocratic Sadducees, the second group we will examine. They were also respected for standing up to the corrupt Hasmonean Dynasty. In 88 BC, some 800 Pharisees were crucified for opposing that regime.

The Pharisees were the only major group that survived the devastating First Jewish War (AD 66–73). The rabbinic Judaism of the Pharisees continues to this day.

Sadducees

As descendants of Zadok (2 Samuel 15:24; 1 Kings 4:4; Ezekiel 40:46), the most faithful of the Levites, the Sadducees took pride in their heritage even while cherishing their status as a wealthy caste of priests. Archaeological evidence from the destruction of Jerusalem in AD 70 has revealed the opulence of their lifestyles. There were fewer than 1000 Sadducees in the time of Christ (there isn't a lot of room at the top). Not surprisingly, they were also held in suspicion by the common people for their collaboration with the Romans. They rejected the Pharisees' oral law and diverged from them on a variety of subjects (including ritual purity, torts, and inheritance law). These are a few of the most famous ways the Sadducees disagreed with the Pharisees:

- They believed the Torah alone carried divine authority (not the Prophets or the Writings).

- They rejected the notion of life after death.

- They denied the existence of angels and demons.

- They rejected the resurrection of the dead (Matthew 22:23; Acts 23:8).

- They believed that humans have completely free will.

Like the Pharisees, the Sadducees were generally hostile toward the Jesus movement, but with notable exceptions. The upper-class Joseph of Arimathea, the one who asked permission to care for the corpse of Jesus, may have been a Sadducee (Luke 23:50-53). In the early years of Christianity, many priests were converted to the faith (Acts 6:7).

Essenes

In contrast to the Pharisees and Sadducees, the Essenes gave up on the temple system. Most of them withdrew into a monastic life of studying the Jewish Scriptures, sharing everything in common, and following a strict code of conduct. They are not mentioned in the New Testament, so their history is largely provided by Josephus and Philo in the first century and by Pliny the Elder and Hippolytus in the second. Although there is evidence of Essene communities in Jerusalem—one of the ancient gates was named the Essene Gate—and elsewhere around Palestine, many of them took to the desert. Members of the well-known monastery at Qumran, near the northwest corner of the Dead Sea, secreted the Dead Sea Scrolls in nearby caves in approximately AD 68 as the Roman forces were closing in. Thanks to the Essenes, copies of prophecies about Jesus Christ have survived from a century or more before his lifetime—a great boon to Christianity.

They claimed that the priesthood had become corrupt—a claim that was certainly true, based on the testimony of Jewish and Christian writers. Their writings are apocalyptic, anticipating a cosmic showdown between the forces of good and evil. They also believed in two messiahs, one of whom appears to have been their leader at Qumran.

Many have tried to make John the Baptist an Essene, and some even claim Jesus was influenced by this sect, but the evidence is thin. What John, Jesus, and the Essenes do have in common is the pursuit of holiness and the willingness to speak truth to people in power.

Herodians

The Herodians were supporters of Herod the Great (73–4 BC) and his descendants who ruled after him. Notable leaders in New Testament times include Herod Antipas (Mark 6:14-28) and Herod Agrippa (Acts 12:1-4,11,18-23). The Herodians are portrayed as dismissive of the message of Jesus (Mark 3:6).

Scribes

From exilic times—in the absence of the temple—the scribes gradually replaced the priests as teachers of Torah. The NIV refers to scribes as "teachers of the law." This parallels developments after the second temple was destroyed in AD 70, when Jewish life stopped centering on the temple sacrifices, focusing instead on the study of Torah. In ancient times, Ezra was the most illustrious scribe (Ezra 7:6,10; Nehemiah 8:1-8), a man of faith and learning who devoted his life to cultivating biblical literacy in the people.

The two most famous first-century scribes were rivals: the liberal Hillel and the more conservative Shammai. Hillel's grandson was the Pharisee Gamaliel, mentor of Saul of Tarsus (the apostle Paul). Though the scribes as a whole opposed Jesus, not all rejected his message. In Mark 12:34 we meet a scribe who was "not far from the kingdom of God"—yet another member of the Jewish leadership favorable to Jesus.

Samaritans

The Samaritans originated in the eighth century BC as the offspring of three patriarchs (Ephraim, Manasseh, and Levi—their claim now confirmed by DNA analysis) and the foreigners settled by the Assyrians in Israel (2 Kings 17:24). As antagonists to the people of God, they were rejected by the Judeans (Jews) in the fifth century BC (Ezra 4:1-24; Nehemiah 4:2). As a result, in the fourth century BC they built their own temple atop Mount Gerizim, but it was destroyed in 129 BC. The Samaritans had their own dialect of Hebrew with its own script, as well as their own customs. They also rewrote the Pentateuch. The most notable change is that a new commandment was added to the Decalogue, mandating that God be worshipped in Mt. Gerizim (see John 4:20). Despite their heterodoxy, Jesus seems often to have made them the heroes of his stories (Luke 10:33; 17:16; John 4:39).

Zealots

Members of this last group not only rejected the Romans' right to rule over God's people but also resorted to violent means to register their protest and foment dissent. In today's parlance, they would be labeled terrorists. Closely related to them, and perhaps a breakaway group, were the *Sicarii* ("dagger-men"), who carried out assassinations. The Zealots were instigators in the unsuccessful revolution that began in Galilee in AD 66 and soon swept up the whole country (the First Jewish War). Although Jerusalem fell in AD 70, the last bastion of the Zealots, Masada, held out until AD 73. The Masada community (nearly 1000 persons at this time, including women and children) preferred mass suicide to capture by the Romans. In this horrific war, more than a million Jews starved in the siege or were killed in battle, crucified, or enslaved. (Those who survived as slaves built Rome's Coliseum, completed in AD 80.)

At least one of Jesus' 12 disciples was a zealot—Simon (Mark 3:18)—though in the presence of the Prince of Peace he obviously changed his tactics. Interestingly, Judas Iscariot, the man who betrayed Jesus to the high priest, to some extent may have bought in to the Zealots' program. It is theorized that Judas gave up on Jesus' peaceful strategy, attempting to force his Master's hand to usher in the kingdom of God. Yet Christ's kingdom is not of this world (John 18:36; see also Luke 17:20-21; John 6:15), and so Judas' ploy failed.

All these sects were players on the stage of first-century Palestine. Only against this dramatic backdrop can we fully appreciate the action of the Gospels and Acts. And although none of the seven groups we have examined supported Christ, nearly all of them supplied individual

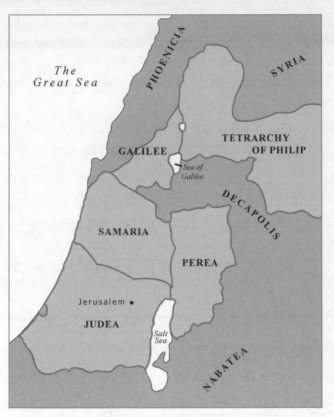

Palestine in the first century.

converts for the fledgling Christian movement. No one is beyond the reach of grace. Anyone can change.

The Emperors

The Roman eclipse of the Greeks began in the second century BC with an enormous power struggle. A century of civil war in Rome ended in the late first century BC after Julius Caesar and his nephew Octavian (Augustus) effectively made Rome an empire.

Jesus Christ was born halfway into the long reign of the emperor Augustus (27 BC–AD 14) and died under his successor, Tiberius (AD 14–37). The emperors were also called caesars, after the dictator Julius Caesar (assassinated 44 BC). Thus a caesar is an emperor.[3] Until the caesars began to demand worship, especially at the end of the first century, there was relatively little conflict between the church and Rome. But once emperor worship was enforced, the Christian church was on a collision course with the state (this is the theme of the book of Revelation).

FIRST-CENTURY ROMAN EMPERORS

Augustus (27 BC–AD 14)	Otto (AD 69)
Tiberius (AD 14–37)	Vitellius (AD 69)
Caligula (AD 37–41)	Vespasian (AD 69–79)
Claudius (AD 41–54)	Titus (AD 79–81)
Nero (AD 54–68)	Domitian (AD 81–96)
Galba (AD 68–69)	

Pax Romana

The period of calm lasting from the late first century BC to the death of the emperor Marcus Aurelius in AD 180 facilitated a time of major economic and cultural growth. There was no major military conflict anywhere in the Roman Empire. This period is called *Pax Romana* (Latin for "Roman peace"). It was characterized by these positive features:

- practical government and political stability
- an absence of warfare
- a vast and effective administrative complex
- economic and cultural growth
- sturdy, extensive, and interconnected roads that were largely cleared of bandits
- sea lanes that were largely cleared of pirates
- secure borders and no need for passports

Other Conditions

Nine other conditions not directly related to the *Pax Romana* should also be briefly noted.

1. Paganism was beginning to lose its credibility, though it would not die easily. The traditional religions were slowly being seen as bankrupt, and the gods were mocked in literature and philosophy.

2. Monotheism was beginning to become fashionable, and the notions of the fatherhood of God and the brotherhood of man were spreading even before Christianity.

3. Providentially, the Jewish Diaspora had led to the existence of synagogues all over the empire, and these served as beachheads for the Christian proclamation (Acts 9:20; 13:5,14; 14:1; 15:21; 17:1,10,17; 18:4,19,26; 19:8; Romans 1:16-17). Judaism had already planted the notion of monotheism as well as the organic connection between religion and ethics (a connection not part of paganism, as we observed in chapter 8). Many Gentiles were attracted to the Jewish faith. Those who identified with the Jews but never took the final step of conversion (circumcision) were called "God-fearers" (Acts 10:2,22; 13:43; 17:4,17).

4. Rome normally required its subjects to acknowledge the divinity of the gods or (later) the emperor himself, but the Jews were exempted. The Romans had learned from the Maccabean revolt that the Jews would not easily be coerced into relinquishing their monotheism. As a result, imperial protection and privileges were extended to the Jews. Christianity was initially viewed as a sect of Judaism—after all, every major leader was Jewish, including Jesus Christ—so the same privileges were afforded the first-century church.

5. Another consequence of Judaism was that by the first century, messianic expectation was running high. New Testament evidence includes Matthew 24:24 and Acts 5:36-37, and extrabiblical evidence is abundant.[4]

6. Fatalism was rampant—the unshakable sense that despite all his efforts, man's fate is somehow sealed. This drove many to consider alternative faiths, such as the mystery religions.

7. Anxiety about the future was escalating. People were seeking security in such things as astrology, magic, materialism, and metaphysics.

8. The spread of ideas was accelerated by the excellent infrastructure the Romans had created, including not only the roads but also the superior postal system.

9. Most of the empire spoke Greek, thanks to the Hellenizing program of Alexander in the fourth century BC, so there was little need for translators. Greek was the *lingua franca* of the empire, and the entire New Testament was composed in Koine Greek. (*Koine* means "common." This was the language of the people, as opposed to the more complex and subtle dialect of the philosophers and historians, Classical [Attic] Greek.) The entire Hebrew Bible had been translated into Greek (the Septuagint) in the third and second centuries BC, and this was the preferred version of most Jews and early Christians.

In combination with the *Pax Romana*, these conditions significantly prepared the way for the Christian message. One might ask, Why didn't Jesus come earlier? As we see, God was laying the groundwork for the Christian movement. Through his relations with the Jews, he was preparing a people (Galatians 3:24) and progressively revealing his will (Hebrews 1:1). As the New Testament claims, Christ came at just the right time (1 Corinthians 10:11; Galatians 4:4; Ephesians 1:10; 1 Timothy 2:6).

Pax Moderna?

It doesn't take much imagination to see the many parallels between the Roman Empire and our modern world. Absence of world wars, stable government (in many nations, at any rate), simplicity of air travel, technology, instantaneous communication, the translation of the Bible into thousands of languages, the vast spread of English, the Internet—how easy it is to get the word out today! But there's more: the postal system, increasing openness to diversity, disillusionment with traditional religions, the valuation of authenticity, the concentration of an enormous amount of wealth in a relatively small number of Christianized nations (such as the United States, Canada, and the United Kingdom) with citizens who may be willing to invest in missions, the growth of Christianity in so many nations of the developing world…Could the time ever be better? Could it be that we're living in the best time for the spread of the gospel since the first century?

---

10 KEY EVENTS AND DATES

Christ is born (6 BC)

Pilate becomes governor of Judea (AD 26)

Christ begins his public ministry (27)

Christ is crucified and resurrected, and the church of Christ is begun (30)

Saul (Paul) is converted (33)

Paul's first missionary journey (48)

the council of Jerusalem (49)

Nero blames Christians for the great fire of Rome (64)

Rome destroys Jerusalem (70)

emperor worship grows, threatening the legality of Christianity (95)

A Quick Review

Most New Testament history takes place between the beginning of the ministry of Christ (AD 27) and the Roman destruction of Jerusalem (AD 70). Unlike the Old Testament, the New Testament witnesses no procession of empires, so we need only concern ourselves with the Roman Empire. Secular history provides us with many opportunities to cross-check biblical dates and events, just as most of the many places referred to in the New Testament can be found on a map.

It is of great benefit to familiarize yourself with a little history and geography. Learn the ten key dates in the list above. Refer to the maps of first-century Palestine (page 181) and the Roman Empire (page 175). Once unfamiliar places, persons, and events become familiar, you will navigate the life-changing pages of the New Testament much more easily and effectively. Things will make sense. In short, your Bible study will be turbocharged.

18

JESUS CHRIST

Anyone who has seen me has seen the Father.

JOHN 14:9

Jesus Christ is the central figure of the Bible, and indeed of all history. He was highly literate, yet he left us no letters. He is the Word of God (as God in the flesh), yet he didn't write a single word in the word of God (the Scriptures). In fact, the only reminiscence of him ever writing was a few words scribbled in the dirt (John 8:6,8). Nevertheless, we know more about Jesus than any other person in the Bible. No figure in the Bible has 90 continuous chapters devoted to him (Matthew 1– Acts 1). No other person appears as frequently in Scripture (more than 1200 times, named as Jesus, Christ, Christ Jesus, and Jesus Christ). And no one in history has touched and transformed as many lives as he has.

Even though he has not left us a diary, autobiography, or anything in writing at all, his followers have, for he entrusted his life-saving message to them. Nowhere do we catch a better glimpse of this message and the Man who generated it than in the four Gospels. This chapter provides a panorama of the four Gospels. We will begin by zooming in on the life of Jesus Christ.

His Name

Jesus, or *Yeshua* (Hebrew and Aramaic), was born in the late first century BC. Interestingly, five of the ten most common names of the time were given to members of his family, as we read in the Gospels. Based on grave inscriptions and other literary sources, the most

187

common names in first-century Palestine were, in order: Salome, Simon, Mary, Joseph, Judas, Lazarus, Joezer, John, Martha, and Jesus. The meaning of *Yeshua* is "God saves," an appropriate name for the Lord.

Another name for Jesus Christ was Immanuel, or "God with us" (Matthew 1:23; see Isaiah 7:14; 8:8). Both epithets denote his deity. The unexpected entrance of deity into humanity—what theologians call the *incarnation* (the physical embodiment of God)—took place in fulfillment of prophecy. We shall return to this crucial theme at the end of this chapter.

His Birth

Although Jesus grew up in Galilee, in the northern part of Palestine, the town of his birth was Bethlehem, in the south. Significantly, Bethlehem was the birthplace of Jesus' ancestor David, the most revered of all the Jewish kings.

Jesus was born probably no later than 6 BC. This deduction is based on two facts. First, Josephus tells us that Herod the Great died in 4 BC.[1] And second, Matthew 2:13-19 records Herod's attempt to do away with the infant Jesus. In that account, Herod feels threatened when he learns from gift-bearing "Magi from the East" of the birth of a potential usurper to his throne—someone they refer to as "the king of the Jews" (Matthew 2:2-12).[2]

Herod is known for his paranoia, brutality, and ruthlessness as king, as evidenced by his execution of three of his sons, two brothers-in-law, an uncle, many rabbis, and his favorite wife Mariamne I. But it is noteworthy *why* he killed one of those two brothers-in-law, Aristobulus III. In 37 BC, Herod installed the 17-year-old Aristobulus as the Jewish high priest. But the Jews did not trust Herod's claim of being a believing Jew, and Herod began to fear that the Jews might declare Aristobulus to be the "King of the Jews" in his place. Consequently, Herod had Aristobulus drowned in 36 BC. Therefore it is no surprise that Herod ordered all male children two years of age or younger in and around Bethlehem killed after encountering the Magi.

There are no historical accounts of Herod ordering any other mass murder. Jesus may have reached the age of two, so he would have been born no later than 6 BC.

His Family

Jesus' supposed father was Joseph (*Yosef* in Hebrew), named after the great patriarch who dominates Genesis 37–50. Jesus' mother, Mary (or Miriam) was named after Moses' sister, a powerful leader and prophetess in her own right. As we have seen, these were common names at the turn of the millennium.

The New Testament repeatedly refers to Jesus' brothers and sisters (Matthew 13:55-56). The brothers' names were James, Joseph, Judah (Judas), and Simon, but the text mentions "all his sisters" as well, indicating a large family. The notion that his brothers were cousins or children of Joseph by a previous marriage arose in the second century, apparently as an attempt to preserve the perpetual virginity of Mary. However, the natural reading of such texts as Matthew 1:25 is that Mary began sexual relations with Joseph after the birth of Jesus. This most easily explains the birth of seven or more of Jesus' siblings.

Jesus was raised in a Jewish family. Technically speaking, Jesus was not a Christian—as odd as that may sound to Western ears. He was a zealous and faithful Jew. After Joseph's death, he would have had significant family responsibilities, which he carried out for several decades before he began his public ministry.

His Appearance and Personality

Of course, we have no photographs or paintings of Jesus. In all likelihood, he looked like a typical male Jew. He would have worn a beard, though after the Jewish fashion of the first century, it may have been trimmed. As a Middle Easterner, he would have had dark skin. Having been a manual laborer and then walking everywhere during his three-year ministry, he would have been muscular and fit. We know one thing for sure: He wasn't Anglo-Saxon. No blond hair, no blue eyes. He probably wasn't exceptionally tall. The average height for a man of his time was less than five and a half feet.

In Mark 14:44, Judas guides the arrest party to the Garden of

Gethsemane. It is nighttime, and the high priest and his detachment of guards don't seem to know which one they are to arrest. Judas helps them by pointing out the suspect with a kiss. If Jesus were six feet tall, he could have referred to Jesus as "the tall guy by the tree." (And if he were a blue-eyed blond...well, even less need for the kiss.)

We know little about how Jesus looked, but we know a lot about how he lived. The Bible freely records the sins and weaknesses of all its major characters—Abraham's lies, Sarah's meanness, Rebekah's deceit, David's adultery, the initial lack of faith on the part of Jesus' own family members, and so on (Genesis 20:2; 16:6; 27:2-13; 2 Samuel 11; Mark 3:21; John 7:5). Yet at no point is sin attributed to Jesus (Matthew 5:17; 26:59-60; Luke 4:13). Even his enemies were unable to convict him of sin (John 8:46)—not to say they all accepted him. Some charged him with being a fraud (Matthew 12:2,38; 13:53-57), or of being demon-possessed (Luke 11:15), or of making political threats against the Romans (Luke 23:2,10,13-15), yet none of these charges was substantiated. Could it be that one human perfectly fulfilled God's plan for his life, never sinning? This is the audacious claim of the New Testament.

Jesus' strengths were many: courage, kindness, insight, service, joyfulness, serenity, intensity, patience, gentleness, and an astounding degree of self-control. In one sense, no single trait stands out more than any other. His personality shows perfect balance. Like the brilliance of the sun, all parts of his character were dazzlingly impressive. No one ever comments on how bright the top left quadrant of the sun is (though it is). The other quadrants of our nearest star are equally bright. We perceive it as a unified whole. But this unity of Jesus' character may lead us to miss some of his qualities.

For example, Jesus was highly intelligent—not just as a scholar of the Scriptures (Luke 2:41-47) but also as a student of human nature (John 2:25). As you read the Gospels, try to see how his mind works when he is in a tight spot (Matthew 21:23-27; 22:16-21). His logical mind is truly brilliant. Yet he never bullies others with his intellect, but rather remains humble in every interaction.

Another trait many read right over is his intensity. In the Gospels we have a picture of how much one man can pack into a day, how one can keep giving even though emotionally spent (Mark 3:20-21; 6:30-56). His drive was phenomenal, and the New Testament invites those who follow him to lead zealous and passionate lives (Luke 13:32-33; 24:19; Titus 2:11-14; 1 John 2:3-6). This is the shape of holiness.

His Vocation

Often people ask, if Jesus was the Savior of the world—if salvation depended on him—why did he wait until his thirties before launching his ministry? Christians believe that the cross reached both forward and backward in time, covering the sins of all who put their faith in God, so in one sense nothing was lost by waiting. Yet there are other clues in the Scriptures. The last time Joseph is mentioned is during a family visit to Jerusalem (Luke 2:41-48). Scholars suspect that Joseph died before Jesus' public ministry began. If he passed away around AD 20, he would have left behind a family of at least nine (Mary plus the eight or more children). It would then have fallen on Jesus, as eldest male, to assume leadership of the family. In other words, leaving his family to fend for themselves would have been a dereliction of duty—an action that would have disqualified his character and claims. In time, of course, James (the second-born male) would transition into the head of the family.

Here are three more reasons Jesus may have waited so long to begin his ministry. First, he knew from Scripture that a forerunner would come (Isaiah 40:3-5; Malachi 3:1). Not until John the Baptist presented the Messiah did Jesus commence his special work. Second, Jesus was righteous. The Bible urges us to defend the cause of the widow (Deuteronomy 10:18). If Mary was widowed, Jesus had a special obligation, and especially if Joseph died when Jesus was still in his teens. Third, would he have succeeded in his important work if he began at, say, age 17? Who would follow a 17-year-old Messiah?

If Jesus followed in his father's vocational footsteps, he too would have labored as a *tekton*. This Greek word (Mark 6:3) denotes one who works with wood or stone—a builder. The English word *architect* ("master builder") comes from this word. Thus there is reason to believe that from boyhood until his early thirties Jesus worked as a carpenter or stonemason. In addition to enabling him to provide for the family, such work would also have helped him to relate to common folk and build strength of character through consistent work.

Though Jesus' mission was urgent, he did not rush to begin his ministry. Always he proceeded with a keen sense of divine timing (John 2:4; 7:6,8,30; 8:20; 12:23,27; 13:1; 17:1; 19:30).

To Marry or Not to Marry

Both Jesus and Paul advocated remaining single as an effective path of service to God, although they conceded that only a few had the gift of celibacy (Matthew 19:10-12; 1 Corinthians 7:1-9). Yet neither taught that there was anything inherently sinful or unclean about sex and marriage. Jesus knew, and often predicted, that he would die in the cause of his mission (Matthew 16:21). Had he married, he would have left behind a young widow and fatherless children. Perhaps this is why he never married. Or it may be that his intention was not to establish a dynasty. Imagine the elitism that could be spawned by membership in the literal family of God!

His Ministry

After Jesus' baptism and temptation, he embarked on a three-year teaching ministry.[3] In John's Gospel we learn that he returned to Jerusalem for three Passovers (2:23; 6:4; 12:1). Thus if he began work in AD 27 or 28 (according to the chronology of Luke 3:1-2,23; 4:14-16), he would have been executed in AD 30.

Jesus began in Galilee, working among the towns of present-day Lebanon, Syria, Jordan, and Israel. Once the disciples began to understand his identity as the Messiah, he proceeded to Jerusalem, where he came into direct conflict with the religious establishment and was summarily dispatched by them (Luke 9:21-22,51-53; 22:52–23:2). His ministry included several components: proclaiming the gospel of the kingdom, teaching, healing, exorcizing, training the 12, and most important, giving his life for the sins of the world (Mark 10:45).

His Miracles

Jesus worked numerous miracles. Their purpose was not to impress the crowds, but to demonstrate the presence of the kingdom of God (Matthew 12:28; Luke 10:9,11; 11:20; 17:20-21). His miracles are credible, unlike these apocryphal and fanciful wonders attributed to him in specious sources dating from the second to fourth centuries:

- The ox and the donkey worship the baby Jesus. When Mary is hungry, her infant son commands the palm tree to bow down and offer her dates.

- A colt descended from Balaam's donkey salutes Thomas as Christ's twin brother.

- Jesus forms pigeons out of clay on the Sabbath. To avoid suspicion of breaking the Sabbath, he transforms the inanimate figures into real birds, which fly away, thereby eliminating the evidence.

- Jesus strikes dead a boy for accidentally bumping into him. He curses another child: "You cheeky, godless blockhead...now you also shall wither like a tree."

This is nothing but mythology, next to which the miracles of Christ seem sober and their narration restrained. The later, spurious works differ enormously from the authentic first-century documents of the New Testament. Those who try to explain away Jesus' miracles as legends have not carefully compared the Gospels and the apocryphal writings. Jesus' miracles are neither out of character for him nor sensationalistic. They are recorded for a reason: "that you may believe that Jesus is the Messiah, the Son of God, and that by believing you may have life in his name" (John 20:30-31).

His Message

Jesus' central message was the kingdom of God (Matthew 4:17; Mark 1:15; Luke 4:43). The day of the Lord was dawning even in the present; the future messianic age of righteousness was breaking into our world. This means that forgiveness, freedom, and participation in the abundant life brought by the Messiah are available now—not only in the hereafter. Jesus also called his followers to a radical standard of holiness, even higher than that of the Law (Matthew 5:21-48). The 12 apostles are sometimes called the disciples, but actually, all who follow Christ are disciples (Matthew 28:19; Acts 11:26). Jesus said that we are his disciples if we hold to his teaching, love one another as he loved us, and bear fruit that lasts (John 8:31-32; 13:34-35; 15:16). In another sense, the man *is* the message. Jesus not only pointed people to the way (Matthew 7:13-14) but also *is* the way (John 14:6).

His Death

Clashing with the leaders of a complacent and inert religious establishment, Jesus was arrested, abused, and executed. The final week of Jesus' life is called the Passion Week. *Passion* has another sense besides "zeal"; its original meaning is "suffering." His passion culminates in his crucifixion, a gruesome and humiliating form of torture and death perfected by the Romans. Originally only corpses were nailed up on crosses, but the Romans began crucifying live persons. And yet as horrific and gory as such a punishment was, the New Testament never emphasizes the details.

The scandal of the cross (a stumbling block—1 Corinthians 1:23) has nothing to do with the degree of pain, but rather the shame of the event. This execution was normally reserved for slaves, never for Roman citizens (except perhaps those guilty of treason). The shame of crucifixion might be on a par with registration as a pedophile. Even if the accused were innocent, all would naturally assume he must have done something to deserve the label, and he would not easily lose the stigma. (How would you feel about attending a church where the preacher had been tried for pedophilia?) No wonder the cross was foolishness to Greeks and a stumbling block—scandalous nonsense—to the Jews.

DATING THE CRUCIFIXION

How do we know the year Jesus was put to death or how old he was at the time? Consider these facts:

- John the Baptist's ministry began in the fifteenth year of the reign of Tiberius Caesar (Luke 3:1-3). Tiberius came to the throne in AD 14, so John must have started preaching in AD 27 or 28 (partial years counted as full years in inclusive reckoning).

- Jesus' ministry started when he was "about thirty" (Luke 3:23). Note that Luke does not assign a precise age. If Jesus was born as late as 6 BC, he would be around 32 when he entered into his public ministry.

- John's chronology, with Jesus attending three Passovers, suggests a three-year ministry.

- Pontius Pilate was removed from office in AD 36, so the crucifixion must have occurred before then.

- Herod the Tetrarch (son of Herod the Great), who met Jesus, died in AD 34, narrowing the range even further.

- Passover fell on a Friday during only two years: AD 30 and 33. In this case, the Passovers mentioned in John are those of AD 28, 29, and 30.

- Jesus' ministry gained traction immediately after John's ministry (AD 28). If so, AD 33 may be too late for Jesus' death.

- April 7, AD 30 would have been the Passover date marking Jesus' execution.

- Thus Jesus had reached 35 years of age by the time of his crucifixion and may have been older.

After His Death

The Bible teaches that death was not the end for Jesus. Rather, he...

- descended to the realm of the dead and preached there (Ephesians 4:9; 1 Peter 3:19)

- was resurrected on the third day (1 Corinthians 15:4-8)

- appeared to many of his disciples over a 40-day period (Acts 1:3)

- ascended to heaven, where he lives to make intercession for God's people (Acts 1:9; Hebrews 7:25)

- will return one day in glory, initiating the resurrection

of the dead and the last judgment (John 14:2-3; Acts 1:
11; Philippians 3:20)

As a result of the cross, Christ has provided reconciliation, redemption, ransom, atonement, reconciliation, and sacrifice for sins (Romans 5:11; Ephesians 1:7; 1 Timothy 2:6; Hebrews 2:17; 1 John 2:2). Those who respond to his message are therefore redeemed, born again, ransomed, adopted, transferred into the kingdom of God, saved, justified, reconciled…a torrent of metaphors cascades through the pages of the New Testament. Yet no single image can capture the wonder and awe of what took place at Calvary.

It Was Prophesied

The testaments are inextricably connected. The institutions of king, prophet, and priest all point toward Christ. *Christ* (*Christos* in Greek) and *Messiah* (*Mashiach* in Hebrew) mean "the anointed one." In the Old Testament, anointing was for prophets, priests, and kings. Scores of messianic chapters point to Jesus Christ in all three divisions of the Hebrew Bible.[4] Messianic prophecy was therefore heavily emphasized in the teaching of the early church.[5]

Of course the Scriptures point to Jesus in different ways. Some passages only foreshadow Christ. For example, Genesis 22:1-18 contains nine parallels between the sacrifice of Isaac and sacrifice of Jesus. Other passages, such as Psalm 22, are not direct prophecies but find deeper fulfillment in the events surrounding Jesus. And then there is strict prophecy, such as Isaiah 52:13–53:12, which foretells that the Messiah would suffer before he triumphed.

This concept was especially difficult to grasp for the Jewish people, who focused on the prophetic images of the Messiah as conquering king and paid less attention to the passages where he is a suffering servant. They tended to equate the coming of Messiah with the full appearance of the kingdom of God (John 6:15). To people who were expecting glory, the cross was not only counterintuitive but also seemingly unscriptural.

The New Testament makes it clear that the Lamb that was slain is none other than the Lion of the Tribe of Judah (Revelation 5:5-6). The cross and the crown are united. Isaiah contains the greatest number of messianic texts, so let's list seven of the remarkable facts about this book and its longest messianic prophecy, Isaiah 52:13–53:12.

1. Isaiah is the prophetic book most quoted in the New Testament.

2. In Acts 8:26-28, the Ethiopian eunuch has been reading Isaiah 53. Once Philip the Evangelist teaches him that Jesus is the subject of the text, he cannot wait to be baptized and become a follower of the Messiah.

3. Isaiah is the prophetic book found most in the Dead Sea Scrolls, constituting 17 partial and 2 complete manuscripts.

4. The prize scroll of the lot, 1QIsaᵃ, proves that the prophecy of Christ in chapter 53 cannot have been written after the fact. The scroll dates to at least 100 years before Christ. Because it is so long and so well preserved, this single scroll constitutes a quarter of the biblical scrolls among the Dead Sea Scrolls!

5. In one of the Dead Sea Scrolls, an Aramaic targum (a translation with interpretation) refers to "My servant Messiah."[6] So there was a strand within Judaism that recognized the suffering of the Christ.

6. Moreover, the Babylonian Talmud (from the third to fifth centuries AD) says explicitly of the Messiah that "he bore our sickness."[7]

7. Finally, the medieval rabbis applied Isaiah 53 to the Messiah.[8]

Here are some of the most specific and best-known Old Testament prophecies of the Christ.

PROPHECIES OF JESUS' BIRTH
- born at Bethlehem (Micah 5:2; compare John 7:41-42)
- born of a virgin (Isaiah 7:14)
- God to become man (Psalm 110:1; Isaiah 9:6)

PROPHECIES OF HIS MINISTRY
- heralded by John the Baptist (Isaiah 40:3-5; Malachi 3:1; 4:5-6)
- ministered in Galilee (Isaiah 9:1-2)
- a wise counselor (Isaiah 9:6) and champion of the needy (Isaiah 11:1-10)

- a shepherd in the spirit of David (Ezekiel 34:11-16,20-31)
- healed the sick (Isaiah 53:4)

PROPHECIES CONCERNING HIS DEATH

- entered Jerusalem on a donkey (Zechariah 9:9)
- betrayed by a close friend (Psalm 41:9)
- abandoned by his disciples (Zechariah 13:7)
- lots were cast for his clothes (Psalm 22:18)
- crucified (Psalm 22:14-16)
- pierced (Zechariah 12:10; Isaiah 53:5)
- bore our sins on the cross (Isaiah 53:6,8,12)

PROPHECIES CONCERNING HIS RESURRECTION AND ASCENSION

- divinely rescued (Psalm 22:22-24; Isaiah 53:11)
- resurrected (Psalm 16:10)
- ascended to God and received everlasting dominion (Daniel 7:13-14). (It is remarkable that the divine Judge in this passage is a human being—the resurrected and ascended Jesus.)
- served as an intercessor (priest) in the order of Melchizedek (Psalm 110:4)

Interpretation of prophecy is complicated. Yet taken all together, the implications are inescapable. Jesus was the Messiah predicted in the Old Testament, centuries in advance.

A Quick Review

We do not know what he looked like, yet we recognize his image in all who are born of God. He left us nothing in writing, yet he is the Word of God, and through his Spirit the New Testament was inspired and given to us as a precious gift. He told us he is coming back, yet we don't know when—which means we must strive to live in a state of expectation and preparation. For as the Lord asked, "When the Son of Man comes, will he find faith on the earth?" (Luke 18:8).

THE GOSPELS

Jesus performed many other signs in the presence of his
disciples, which are not recorded in this book. But these are
written that you may believe that Jesus is the Messiah, the Son
of God, and that by believing you may have life in his name.

JOHN 20:30-31

Having met the central character of the Bible, Jesus Christ, we are now prepared to inspect the New Testament, which has four sections: the Gospels, Acts, the epistles, and the Apocalypse. In this chapter we will survey the four Gospels.

The word *gospel* is used in two senses when referring to the New Testament. First, it refers to the good news (Greek *euangelion,* from which comes the word *evangelical*). In this book, we use a lowercase *g* when referring to the gospel in this sense. Paul provides one perspective of the gospel in his first letter to the Corinthians.

> Now, brothers and sisters, I want to remind you of the gospel I preached to you, which you received and on which you have taken your stand. By this gospel you are saved, if you hold firmly to the word I preached to you. Otherwise, you have believed in vain.
>
> For what I received I passed on to you as of first importance: that Christ died for our sins according to the Scriptures, that he was buried, that he was raised on the third day according to the Scriptures, and that he appeared (1 Corinthians 15:1-5).

In this sense, the gospel is the good news about Jesus—that through his death and resurrection, we are saved from our sins.

Second, the word also refers to the four Bible books that record the story of Jesus' life—Matthew, Mark, Luke, and John. In this book, we use an uppercase *G* when referring to these four Gospels. In this second sense, the Gospels are selective stories about the life of Jesus. The message is good news, so the authors of the four Gospels are accordingly called evangelists. Our focus in this chapter is on the Gospels in this second sense: accounts of the life of Jesus.

Authorship, Language, and Date

Traditionally two of the Gospels are attributed to apostles (Matthew and John) and two to companions of apostles (Mark, a companion of Peter, and Luke, a companion of Paul). All the Gospels are anonymous, but the evidence for the traditional authorship is strong.[1] Presumably the human medium of the message is less important than its divine origin.

As for the dates of the Gospels, most scholars put Mark first, followed by Matthew and Luke, with John being written last.[2] In general, the New Testament epistles (beginning in the late 40s) preceded the Gospels. Two key years in first-century history for understanding the New Testament are AD 30 and 70. The first marks the death and resurrection of Christ—the pivotal point of human history. As for AD 70, this is the year the Roman army destroyed Jerusalem and its temple, a devastating event Jesus prophesied in Matthew 24, Mark 13, and Luke 21, and which we discussed in chapter 17.

The language of the Gospels is Koine (common) Greek, though it should be said that the language of Luke (author of Luke–Acts, a double work) is far from common. Luke and the unknown author of Hebrews display the finest Greek in the New Testament. There is an early tradition that Matthew was originally written in Hebrew, and some scholars accept this conclusion. It is certainly true that all Jesus' apostles were Jews, and regardless of whether they spoke more Aramaic or Greek, they were deeply immersed in the Hebraic world, so their thoughts would conform to the patterns of Semitic language.

Genre: *Bios*

A Gospel is not a biography in the modern sense. Jesus' birth is discussed in two of the four Gospels, yet except for a single glimpse of the 12-year-old Jesus, his childhood is wholly skipped over. There is little interest in his family. His thoughts are almost never related. Nor are the Gospel episodes always strictly chronological. Consider the words of a second-century writer.

> Mark, having become the interpreter of Peter, wrote down accurately whatever he remembered. It was not, however, in exact order that he related the sayings or deeds of Christ. For he neither heard the Lord nor accompanied Him. But afterwards, as I said, he accompanied Peter, who accommodated his instructions to the necessities [of his hearers], but with no intention of giving a regular narrative of the Lord's sayings…He took special care not to omit anything he had heard, and not to put anything fictitious into the statements (Papias, AD 125).

Papias notes that the Gospel of Mark is a truthful account, though not strictly chronological. This may offend modern journalistic sensibilities, but it was standard among ancient writers of biography. What's going on here?

Nothing strange, once we identify the literary genre of the four Gospels. All fall into the ancient genre of *bios,* or "life."[3] Yet it's not like modern biography, as *bios* does not cover one's entire life. Rather, it is quite selective. Many ancient *bioi* (and *vitae*) have survived, so the genre is well understood. These are some of the typical characteristics of *bios*:

- continuous prose narrative style
- three-part structure:
  1. introduction of the subject by name, sometimes including a birth account or genealogy, and then his public appearance
  2. narrative of words and deeds that reveal the character
  3. death and vindication

- material grouped by subject with a somewhat flexible chronology
- discourse (sayings, stories, speeches, and conversations) crafted to express the character's teachings and beliefs
- lack of interest in analyzing the subject's inner life
- life held up as an example to emulate

How do the Gospels measure up to this description?

Continuous prose narrative. In all four Gospels, the events of Jesus' life are presented as a continuous sequence. The Gospels are mainly prose, although occasional sections are more stylized or even apocalyptic (such as Matthew 23–25).

Tripartite biography. Matthew and Luke have birth narratives as well as genealogies, whereas John's theological prologue ("In the beginning was the Word...") takes the place of the birth narrative. Mark begins with the name of Jesus and the subject matter of the Gospel. In all four Gospels the middle section is the largest. It is followed by a substantial death and vindication account that includes Jesus' suffering, death, resurrection, and appearances.

Material grouped by subject matter. Matthew is arranged into five major discourses (5–7; 10; 13; 18; 24–25), thus mirroring the five books of the Torah (the Pentateuch) and the five books of Psalms. John is structured around three sevens: seven "signs," or miracles, seven "I am" statements, and seven testimonies that Jesus is the Messiah.

Discourse represents the character. There are differences in the wording of various interactions across the Gospels, but all portray a consistent picture of Jesus as a virtuous and divine Messiah whose life and mission fulfill Old Testament prophecy. The speeches in the Bible are usually condensed and paraphrased. Biblical writers did not feel a burden to report the exact words when they recorded a conversation. In fact, everything Jesus said that is recorded in the Bible can be read aloud in just a couple of hours. Surely Jesus spoke for more than two hours during his three-year ministry, but how fortunate it is that the Bible didn't record everything he said—the Gospels alone would be tens of thousands of pages long.

Jesus' inner thoughts are seldom represented. There are exceptions, however, as in the temptation scene, Jesus' Gethsemane prayer, and his occasional frustration with the disciples.

The life of Christ is held up for our sake. Jesus is both an example for us to imitate and a divine revelation who leads us to saving faith (John 13:15; 21:19; 20:30-31). And yet we are not just to admire Jesus for his virtue; we are also to worship him for who he is—God incarnate.

The Gospels were written primarily for believers, whereas *bios* was intended for the general public. But this is a small difference. In most respects, the Gospels fit the genre of *bios*.

As for Jesus' words, many sayings circulated orally for a generation or two. In the oral culture of the first century, audiences and especially the 12 disciples may have memorized Jesus' exact words. Oral transmission is a well-trodden field, and it is impressive how accurately information in ancient times was transmitted. But there seems to be more going on here, for other words are attributed to Jesus in accordance with the accepted style of the *bios*. This is not to say that "words have been put into his mouth." If you have ever been in a heated discussion and told the other person that he was putting words into your mouth, you were accusing the person of misrepresenting you. We do not, however, object when others paraphrase, reword, or summarize us, provided our intention has been preserved. Paraphrasing is not misrepresentation.

Thus we see that the Gospels are best understood as examples of ancient *bioi*.

Gospel Discrepancies?

Critics point out minor discrepancies among the four Gospels. These are usually chronological variations, alternate wordings in conversations, and other petty differences. Yet once we take account of the genre, ancient *bios*, we can easily account for such differences.

Moreover, I would argue that if all four accounts matched perfectly, we would have real grounds for suspicion. Try this: Sign your own name the same way twice. (Go ahead—it can't be done.) Identical signatures suggest at least one of them is counterfeit. Or, resorting to another analogy, eyewitnesses may provide different details of an accident. Perhaps not every statement can be harmonized with the report of the next witness. Thus certain questions may remain, but the reasonable conclusion is certainly not that the accident never occurred. However, if the witnesses gave the same testimony word for word, you would assume some kind of collusion had taken place between them.

The fact that the copyists of the biblical documents let the minor discrepancies stand is a testimony to their integrity. They did not feel at liberty to alter what they had received. Rather than bringing into question the divine inspiration of the Gospel accounts, this is more of an affirmation that imperfect men were involved. In fact, we are quite likely to find that the discrepancies between the Gospels help us to better understand the authors—who each was, how he thought, who his intended audience was, and what he (and the Holy Spirit) wanted to accomplish with his particular Gospel.

GOSPEL ELEMENTS AND EXAMPLES

apocalypses (Mark 13)	parables (Luke 15)
beatitudes (Luke 6)	passion narratives
birth narratives (Matthew 2)	(Mark 14–15)
conversations (John 4)	prayers (John 17)
discourses (Matthew 23)	sayings (Mark 2)
genealogies (Luke 3)	sermons (Matthew 5–7)
miracle stories (Matthew 14)	theological reflections
Old Testament fulfillment	(John 1)
stories (Mark 1)	

Gospel Themes

What themes and emphases do we find in the four Gospels? The synoptic Gospels (Matthew, Mark, and Luke) share common stylistic elements, such as short conversations, clear literary connections, common material, and this common framework:

1. Jesus' Galilean ministry, culminating in
2. Peter's confession of Jesus' identity as Messiah (or Christ), followed by
3. the long trek south to Jerusalem, where
4. the passion week takes place, followed by
5. the resurrection, postresurrection appearances, and final charge to his disciples.

In John, on the other hand, conversations may dominate entire chapters (as in chapters 4 and 9). Jesus' teaching and healing ministries center in Jerusalem. Of course the two viewpoints are not exclusive; Jesus and his band walked all over the small country of Palestine.

Here are some of the emphases of the four Gospels, beginning with the oldest, Mark.

Mark

Mark is the shortest of the Gospels and gets right to the point. One of its most common words is *immediately*. This is a Gospel of swift action.

Mark targeted a Roman audience of (mostly Gentile) believers. He emphasized Jesus' power and demonstrated his deity through his miracles of healing people, controlling nature, driving out demons, bringing dead people back to life, prophesying, and rising from the dead.

Jesus is the kingly Messiah and the suffering servant of Isaiah. This has implications for the kingdom of God, which is now breaking into the present age.

Jesus' identity is to be concealed (for a while) and then broadcast.

Discipleship entails taking up the cross and accepting God's plan for our lives.

Jesus trains the 12 in Galilee. Once his identity begins to dawn on them, he heads south to Jerusalem, where he will be executed by the religious powers of the day.

His ministry is telescoped into a single year.

Israel is to undergo a new exodus (another motif of Isaiah).

Matthew

Matthew utilized nearly all of Mark's Gospel but with a number of changes. This was the Gospel most used by the church fathers (writers and leaders in the centuries immediately following Christ).

Matthew, also called Levi, targeted a Jewish audience and demonstrated that Jesus is the Messiah foretold by Old Testament prophets. Matthew's work as a tax collector, requiring accurate records and note taking, made him an ideal person for the Holy Spirit to use in preserving precisely Jesus' teaching, sermons, and discourses for all generations.

Matthew's genealogy (1:1-17) moves forward from Abraham to Joseph, establishing Jesus' legal claim to the throne of David through Joseph's ancestral descent from Solomon. Joseph is identified as the husband of Mary, not Jesus' biological father.

The presence of three Gentiles in the bloodline demonstrate God's will to save all nations. The Gospel ends with Jesus commanding that his followers make disciples of everyone, thus fulfilling God's promise to Abraham (Genesis 12:2-3).

Matthew used Old Testament fulfillment formulae 11 times.

Jesus is a teacher and lawgiver like Moses, yet Jesus brings something even better than the Torah.

Luke

Luke was a historian, a medical doctor, an associate of Paul, and the only Gentile author in the New Testament. He utilized a good deal of Mark and possibly Matthew as well, writing for the Gentiles (Greeks).

Luke emphasized Jesus' humanity with stories of his caring for the weak, the suffering, the aliens, and the outcasts. Jesus' close relationship with the family of Lazarus and his respect and love for many different women from all strata of society are uniquely portrayed in this Gospel.

Luke's genealogy (3:23-37) moves backward from Jesus to Adam, establishing Jesus' physical descent from David and his claim of kingship. Saying, "He was the son, so it was thought, of Joseph" (3:23), Luke traces Jesus' lineage through Mary's ancestor Nathan rather than Joseph's ancestor Solomon. This designation fulfills the angel's prophecy of Luke 1:32-33: "He will be great and will be called the Son of the Most High. The Lord God will give him the throne of his father David, and he will reign over Jacob's descendants forever; his kingdom will never end."

Luke claims to have done his research carefully (Luke 1:1-4).

In Luke, salvation is for all strata of society, every class from slave to royal. In Acts, salvation is for all geographical regions.

In Luke, the gospel must go from Galilee to Jerusalem; in Acts, from Jerusalem to Rome. (More on this in the next chapter.)

Jesus displays God's care for the marginalized (women, the poor, slaves, aliens, the sick, the suffering, and outcasts).

The Spirit, prayer, repentance, and other components of spirituality are heavily emphasized.

John

John's story is told from the perspective of time *after* the resurrection and the outpouring of the Spirit, and it spans several years. Unlike the first three (synoptic) Gospels, there is no mention of Jesus' baptism, exorcisms, transfiguration, or parables, and there is no prediction of Jerusalem's destruction. More than 90 percent of John's material is unique to him; it is not found in the synoptics.

John emphasized Jesus' deity. His target audience was all those who are or will someday be disciples of Christ. The strongest Christian traditions acknowledge that John was "the disciple whom Jesus loved" and the one whom Jesus entrusted with Mary while on the cross.

Like the letter of 1 John, John's Gospel emphasizes Jesus' humanity. He is the incarnate Word, as laid out in the philosophical prologue.

Whereas Matthew's genealogy runs from Abraham to Jesus, and Luke's from Jesus to Adam, John goes back further still—before the beginning of time.

Jesus' ministry is set primarily in Jerusalem, not Galilee.

John makes effective use of paired opposites: flesh and spirit, light and dark, heaven and earth, love and hate. Other words are imbued with special meaning (including *know*, *send*, *receive*, *world*, and *word*). Moreover, many words have double meanings (such as *again*, which can also mean "from above," as in John 3:3-7).

John records seven "I am" statements, seven signs, and seven testimonies to Jesus' deity. Seven is the number of perfection, and three is the number of God.

THE TWELVE APOSTLES
(MATTHEW 10:2-4; MARK 3:16-18; LUKE 6:14-16)

Simeon (Simon, Peter, son of John, Cephas)

Andrew (brother of Peter)

James (son of Zebedee, son of thunder, brother of John)

John (son of Zebedee, son of thunder, brother of James)

Philip

Bartholomew (Nathanael)

Matthew (Levi)

Thomas (Didymus, or twin)

James (son of Alphaeus)

Thaddeus (Lebbaeus, Jude, Judas, son of James)

Simon the Zealot

Judas Iscariot

The Apocryphal Gospels

In the centuries following the apostolic era, several persons constructed imaginative gospels and tried to pass them off as genuine. People today seldom investigate the facts, so they are easy targets for bogus claims. For example, *The Da Vinci Code* claimed that Constantine (in the early 300s) helped the church select 4 out of 88 gospels in circulation in his day. Of course, this is far from the truth. The four canonical Gospels were circulating as a unit by the early 100s, whereas the spurious documents weren't even written until the late second and third centuries. And even if we counted all the Gnostic gospels, there still weren't anywhere near 88 by Constantine's time.

Not surprisingly, these works contradict the teaching of the authentic Gospels. Many were nothing more than propaganda for sectarian groups that denied Jesus' crucifixion and resurrection, as reflected in such documents as the Gospel of Judas. They also contain a great deal that is mythological. Various wonders are ascribed to Jesus' apostles in such documents as Pseudo-Matthew, the Acts of Thomas, the Infancy Gospel of Thomas, the Acts of Peter, and the Acts of Paul.

- When Peter and Simon the sorcerer have their showdown in Rome, Peter commands a dog to lecture Simon on the hellfire awaiting him. The dog delivers the message and then dies.

- Peter repairs a broken statue simply by sprinkling holy water on it.

- Peter also makes a piece of smoked fish come back to life, whereupon it swims away.

- Paul baptizes a lion.

Have you heard of the Lost Letter of St. Paul, the Gospel of Philip, the Gospel of Peter, the Gospel of Truth, or the Acts of Pilate? Better known is the Gospel of Thomas (late second century), whose theology, if there is one, is Gnostic. In other words, insight (*gnosis,* Greek for "knowledge") is more important than morality. The goal is liberation from ignorance, enabling one to discover the god in himself, not liberation from sin that we may know the true God. Here are a few examples.

- "A person cannot mount two horses or bend two bows, and a servant cannot serve two lords" (saying 47).

- "Business people and merchants will not enter the realm of my Father" (saying 64).

- "Simon Peter said to them, 'Let Mary leave us, because women are not worthy of life.' Jesus said, 'Behold, I shall guide her so as to make her male, so that she may become a living spirit like you men. For every woman who makes herself male will enter the kingdom of heaven'" (saying 113/114).

Not surprisingly, all of these writings and false teachings were foretold and warned about by Jesus, Paul, Peter, and John (Matthew 24:4-5,11,24-25; Mark 13:22-23; Luke 21:8; Galatians 1:6-9; 2 Thessalonians 2:1-3; 1 Timothy 4:1; 2 Timothy 4:2-4; Titus 1:9; 2 Peter 2:1-22; 1 John 2:18-27; 4:1).

Is the New Testament missing any books? Not at all. Nothing is missing because nothing was removed or lost. The early church did not recognize the authority of this spurious gospel, and neither should we. Next time your friends or workmates drop comments about the Gospel of Thomas, I hope you will be well equipped to respond. Exaggerations and embellishments appear throughout all the spurious books, known as the New Testament Apocrypha.

Reading Tips

How can we get the most out of the Gospels? Here are seven suggestions.

1. Don't "homogenize" them. It is not necessarily wrong to harmonize, but the reason we have four documents and not just one is surely that the Holy Spirit wants to emphasize different things. The differences among the accounts reveal a lot of theology as well as the richness and texture of the Gospels. This richness is eliminated when we homogenize, but it becomes available to enhance and energize our study when we appreciate the differences.

2. The Gospels, just like the epistles, were composed primarily for Christians. They were written for insiders, not outsiders. This being the case, it is appropriate to read between the lines. What were the specific needs in the communities for which Matthew, Mark, Luke, and John were produced?

3. A good working knowledge of the Old Testament is

essential, for the Old Testament is constantly in the background. Without this, many reference points are lost and the Gospels may appear more enigmatic than they actually are.

4. Understand that Matthew is the Gospel for the Jews. It is concerned with the messianic connections between the Old Testament and the new covenant.

5. Remember that Mark is written for those in the Roman Empire who had less biblical background. It is a Gospel of action.

6. Know that Luke is written for those most comfortable in the Greek culture. Luke has the finest Greek and the greatest literary quality of the four Gospels.

7. Keep in mind that John has the most universal focus. It is also the most "spiritual" and theological of the Gospels. (Consider its prologue.) We also hear the constant refrain of misunderstanding—Jesus speaks on the spiritual level, but his listeners misunderstand him, taking him literally.

A Quick Review

The gospel message (the good news of the kingdom) could have been presented in a single evangelistic account. But it was not. Rather, Jesus' words and deeds are presented, each with its own emphases. These are difficult waters to navigate. The Holy Spirit gave us the Gospels just as he wanted us to have them.

Four portraits of Jesus—from four different angles—are better than one single Gospel, for they afford us a four-dimensional perspective. All students of the Bible must resist the temptation to combine the four Gospels into one harmonized Gospel by attempting to explain away their differences. Theologically inconsequential details are more properly called "human recollections" influenced by the writers' personal life experiences and perspectives. Savor them.

Although later writers penned numerous gospels, none of these can be credited with the validity and God-breathed authority of the genuine first-century Gospels. The later writings are replete with inaccuracies, mythology, and skewed theology. They were never part of the New Testament canon. We can trust the ancient biographies of the life of Jesus Christ. They accurately preserve genuine words, deeds, reminiscences, and records of the most powerful figure in all of history, Jesus Christ.

20

ACTS

*They devoted themselves to the apostles' teaching and
to fellowship, to the breaking of bread and to prayer.*

ACTS 2:42

Moving from the first section of the New Testament, the Gospels, we now arrive at the second section. Acts is generally thought of as a history book, yet properly speaking, it is not, as it focuses only on a few persons working in a narrow geographical area, and it covers only about 30 years. Nor is it actually the "Acts of the Apostles," as it is commonly called. Nothing is said about most of the apostles, and only a little is relayed about James and John. The author focuses instead on the earlier years of Peter and the middle years of Paul. Like the Gospels we examined in the previous chapter—a genre called *bios*—Acts is its own genre.

In the ancient world, *Acts* refers to a record of deeds, intended to popularize the regime or memorialize the departed.[1] Later some spurious Acts were created, such as the apocryphal Acts of Pilate, Acts of Peter, and Acts of Paul and Thecla. (In this last document, invented a century after Paul's death—long after he was around to deny its preposterous claims—Paul baptizes a talking lion.)

Acts is the companion volume to Luke and is dedicated to the same Theophilus (Luke 1:3; Acts 1:1-2). They are clearly written by the same author. This man is a traveling companion of Paul (in Acts the writer often claims to have been present with the apostle), and considering the writer's interest in medical things, the conclusion that he is Luke the physician seems justified (Colossians 4:14). Acts picks up where Luke ends off with only minimal overlap. Luke ends with the ascension of Christ from Bethany, and Acts resumes the action after its short prologue. The Gospel takes the story of Jesus from Galilee to Jerusalem; Acts takes it from Jerusalem to Rome.

Structure

Acts gives its own outline in Acts 1:8. After the Spirit came and the nuclear church began, the gospel was proclaimed (1) in Jerusalem, (2) in Judea and Samaria, and (3) to the ends of the earth (see Isaiah 49:6). Yet the evangelistic outline can be amplified:

- Jerusalem (1:1–6:7)
- Judea and Samaria (6:8–9:31)
- the Gentiles and Paul's conversion (9:32–12:24)
- Asia (12:25–16:5)
- Europe (16:6–19:20)
- Rome, the capital of the Gentile world (19:21–28:31)

Another structural consideration is that Peter dominates chapters 1–12, and chapters 13–28 focus on Paul. Peter was one of the 12, while Paul (baptized in AD 32 or 33) joined the apostolic group a few years after Pentecost. Their lives share multiple parallels. Both are Jews who preach to Gentiles, defeat a sorcerer, heal a lame man, raise the dead, heal the sick indirectly, impart the Spirit, and escape from prison. (In chapters 21 and 22, we will concentrate on Paul and his letters.)

Even within the part of Acts detailing the preaching and church planting of Paul, there are four missionary journeys—yet another way to dissect Acts. Overall, Luke's point is to emphasize the successful transition of the Christian movement from Judaism into the Gentile world, without belittling Jewish or Gentile Christians. This accounts for the parity between Peter and Paul.

Themes

The themes of Acts are mostly the same ones we encounter in Luke.

Some of these arise in the sermons of Acts, others in the narrative material.

The resurrection. In Acts, this is emphasized in nearly every speech, even more than the crucifixion.

Old Testament fulfillment. The coming of the Messiah, the beginning of the age of the Spirit, and the Gentile mission all unfold according to plan.

The kingdom of God. Already in this world we may taste of the heavenly kingdom, and one day we will enjoy a time of uninterrupted worship and fellowship.

Repentance. The proper response to the message of the kingdom is not just a sense of awe or even faith but a heartfelt and thorough turning from the fleshly desires of self to the spiritually discerned will, commands, and purposes of God.

Smashing through barriers. The gospel unites us all, overcoming the obstacles to fellowship that destroy relationship. Whether ministering to a neglected minority (Acts 6) or making the conceptual leap to receiving Gentiles into the fellowship on the basis of faith in Christ (Acts 10–11; 15), only through the Spirit can the vision of a united humanity be achieved. In Acts 15 a dispute within the church is resolved by elders collectively—not by a preacher, a majority vote, a committee of deacons, or an influential member. Group process makes for group unity.[2]

Concern for the marginalized. Luke cares specially for those without a voice: the poor, foreigners, women, and children.

The Holy Spirit. Everything that happens in Acts is through the power of the Spirit. The Holy Spirit is poured out only after Jesus has ascended (2:30,33), signaling the new covenant (Jeremiah 31:31-34; John 7:38-39; Acts 2:17-38). The Spirit is poured out in four remarkable manifestations, each with an important historical significance.

- in Jerusalem (chapter 2), signaling the beginning of the age of the Spirit
- in Samaria (chapter 8), as those who are part Jew and part Gentile are received into the fellowship

- in Caesarea (chapter 10), where full Gentiles are baptized, not circumcised

- in Ephesus (chapter 19), enlightening and empowering doctrinally wayward followers of Christ who had no clue about the spiritual revolution wrought by Jesus

Prayer. From the timorous petitions in the upper room to the earth-moving entreaties after the release of Peter and John (1:14; 4:23-31), prayer connects believers to their Lord and unleashes the power of the Spirit.

Possessions and wealth. Jesus requires his followers not only to share their goods with others but also to put all their wealth at his disposal.

Breaking of bread. As in Luke 24, the Lord makes himself known in the breaking of bread.

Apostolic miracles. In 2:17, again in 2:43, and on throughout the book, every miracle is done by, in connection with, or in the presence of an apostle of Christ. Thus miracles characterized the apostolic age, the foundational period of the church (Ephesians 2:20).

Relationship to authorities. Christ-followers strove to be respectful and obedient to the Jewish leaders and to the ruling Romans. Believers had to make an exception to obedience when they were required to violate the law of God (Acts 4:19; 5:29).

Persecution. The radical message of the kingdom was bound to be opposed by the world.

Proclamation of the gospel. Through the bold preaching of the apostles and evangelists, the world hears the good news. The speeches, which appear at crucial points in Acts, show how the gospel is presented and defended in a variety of settings (compare 13:13-52 with 17:16-34). In the end, Paul carries the gospel to Rome.

We can enhance our reading considerably by being sensitive to these major themes. If you make notes in your Bible while reading, you might consider using different colored highlighters for the main themes. This makes it even easier to recognize them next time you're reading the book.

Words for Christians in the New Testament			
Name	Greek meaning	Occur-rences	Emphasis
brother	brother or sister	79	a member of the spiritual family
Christian	Christ-follower	3	a committed imitator of Christ
church	assembly	112	a community of believers
disciple	student	271	a learner
friend	friend	2	an esteemed companion
saint	holy one	60	one who has been made pure
believer	believer	12	one who has faith in Christ
the Way	road	4	the path to following Christ

Interpretation

How are we to interpret Acts? There's so much to learn. Here are some keys to healthy interpretation:

Keep one eye on the Gospel of Luke. Remember that Acts is the complement to Luke. In the Gospel, the good news is for every social stratum, from the lowborn servant all the way to Caesar and his governors. In Acts, the gospel is for every region, as the message ripples out from Jerusalem to the far reaches of the empire.

Distinguish between the covenants. In Acts the age of the Spirit breaks in to the present; the kingdom to come is tasted even in this world. This had been prophesied in the Old Testament (Isaiah 59:21; Ezekiel 11:19; 36:26; 37:14; Jeremiah 31:31-34). The mark of the new covenant is the Holy Spirit (John 7:38-39; Acts 2:17-18,38; 5:32). On a related note, keep in mind that there are no Christians (strictly speaking) in the Gospels, for the possession of the Spirit is the mark of a Christian (Romans 8:9). With respect to becoming Christians, there are three temporal angles in the New Testament. The Gospels *anticipate* the new age (it is yet to come), Acts *records* the beginning of the new age (people become Christians from Pentecost on), and the epistles and the Apocalypse *assume* the new age has come (it has already broken in).

Keep an eye on the historical background and Luke's special emphases. Notice his eagerness to depict the Christians as law-abiding citizens. Rome is the capital of the empire, and the empire virtually constitutes the known world. Keep an eye on Luke's attention to medical details. He was, after all, a physician (Colossians 4:14). Note also his focus on women, the needy, and above all, the Holy Spirit.

Correlate events in Acts with the corresponding epistles. Pay special attention to 1 Corinthians, Galatians–2 Thessalonians, and Philemon.

Intend to obey. We should not aim to recapture first-century culture, but we should certainly strive to imbibe the spirit of courage and faith of the early church. Not everything in Acts is easy to apply, and there will always be small areas of disagreement among people of good faith, yet the nonnegotiable areas are clear. One must come to Christ initially (Acts 2:36-41) and then live a life devoted to the apostles' teaching, the fellowship, the breaking of bread, and prayer (Acts 2:42-47). The Lord gives the increase (the joy, awe, togetherness, and growth of 2:43-47).[3] Finally, to obey is to get the word out, pushing through whatever challenges come our way (5:1-11,29-33; 14:26; 16:16-40; 27:27-44).

A Recipe for Christianity?

Many Christians long to imitate or "restore" the early church. Yet is it really a matter of discovering the recipe for "New Testament Christianity"? Are we to cast lots when uncertain (Acts 1:26) or appoint seven deacons at a time (Acts 6:3)? Enter into sharp disputes (Acts 15:39) or take communion on Sunday only (Acts 20:7)? Using the Bible as a strict pattern in this way does not work well, nor is it scripturally required.

There are many such subjects in Scripture: foot-washing, the holy kiss, offering to carry a Roman soldier's pack an extra mile, and so on. Every case includes a principle that carries through to our day (such as humble service, godly greeting, or willingness to be inconvenienced without developing a bitter attitude), yet many of the practical details are different in our day. How exactly are we supposed to reproduce the church of Acts, in the presence of such a confusing matrix of issues? Using the book of Acts as a strict pattern for the church today is problematic.

What we can imitate is faith (1 Corinthians 11:1; Hebrews 12:2-3; 13:7)—and the spirit of faith among the early Christians is supremely inspiring. This is something all Christians can and should aim to restore.

Interpretation is no mere academic exercise, though we do need to *think* as we read. This is an opportunity to love the Lord our God with all our mind (Matthew 22:37). Interpretation must move from head knowledge to heart knowledge, from understanding to action.

Beyond Acts

After the time frame of the book of Acts (from about AD 30 to about 60), many other important events took place that are beyond the scope of this overview. Perhaps, however, this list will stimulate you to further exploration.

1. During the time frame of Acts, Paul wrote all of his letters but three, which he wrote after his release from Roman imprisonment. Peter, John, and Jude wrote their epistles after AD 60.

2. According to tradition, Paul eventually reached the extreme west—Spain (Romans 15:24,28). Thomas began his mission in southern India in 52.

3. Both Peter and Paul were executed under Nero by 68, the year of Nero's death, and most of the other apostles also met violent deaths.

4. Jerusalem was destroyed by the Romans in AD 70, forever transforming what till then had been a Jewish-flavored Christianity.

5. In the final decade of the first century, persecution heated up in Asia Minor as the wicked emperor Domitian (AD 81–96) demanded worship as "Lord and God." This brought the church into direct conflict with the Roman state for the first time since July 64, when Nero blamed the fire of Rome on the Christians. For more than two centuries, being a Christian would remain illegal.

A Quick Review

The double volume of Luke–Acts constitutes a quarter of the New Testament. The message of Jesus Christ is preached from Jerusalem all the way to Rome, foreshadowing a major shift as the church inched from its Jewish roots to a more Gentile expression of faith. This demonstrates the wisdom of Luke's approach, lifting up Peter, the apostle to the Jews, as well as Paul, the apostle to the Gentiles (Galatians 2:8).

Acts is to be read with the intention to obey. We too can be injected with the spirit of faith that animated the early church. And we will need it, for the road is long. Some drop out of the race early on, like Ananias and Sapphira or Simon the Sorcerer (Acts 5; 8). Others finish gloriously, yet that end comes early, as in the case of the martyrs Stephen and James (Acts 7; 12). Others run the race with perseverance to the end, though in time they may be eclipsed by other powerful men of God, as Barnabas and Peter were by Paul (Acts 11; 13). Many walk by faith for decades but may still suffer hardship along the way to their destination, just as Luke and Paul suffered shipwreck (Acts 27–28). The important thing is to persevere, for "it is necessary to pass through many troubles on our way into the kingdom of God" (Acts 14:22 HCSB).

THE APOSTLE PAUL

For I am the least of the apostles and do not even deserve
to be called an apostle, because I persecuted the church of
God. But by the grace of God I am what I am, and his grace
to me was not without effect. No, I worked harder than all of
them—yet not I, but the grace of God that was with me.

1 CORINTHIANS 15:9-10

O ur survey of the New Testament has taken us through the first
two sections, the Gospels and Acts. We now arrive at the third
section, the epistles, which cannot be understood without knowing
something about their dominant writer.

Jesus and Paul are beyond question the two most familiar persons
in the New Testament. Paul wrote 13 of the 27 New Testament documents (87 chapters—nearly as many as the 89 of the four Gospels). He
thought, taught, and wrote at a deeper theological level than any of the
other biblical writers. But as we have seen, Jesus left nothing directly
to us in writing. In Paul's case, we are able to coordinate his missionary activities (in Acts) with his writing and follow-up ministry (in the
epistles). This affords a kind of triangulation, a perspective that brings
the man to life.

Roman Citizen and Pharisee

Paul was a Jew, though not from Palestine. He was a citizen of Tarsus, capital of the Roman province of Cilicia, which was located in
modern southern Turkey (Acts 9:11; 21:39). He was trained as a rabbi

under the distinguished Gamaliel (Acts 22:3). His secular profession was tent making (Acts 18:3). Paul was also born of the purest Jewish blood, a descendant of the patriarch Benjamin (Philippians 3:5), at a time when few Jews would have been able to trace their descent because of the exiles. He was named after Israel's first king, Saul—though sometime after his conversion, his name changed to the less Jewish, more Gentile-sounding Paul (Acts 13:9).

Paul was born a Roman citizen (Acts 16:37; 22:25-29)—a privilege shared by a minority of those residing within the Roman Empire. The combination of pure pedigree, tutelage under Gamaliel, and Roman citizenship would have brought him great prestige—somewhat like a person today with degrees from both Oxford and Cambridge.

In addition, he was an intensely focused Pharisee (Acts 22:3; 23:6; 26:5; Philippians 3:5—for more on the Pharisees, please review our discussion in chapter 14). A driven man, Paul claimed to have advanced beyond many of his contemporaries (Galatians 1:13-14). Certain that the Christians were dangerous heretics, he hounded, imprisoned, tortured, and killed them (1 Corinthians 15:9; 1 Timothy 1:13). Commentators sometimes assert that Saul was troubled during his pre-Christian days by his active persecution of the Christians, but he himself insists that he always had a clear conscience (Acts 23:1). Paul's training as a Pharisee would have equipped him to think long and hard about the relationship of Torah to believers in Christ—appropriate for the one who was divinely appointed to be the apostle to the Gentiles (Romans 11:13; Galatians 2:8).

Paul's Celibacy

It is unknown whether Paul had a wife (1 Corinthians 9:5). Many rabbis were married, though it is unclear whether marriage was required, and even then, whether Paul was an exception to the rule or his wife had died or left him. The fourth-century historian Eusebius claims that Clement of Alexandria (150–215) said Paul was married, but I'm not confident this relatively late evidence is reliable.[1] Paul had received the gift of celibacy (1 Corinthians 7:7), and this freed him to focus on his service for Christ.

From Saul of Tarsus to Paul the Apostle

Saul of Tarsus had left Jerusalem for Damascus, but the one who had arrested so many was himself arrested in his tracks, temporarily blinded, and stunned beyond belief by the risen Lord. His Damascus Road experience is recounted three times (Acts 9; 22; 26).

After he arrived in Damascus, he had several days to think over his situation (Acts 9:9), and finally his sins were washed away (Acts 9:18; 22:16). He was commissioned as an apostle by the resurrected Jesus (1 Corinthians 9:1; 15:8-9). The word *apostle* has the sense of "one who is sent," or "missionary." Used in a technical sense, an apostle was an eyewitness of the resurrected Jesus, specially chosen to receive the words of Christ through the Holy Spirit (Acts 22:14-15; Galatians 1:11-12) as Jesus promised (John 14:25-26; 16:12-15). Apostles also had the ability to work miracles (Luke 9:1; 2 Corinthians 12:12; Hebrews 2:4). He joined the 12 after the earthly ministry of Jesus, so he describes himself as "one abnormally born" (1 Corinthians 15:8). Occasionally the word *apostle* appears in the New Testament in the general sense of missionary, or one who is sent, but this does not indicate the same level of authority as an apostle in the technical sense.[2] We also read that Paul spent three years in Arabia (Galatians 1:18).[3] Perhaps this time of personal growth and instruction from the Lord parallels the three years the first apostles spent with Jesus in his earthly ministry.

As an apostle, Saul worked at large in the Gentile world. This may be the reason he used a Roman name, Paul, instead of his original Hebrew name, Saul. Besides, in Greek, *saulos* meant "conceited, affected, walking in a suggestive way (like a prostitute)"—not the kind of name a Christ-follower wants to have. Moreover, apostleship clearly did not go to his head, and in fact we discern a progression of humility in Paul's life.[4]

Before Christ, Saul was sincere—but sincerely wrong (see Romans 10:2). After Christ, he kept up the same sincerity and intensity as before, placing his entire life at the disposal of his new Lord. Though physically resilient (1 Corinthians 9:24-27; 2 Corinthians 11:23-27; 2 Thessalonians 3:7-10) and practically exploding with conviction, he was a winsome character. Paul was full of tenderness and compassion for others (Philippians 1:7-8; 1 Thessalonians 2:1-12). He was relatable and versatile, becoming "all things to all men" (1 Corinthians 9:19-22). He was as effective as he was, not because of his many natural gifts, but because he relied on the Lord (2 Corinthians 1:8-9). For example, many thought he was unimpressive in appearance (2 Corinthians 10:10), and Paul himself admits that he was far from a polished speaker (1 Corinthians 2:1-5). But never mind—his power came from God's Spirit, and his effectual labor flowed from a deep appreciation of how much he had been forgiven (1 Corinthians 15:9-10).

Paul internalized the Spirit of Christ and knew how to make it real to others. Yet we must be careful. Since the Protestant Reformation, many have concluded, in so many words, that Paul is the key to understanding Jesus. Surely this is backward. Jesus' life and teaching form the filter through which we understand Paul, not the other way around. Paul himself would be outraged with this teaching (1 Corinthians 1:13-17). He had a brilliant mind—but not in comparison to Jesus. And as passionately as he strove to live a holy life, he admits to frequent failure. Jesus is the key to understanding Paul, which means that the Gospels, not Paul's epistles, are the entrance point to grasping the message of the New Testament.

A Chronology of Paul's Life

Paul was baptized within a few years of Jesus' resurrection, between AD 32 and 34 (Acts 9:18; 22:16). This is a deduction from Galatians 2:1. Paul wrote Galatians, his first epistle, in AD 48, and so 34 would be the latest possible date for his second Jerusalem visit. If Paul can call himself an "old man" by the time of Philemon 9 (about AD 60)—presumably 60 years old—then he was born by AD 1.[5]

He was executed under Nero, who himself committed suicide in AD 68, which is therefore the latest date for Paul's death. One tradition says he was beheaded—the standard form of execution for Roman citizens—at *Aquae Salviae*, along the Appian Way just outside Rome. Death is imminent when he writes his last letter (2 Timothy 4:6).

The following chart assumes that Paul was baptized in the year 32. The dates are based on information from Acts and Paul's epistles, though some dates are speculative.

Dates in the life of Paul	
1 BC	born in Tarsus
AD 13–16	trained by Gamaliel in Jerusalem
31	presided over Stephen's martyrdom (Acts 8)
32	baptized in Damascus
33–36	ministered in Damascus and Arabia; received further revelation from Jesus Christ in Arabia (Acts 9:19-22; 26:20; Galatians 1:16-17)
36	first Jerusalem visit (Acts 9:26-29; Galatians 1:18)
36–45	ministered in Syria and Cilicia (Acts 9:30; Galatians 1:21)
46	second Jerusalem visit (Acts 11:27-30; Galatians 2:1-10); returned to Tarsus
47	return to Antioch (required by Acts 11:25)
48	first missionary journey (Acts 13:1–14:28)
49	Jerusalem council (Acts 15:1-35)
50	second missionary journey (Acts 15:36–18:22); wrote 1–2 Thessalonians from Corinth
57	third missionary journey (Acts 18:23–21:16); wrote 1 Corinthians from Ephesus, 2 Corinthians from Macedonia, Romans from Corinth
56–58	in custody in Caesarea
58–60	Roman imprisonment; wrote prison epistles
60	released from prison; resumed mission
63–65	wrote 1 Timothy from Macedonia and Titus from Nicopolis
64	fire of Rome; many Christians were seized and killed; Paul was rearrested
63–67	wrote 2 Timothy from Rome
67	executed

Paul the Church Planter

Paul was a church planter. Much of his work was accomplished during his three missionary journeys. During the fourth journey he

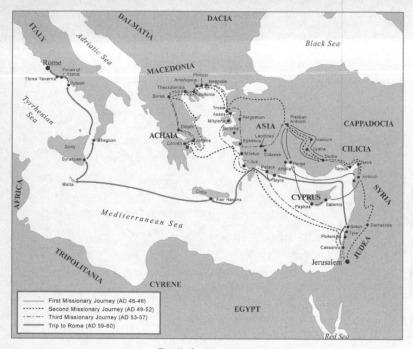

Paul's four journeys.

was under arrest, sailing to Rome to be tried before Nero. We would be greatly mistaken if we took this man for a loner. He had plenty of fellow workers (for example, see Acts 20:4), and he names many at the close of some of his letters.

Paul concentrated on the larger cities. At this time Rome itself had about a million inhabitants, and the next-largest cities in the empire had only a few hundred thousand residents. He preached first to his fellow Jews and afterward to the Gentiles (Acts 18:4-7; Romans 1:16). Thus he established a beachhead for the gospel in each locality.

Once the churches had existed for a few years, he appointed local leadership. His goal was not to create a superstructure of control, but to entrust the direction of the churches to spiritual and respected elders. He understood that missions work takes money and was frequently concerned about financial support for himself and the other workers (1 Corinthians 9:12; 2 Corinthians 11:8). Finally, his ambition was to preach in fresh territory if possible, validating the work of those who evangelized before him and respecting their spheres of influence (Romans 15:19-24).

Paul would not leave young churches to fend for themselves, so he used three methods of follow-up: visiting in person, sending a trusted colleague, and sending a letter (the second and third methods were normally combined).

Paul the Writer

In addition to Paul's 13 canonical letters (or epistles), he refers to many others. He preached in dozens of towns, so he could have penned more than a hundred letters. Yet even if they all survived, the expanded corpus of his writings would not be likely to contain any new doctrines. We trust that through the superintendence of the Holy Spirit, the documents needed to constitute the New Testament were written and preserved (as we saw in chapter 3).

We must keep in mind when reading the letters that we are hearing only one side of a conversation. As when we overhear a friend on the telephone, we can easily make assumptions that are later proven incorrect. Letters were written in response to critical situations and pressing questions. One example will have to suffice.

Paul established the church in Corinth in AD 50–52. We read about his time there in Acts 18. He leaves Corinth for Ephesus, where he writes 1 Corinthians (1 Corinthians 16:8). This letter responds to a verbal report delivered by Chloe (1 Corinthians 1:11—addressed in chapters 1–6) as well as a series of questions from the Corinthians (7:1; 8:1; and so on).

And yet in 1 Corinthians 5:9 he refers to an even earlier letter—in effect making 1 Corinthians the second letter (at least) to the church at Corinth. And 2 Corinthians refers to a previous letter as well (2 Corinthians 7:8). However, as the situation referred to in 2 Corinthians 2 and 7 does not fit well with the context of 1 Corinthians, this appears to be an intermediate letter, thus making 2 Corinthians in effect "4 Corinthians." Finally, once we leave the apostolic period, a leadership issue in Corinth led to Clement of Rome writing a letter to the Corinthians (AD 96). This is known as 1 Clement—a noncanonical letter, copies of which have survived. In short, we know a lot about the Christian community at Corinth. No fewer than five letters were written to the Corinthians, at least four by Paul.

Paul's original audience labored to understand his letters (2 Timothy 2:7). Some parts were difficult, but none were opaque (2 Corinthians 1:13; 2 Peter 3:16). If those in the first century had to work to understand, certainly we in the twenty-first need all the help we can get to follow his train of thought.

Finally, these letters are practical. They offer help in spiritual growth, grasping God's grace, personal discipline, marriage and family, leadership, and a host of other areas.

Early Letters

Paul's earliest letter, Galatians, dates to just before the Jerusalem Council (Acts 15), which settled the issue that was so troublesome to the churches of Galatia and elsewhere. He often wrote from one city to the church he had established in the previous city. Thus 1 Thessalonians was written from Corinth, and 1 Corinthians was written from Ephesus (Acts 18–19).

Galatians. Paul addressed the erroneous teaching of the Judaizers, who claimed that Gentile converts must be circumcised before they are baptized. Paul was irate, for the Galatians' very salvation was at stake. Salvation is through faith, not obsessing over passé regulations of the old covenant. The Judaizers' legalism pandered to their flesh. Paul encouraged the Galatians to live in the freedom of the Spirit.

First Thessalonians. Paul addressed the mistaken notion that there is little point in continuing with normal life because Christ may return at any time. Holiness, suffering, and fellowship are just a few of the emphases of the apostle in 1–2 Thessalonians. Though the day of judgment is on the way for those who persecute Christians, we must focus on such things as faith, sexual purity, and productive living.

Second Thessalonians. This letter corrects misunderstandings arising in connection with the reception of 1 Thessalonians.

First Corinthians. This was written in response to a report from some of the Corinthian leaders about disunity and sectarianism in the church. The crucified Messiah is the central message of the gospel.

Second Corinthians. Paul wrote this letter after a crisis of confidence in which a challenge to Paul's authority had led to the Corinthians overcorrecting an offender. Paul argued that the true credential of an apostle is suffering, for Christian ministry and leadership are characterized by servanthood.

Romans. Fearing disunity in the most influential city of the empire, Paul laid out his gospel in this strategic epistle, emphasizing that Jews are no better than Gentiles, and Gentiles no better than Jews. Jews and Gentiles must be unified as the people of God, and this is possible only on the basis of grace.

Prison Epistles

Paul spent quite a few years in prison. Many scholars believe he wrote his prison epistles from Rome, but Caesarea and Ephesus are also possibilities.

Philippians. Paul appealed for unity in a community where the level of mutual service had fallen. He urged his readers to emulate Christ—as well as Timothy and Epaphroditus. With Christ as the key to all of life, we can joyfully persevere through suffering and grow in character.

Colossians. The source of life is Christ, not external rule-keeping, Gnosticism, astrology, or Judaism. Christ alone is supreme and all-sufficient. Religious regulations are powerless, unable to effect the ethical Christian life that lies at the heart of the faith.

Philemon. Paul appealed to a house-church leader, Philemon, to accept and forgive his runaway slave Onesimus, who became a Christian when he met Paul in prison. Through the gospel we can all be reconciled. As a result we are to treat one another with grace and respect. This short letter may have been delivered along with Colossians.

Ephesians. This letter is similar to Colossians in its scope. Some preachers in Asia were pressuring Gentile Christians to conform to Judaism. There was also confusion about fate and the astrological powers. Yet the cosmic scope of the work of Christ, especially in his church, brings all the world together.

Pastoral Epistles

To fit the chronology of the missions work indicated in these letters, which does not easily fit into the framework of Acts, we may assume they were written after Paul's release from confinement in Rome. The maximum length of time a prisoner could be held without trial under Roman law was two years, so Acts 28:31 implies a release from custody (see also Acts 24:27).

First Timothy. In Acts 20 Paul warned the Ephesians of the rise of false teachers, and by the time of 1 Timothy these "wolves" had begun to ravage the flock. Paul encouraged Timothy to maintain high standards of leadership. Spiritual Christian leadership is vital for the order and progress of the church.

Titus. After work on the Mediterranean island of Crete, Paul established elderships, for false teachers (the circumcision group) had caused much confusion. God's people, and especially leaders, must do what is good, standing firm against the error of false teachers.

Second Timothy. Written shortly before his execution, this most personal of all Paul's letters exhorts Timothy to imitate Paul's faith—even though this is certain to lead to suffering. Leaders must persevere till the end, just as Christ and Paul did, against sin, theological error, and temptations to compromise.

Background Information

To understand the Pauline epistles, and in fact any letter, we need certain background information. Sometimes indirect evidence from Acts sheds light on an epistle. For example, Galatians deals with the Judaizing doctrine that one must be circumcised and made into a Jew before he can become a Christian. The acuteness of the crisis (Galatians 1:6), the fact that the churches in Galatia had been established during Paul's first missionary journey (Acts 14, about AD 48), and the lack of any reference to the decision of the Jerusalem Council of Acts 15—which would have been handy as Paul strove to reason with Galatians who had come under the spell of the circumcision party—seem to indicate that Galatians was written shortly before the Jerusalem Council. Thus we can assign provisional dates to the Council of AD 49 and to Galatians of AD 48. Yet to get the most out of the letters, you will need more than just a working knowledge of the Gospels and Acts. For example, it is helpful to appreciate these topics:

- The history of the Roman Empire helps us understand many letters.

- The geography of the eastern Mediterranean helps us understand most letters.

- The Old Testament is in the background of all the epistles.

- The Apocrypha and Pseudepigrapha (extracanonical writings) help us understand the reference to Jannes and Jambres in 2 Timothy as well as several allusions and citations in Hebrews and Jude.

- Gnosticism, an incipient philosophical heresy, sheds light on Colossians and 1 Timothy (as well as 1–2 John).

- The Jew–Gentile controversy is the backdrop for Romans, 1 Corinthians, Galatians, Ephesians, Colossians, 1 Thessalonians, and Titus (as well as Hebrews and Revelation 2–3). This was the hottest issue in the first-century church.

Red-Letter Letters?

Paul wrote a fourth of the New Testament—nearly half the actual documents—so it is vital that we appreciate his authority. He claimed that he derived it from Jesus. And Peter, the original leader of the apostolic band, appears to accept this authority (2 Peter 3:15-16).

Editions of the New Testament with Jesus' words in red, first appearing in 1899, were intended as an aid to teach the world about Christ and the gospel. The implication, in the minds of many, is that the words of Christ are more inspired than the words in black—implying that the words of Paul and others deserve less study or even that they are trivial. To be sure, Jesus Christ is supreme, but the Spirit works through all Scripture (John 14:26; 2 Timothy 3:16). To separate the words of Christ is to create a false dichotomy. If we want red letters, then every word of the New Testament ought to be printed in red.

Grace and Peace

One last intriguing note. In his letters Paul frequently writes, "Grace and peace." In the East, people wished one another peace, just as the Jews said *shalom,* and the Arabs, *salaam.* In the West, a standard opening word for a letter was "Greetings" (Greek *chairein,* as in Acts 15:23). Paul, the apostle who preached the gospel to Jew and Gentile alike, combines the terms, as in Philippians 1:2. *Charis* ("grace") is similar to the word *chairein.* The Jewish apostle to the Gentiles, so concerned with the unity of the church, makes this greeting phrase an emblem of unity.

A Quick Review

Unlike the case with Jesus Christ, with Paul we have dual sources for understanding his life and message—what others saw (Acts) and what he himself wrote (his 13 epistles). Just as Jesus' work of redemption cannot be appreciated without an understanding of his life, so Paul's letters make much more sense when we know the man.

Letters were primary tools for following up with new Christian communities and confirming them in their faith. They provide a window into the lives, concerns, and struggles of the early believers. They reveal the seeds of the error, sin, and false teaching that plagued the churches in Paul's generation and continue to trouble ours today.

Paul wrote to groups of Christians. He also wrote to individuals (Philemon, Titus, and Timothy), but even then his letters were intended to be read by the larger Christian community. Under the influence and guidance of the Holy Spirit, he was truly writing for posterity. Paul's words, well preserved and thoroughly studied in our time, are life-giving, for like the words of his Master, they are inspired and practical for our daily lives.

22

OTHER LETTERS

I have much to write you, but I do not want to do so with pen
and ink. I hope to see you soon, and we will talk face to face.

3 JOHN 13-14

The epistles account for nearly half the chapters of the New Testament. Two-thirds of these letters were written by the apostle Paul, whose life and letters we surveyed in chapter 21. This chapter overviews the eight letters from Hebrews through Jude. The New Testament also contains a few other letters—seven in Revelation (2–3) and two in Acts (15; 23).

Pen and Ink

Discoveries in the late nineteenth century cast a good deal of light on letter writing in the ancient world. Thousands of letters, memoranda, shopping lists, legal documents, and so on were discovered (especially in Egypt). Letters in the first century were commonly written with pen and ink on papyrus.[1] Most were a single sheet—the size of the one-chapter letters Philemon, 2 John, 3 John, and Jude. The standard format included a greeting, a wish for good health, the letter body, and a farewell. But the New Testament epistles were more than just personal notes or news—though they included those. They were a means of follow-up, encouragement, correction, warning, and instruction. They facilitated unity in a world where the postal system was efficient but personal travel was laborious and occasionally dangerous.

Literacy

Despite many tightly held opinions about the illiteracy of the society in which Jesus ministered during his years on Earth, the evidence paints quite a different picture. A huge percentage of the free population had to read signs, inscriptions on coins, census material, and of course tax information, bills, and receipts. (Not all of those people could write, however.) The archaeological evidence is overwhelming. Yes, professionals were often employed to write—even the learned Paul used a secretary (Romans 16:22; see also Jeremiah 36:4)—but this should not be taken to prove the ignorance or illiteracy of the population at large.

People living in Palestine in the first century spoke Aramaic, but they were also familiar with Greek and Hebrew, not to mention the little bit of Latin that some of the Roman soldiers and politicians must have known. Therefore it is fair to describe this society as trilingual.

Letters were read aloud (Acts 8:30; Colossians 4:16; 1 Thessalonians 5:27), as was the ancient custom (Nehemiah 8:3,8; Jeremiah 36:10,15,21). Words were experienced in a more auditory way than in most modern reading (apart from today's children's literature), so alliteration, rhyme, and rhythm were important. It is nearly impossible to reproduce these effects in translation, so those who read the original languages are at an advantage.

Arrangement

The New Testament documents were written in the first century but collected in the second. That is, early on some communities may have possessed a Gospel or two, Acts, and a handful of letters, but from community to community the collection varied. Most churches did not have all 27 New Testament documents until the second century, and some not until the fourth century.

Interestingly, Hebrews is placed in the Pauline literature by the late second century. In the last ancient collection of Paul's letters I saw (p[46], or papyrus 46, in the Chester Beatty Museum in Dublin), Hebrews immediately followed Romans. This is not to say it was written by Paul. Yet since it is anonymous and has several Pauline connections, it came to rest in the Pauline collection.

Once the New Testament letters began to be collected, the seven general letters (also called the *catholic*, or universal, epistles) circulated as a unit. These were often placed after Acts. Thus one read Matthew, Mark, Luke, John, Acts, James, 1 Peter…This may sound strange indeed if you are a veteran English Bible reader, but not if you read the Scripture in Russian, for in the Bibles of Eastern Europe this order is preserved. Regardless of the arrangement, all the epistles were placed between Acts and Revelation.

In a similar way, the order of the Gospels was fluid for a few centuries. I have examined three Gospel collections in this order: Matthew, John, Luke, Mark.[2] The order of the books is not inspired, and few of us read the Bible straight through, so the various arrangements are really only of academic interest.

Authorship of the New Testament Documents		
Book	Traditional Authorship	Explicit Authorship
Matthew	Matthew	anonymous
Mark	John Mark	anonymous
Luke	Luke	anonymous
John	John	"the disciple Jesus loved"
Acts	Luke	anonymous, though same author as Luke
Romans	Paul	Paul
1 Corinthians	Paul	Paul and Sosthenes
2 Corinthians	Paul	Paul and Timothy
Galatians	Paul	Paul
Ephesians	Paul	Paul
Philippians	Paul	Paul and Timothy
Colossians	Paul	Paul and Timothy
1 Thessalonians	Paul	Paul, Silas, and Timothy
2 Thessalonians	Paul	Paul, Silas, and Timothy
1 Timothy	Paul	Paul

Authorship of the New Testament Documents		
2 Timothy	Paul	Paul
Titus	Paul	Paul
Philemon	Paul	Paul and Timothy
Hebrews	Paul	anonymous
James	James, the brother of Jesus	James
1 Peter	Peter	Peter
2 Peter	Peter	Simon Peter
1 John	John	anonymous
2 John	John	the elder
3 John	John	the elder
Jude	Jude, the brother of Jesus	Jude, the brother of James
Revelation	John	John

Overview of the Epistles

The general epistles (or catholic epistles, from the Greek *katholikos,* which means "universal") are written to clusters of churches rather than to individual congregations, except for 2 and 3 John. As we have mentioned, Hebrews is similar though grouped with neither the catholic nor the Pauline epistles.

Hebrews

• Author: Unknown. Proposals include Luke, Clement, Barnabas, Priscilla, and others. Paul is excluded by 2:3. Apollos is the current front-runner.

• Recipients: Believers from a Jewish Christian background.

• Date: AD 66–68, as the letter was sent to second-generation Christians and the temple system was still operating (Hebrews 13:7; 8:13).

• Location: Palestine, Syria, or another heavily Jewish area of the Mediterranean world.

- Situation: Jewish Christians, fatigued by persecution, were being lured back to Judaism.
- Theme: At every point the new covenant is superior to the old covenant, so why fall away from Christ to return to the old?

James

- Author: James, traditionally James the Just, brother of Jesus Christ (Galatians 1:19).
- Recipients: Jewish Christians (1:1).
- Date: by AD 62 (the date of James' execution), possibly as early as the 40s.
- Location: Palestine.
- Situation: Christians weren't living out their faith.
- Theme: True faith is borne out practically in such areas as charity, speech, and business ethics. James does not contradict Paul's teaching about faith—he complements it.

1 Peter

- Author: The apostle Peter with Silas as scribe.
- Recipients: Believers in Pontus, Galatia, Cappadocia, Asia, and Bithynia—all in Asia Minor (modern Turkey).
- Date: AD 64–68.
- Location: Peter appears to be writing from Rome, which he called Babylon in 1 Peter 5:13.
- Situation: Christians were suffering—possibly in Nero's persecution of AD 64—and this was placing a strain on relationships.
- Theme: To follow in the footsteps of Jesus is to suffer and especially to suffer unjustly.

2 Peter

- Author: The apostle Peter.

- Recipients: Not specified.
- Date: AD 64–68.
- Location: Not specified.
- Situation: False teachers had slipped into the church, advocating licentious living and rebellion against authority.
- Theme: Growth in the knowledge of God is the safeguard against the destructive errors of the false teachers.

1 John

- Author: Anonymous, though apparently the author of 2 John. Traditionally, the apostle John.
- Recipients: Christians living in Asia Minor, where Docetism was being taught.
- Date: AD 90s (possibly earlier).
- Location: Tradition says John was living in Ephesus at this time. He had not yet been exiled to Patmos (Revelation 1:9).
- Situation: Docetists (a variety of Gnostics who deny that Jesus came in the flesh) had left the church and were plaguing it through their false prophecies and worldliness. They also taught that the flesh is evil and only spirit is good.
- Theme: God truly came in the flesh, so believers truly overcome sin and love one another.

2 John

- Author: "The elder." Traditionally, the apostle John.
- Recipients: "The chosen lady." Some commentators think this is a woman, but most believe it is a church.
- Date: 90s.
- Location: Asia Minor.
- Situation: False teachers were denying the incarnation.

They were not in fellowship with the church leaders and seem to have had serious relationship problems.

- Theme: Same as 1 John. The epistle has been called "1 John in miniature."

3 John

- Author: "The elder." Traditionally, the apostle John.
- Recipient: Gaius, a Christian leader.
- Date: 90s.
- Location: Asia Minor.
- Situation: The egotistical and power-hungry Diotrephes is undermining the church. Gaius should assist the godly Demetrius.
- Theme: Ego is a disqualification for leadership. Ego is manifest in poor relationships and lack of hospitality.

Jude

- Author: Jude, brother of James. Traditionally, James' and Jesus' brother Jude.
- Recipients: Unknown.
- Date: late first century.
- Location: Unknown.
- Situation: The church was being assailed by false prophets, who seem to have divorced righteous living from religion.
- Theme: Certain judgment will fall on those who live carelessly and influence others to do the same. Appears to be a condensation of 2 Peter.

Reading Tips

Here are some reading tips for these eight letters—although all apply equally well to the letters of Paul and the other New Testament epistles. Do remember...

- We are hearing only one side of a conversation. The authors and audiences have in most cases already met, or they have been corresponding.

- These letters were read aloud. The hearers took more time to process them than we might in a quick reading.

- The alliteration, nuances, cadences, and more are lost in the transition from Greek to English.

- We need to look up the many unfamiliar Old Testament references.

- The writers are addressing insiders who had been instructed in the life of Christ. The Gospels probably had not yet been written, but reminiscences and some records of Jesus' words and deeds were current and accessible.

Don't assume...

- ...that the letters were written to outsiders. Every epistle was sent to a Christian community. For example, the writer wasn't telling anyone how to become a Christian or presenting the gospel for the first time.

- ...that the same name always refers to the same person. There are many Johns and Marys.

- ...that whatever you don't understand (or like) applies only to the first-century culture. In commenting on homosexuality, Jude was actually going against the loose sexual mores of his time (Jude 7-8). Similarly, in forbidding women to preach to men, Paul was rejecting the culture of Ephesus, where women held prominent roles in religion (1 Timothy 2).

- ...that everything applies directly to our day. Peter tells the people to greet one another with a holy kiss (1 Peter 5:14). Form is not the same as function. The form (the kiss) expressed the function (a warm greeting). In cultures where kissing is not practiced, we need not retain the form, provided the function is preserved. Christians greet one another with affection and respect, whether by an embrace, a handshake, a bow, or a kiss. For one last example, returning to Paul's letters, foot washing, a requirement for widows who received church support (1 Timothy 5:10), was an implementation of the principles of humble service and hospitality in the culture of the day. Sandals were common footwear, and roads were often unimproved and dirty.

A Quick Review

Hebrews and the seven general letters, like the letters of Paul, are eminently practical. They help believers fight worldliness, compromise, and false teaching. Righteous leaders dealt with real issues; nothing was swept under the rug. Though all the normal caveats pertaining to interpretation apply, these letters contain much to learn, much that applies to our lives, both on the individual and congregation level.

The final chapter of our overview brings us to the fourth and final section of the New Testament—the Apocalypse.

THE APOCALYPSE

They triumphed over him by the blood of the Lamb
and by the word of their testimony; they did not love
their lives so much as to shrink from death.

REVELATION 12:11

We have surveyed the entire Old Testament and three of the four sections of the New. We now come to the Apocalypse. The Bible ends, appropriately, with scenes of the end of the world. But not in the sense most people think.

This is not really a book about heaven. Nowhere in Revelation do people go to heaven; the New Jerusalem, the city of God described in the closing chapters, comes down *out of* heaven. Besides, the final vision has non-Christian nations still living on the earth (21:24). True, Revelation speaks of judgment and the ultimate triumph of the kingdom of God over the kingdoms of the world, yet it is not a timetable of end-time events. It doesn't contain a single word about the antichrist or a rapture, nuclear war or bioterrorism. It does, however, make veiled allusions to the Roman Empire, and it incorporates hundreds of images and motifs from little-read parts of the Old Testament.

Popular and sensationalistic religious programs direct our attention to developments in the Middle East, Russia, China, or even to elaborate government conspiracies at home. Yet the book of Revelation itself directs us to faithful Christian living—even at the expense of our lives. There is so much misinformation out there that, for most of us, the first step in making sense of this book is to forget everything we've ever heard about it!

The Meaning of *Apocalypse*

The word *apocalypse* has three meanings. In the popular sense, it is the story of the cataclysmic end of the world inspired by the book of Revelation. Second, the Apocalypse is the alternate name for the last book of the Bible. *Apocalypse* derives from the Greek *apokalypsis,* and *revelation* comes to us unchanged from Latin. Both mean "unveiling," or "revealing." Third, apocalyptic is a literary genre used in both testaments. This genre is poorly understood by most casual Bible readers, and becoming familiar with it will be worth our while.

In brief, the message is an apocalypse because it reveals (unveils) the true nature of Christians' struggles. The saints may appear to be alone, outnumbered, and without hope against the mighty power of Rome. Yet the conflict is not just local, but cosmic—God against Satan. That means that victory for the saints is assured.

The Flow of Revelation

In the first three chapters, the three main characters are introduced: John, Christ, and the church. Chapters 4–7 set the stage for the judgments on Rome, broadly presented in chapters 8–11. Details of the judgment and the triumph of the saints are pictured in chapters 12–22. In chapters 13–14 we meet the two beasts, Rome the political power and Rome the religious power. In 15–16, readers are assured that doom awaits the enemy, and chapters 17–22 speak of two cities opposed in every way. These last chapters also feature glimpses of final judgment and salvation. Chapter 12 is Revelation in miniature, and verses 11-12 state the theme of the entire book:

> They triumphed over him by the blood of the Lamb and by the word of their testimony; they did not love their lives so much as to shrink from death. Therefore rejoice, you heavens and you who dwell in them! But woe to the earth and the sea, because the devil has gone down to you! He is filled with fury, because he knows that his time is short.

Major Views

There are five major views of Revelation.

1. The *preterist* view holds that everything has already been fulfilled. While correctly respecting the historical context, this view seems to ignore the tenor of the book and the note on which it ends: "'Yes, I am coming soon.' Amen. Come, Lord Jesus" (22:20). Thus it does not go far enough.

2. The *idealist* view is that the book contains only general spiritual principles. While the abiding lessons are indeed spiritual principles, too much is lost when the history behind the book is relegated to a footnote.

3. The *historicist* understanding identifies specific periods of church history from the first century to the end. This not only is unsupportable biblically but also ignores context and requires enormous and contrived interpretive leaps.

4. The *futurist* approach insists that most (or all) of the book is still to take place, thus succumbing to the same weakness as the idealist view, which is ignoring context. Further, coordinating Scripture with future events is a doomed enterprise; no one can accurately predict the end (Matthew 24:36; 1 Thessalonians 5:1-2).

5. Perhaps the most rational approach is to understand the apocalypse in the context of both the Roman Empire (and its program of persecution) and Old Testament apocalyptic literature, while taking in the metaphors of judgment and salvation as illuminating events at the end of the world.[1]

Authorship, Location, and Date

Persecution was heating up in Asia Minor (modern Turkey). The center of the troubles was the province of Asia—the extreme western part of Asia Minor—where the seven churches of Ephesus, Smyrna, Pergamum, Sardis, Thyatira, Philadelphia, and Laodicea were located. These were the recipients of this book.[2]

The date of composition is agreed by most to be AD 95 or 96, at the end of the reign of Domitian (81–96). The author was John—apparently the apostle himself—on the remote Aegean island of Patmos. Patmos is just a few hours by motorboat from Ephesus. As beautiful as the island is, its virtue as far as the Romans were concerned was its remoteness. John had been exiled there to punish him for being a Christian and to curtail his influence as a leader.

The message is from Jesus Christ, communicated by an angel to John, to be delivered to seven representative churches in Asia (Revelation 2–3). What did the Apocalypse mean to its original hearers? And what are we supposed to learn? With so many zany interpretations on the radio, TV, and the web, whom are we to believe?

Fortunately, we *can* get the gist of this book (Revelation 1:3). In this chapter we will isolate three keys to understanding Revelation. Not to say that the entire book will then be self-explanatory—there may still be some unanswered questions—but with the assistance of these keys, the pieces come together nicely.

The First Key: Understanding History

Like the other 65 books of the Bible, Revelation is understood in the context of its history and geography. And we don't need to know a lot, just a little. We have already touched on the geography. As for history, the Romans were ruling. Most of the first century was usually calm in Christian–Roman relationships except for the persecution under Nero in 64. The second century, however, during which it was illegal to be a Christian, was a time of brutal persecution.

Domitian was the last of the Flavian emperors. His father, Vespasian, was a better and more level-headed emperor, as was his brother Titus, who succeeded his father. Interestingly, Titus enjoyed one of the biggest military triumphs ever, as he completed the work of quelling the Jewish rebellion and destroyed the temple at Jerusalem. Domitian conferred divine honors on his brother, giving a boost to the emperor cult.

THE FLAVIAN DYNASTY

Vespasian (AD 69–79)

Titus (AD 79–81)

Domitian (AD 81–96)

Domitian may have found it difficult to live in the shadow of his father and brother. Near the end of his reign, he went mad, demanding worship *in his lifetime.* Perviously, emperor worship had taken place after the death of the ruler, not while he was still living. Was this because of the recognition he longed for as a youth?[3] With the power of the empire behind him—and the ease of bumping off enemies or challengers to the throne—he seems to have enjoyed causing suffering for his subjects. He was ruthless, narcissistic, and paranoid. He maintained a network of informers. Domitian is said to have kept the palace marble polished so he could always see if someone was coming to kill him. His fears were evidently well grounded, for his court officials, with the complicity of his wife, eventually assassinated him.

At any rate, Christians refused to participate in the emperor cult, and as a result some were persecuted or executed (Revelation 2:13). Their allegiance was to Jesus as Lord, so they were on a collision course with the state. The state has no right to demand its citizens' ultimate allegiance; it can expect compliance only where the law of God is not violated. Through the Spirit John saw that things would get worse before they got better. Revelation was written to fortify Christians who would suffer under "the beast." In Revelation 17, this individual would be like Nero (one of the first seven kings, or emperors, of Rome—verses 9-10), who persecuted Christians in the capital city in AD 64. Nero died in 68, but Domitian was "Nero Redivivus" (Nero alive again), the "eighth king" (17:11) who reigned from 81 to 96. Jesus revealed this special message to John to help Christians who would suffer at the end of the century in the first Empire-wide persecution of followers of Christ.

The Apocalypse has a historical context. We now know a little Roman history, along with something about Domitian (the beast). This is crucial information for comprehending the message of Revelation. Knowledge of history is the first key.

THE IDENTITY OF JESUS CHRIST

Alpha and Omega	King of kings	Root of Jesse
Branch	King of the Jews	Savior of the world
Bread of life	Lamb of God	Son of David
bright Morning Star	last Adam	Son of God
the carpenter's son	light of the world	Son of Man
Christ	Lion of the tribe of Judah	firstborn over all creation
faithful and true witness	Immanuel	Sun of Righteousness
God	living Stone	vine
good shepherd	Lord	the way and the truth and the life
great high priest	man of suffering	wisdom of God
I Am	Messiah	Wonderful Counselor
Jesus of Nazareth	Prince of Peace	Word
Just One	resurrection and the life	

The Second Key: Understanding the Old Testament

Revelation makes copious allusions to the Old Testament. The 404 verses in Revelation include between 250 and 300 allusions. (The list on the next page provides an expansive sampling.) This means that one cannot understand Revelation without a grounding in the Old Testament. These Scriptures were the Bible of the early Christians, who would have been far more alert to the references than the modern American living in a post-Christian age. This is not meant to discourage the newcomer to the Bible from reading the Apocalypse, but to ensure that interpretation stays on track.

REVELATION—ALLUSIONS TO THE OLD TESTAMENT

God coming in the clouds (Revelation 1:7)—Exodus 13:21;
Deuteronomy 33:26; Psalm 68:4; Isaiah 19:1; Daniel 7:13

Son of Man (Revelation 1:13; 14:14)—Daniel 7:13; 10:16;
Ezekiel 1:26

iron scepter (Revelation 2:27; 12:5; 19:15)—Psalm 2:9; 23:4;
Isaiah 30:31

book of life (Revelation 3:5; 13:8; 17:8; 20:12,15; 21:27)—
Exodus 32:33; Psalm 69:28; Malachi 3:16

living creatures (Revelation 4:6-9; 5:6,8,14)—Genesis 3:24; Isaiah
6:2; Ezekiel 1:5; 10:1

Lamb that was slain (Revelation 5:6,12)—Genesis 22:8;
Isaiah 53:7

Lion of Judah (Revelation 5:5)—Genesis 49:8-10

horses and riders (Revelation 6:2,4,5,8; 19:11)—Psalm 45:4;
Zechariah 1:8; 6:1-8

plagues (Revelation 6; 8–9; 16)—Exodus 7:4-5; 9:14;
Leviticus 26:14-35; Deuteronomy 28:58-59; Amos 4:10

12 tribes of Israel (Revelation 7:4-8; 14:1-5)—Genesis 46:8-24;
Exodus 24:4; Ezekiel 47:13-14

sealing (Revelation 7:3-4)—Genesis 4:15; Ezekiel 9:4,6

angel swearing (Revelation 10:1-6)—Genesis 19:12-13;
Daniel 12:7

Egypt (Revelation 11:8)—Nearly 800 references in the Old
Testament

Sodom (Revelation 11:8)—Genesis 18–19; Isaiah 1:9; 3:9; 13:19;
Ezekiel 16:46-56

national leaders depicted as beasts (Revelation 13; 17; 19–20)—
Daniel 7:12,17; Micah 5:8

two witnesses (Revelation 11)—Deuteronomy 19:15; Isaiah 8:2;
Zechariah 4:14

measuring the temple (Revelation 11:1-2; 21:15-17)—
Ezekiel 40–43; 45:1-6; 47:3-5

woman, child, dragon (Revelation 12)—Genesis 3:1; Psalm 2:7

beast out of the sea (Revelation 13)—Daniel 7:1-7

winepress (Revelation 14:19-20)—Isaiah 63:1-6;
    Lamentations 1:15; Joel 3:13

eternal smoke (Revelation 14:11; 19:3)— Psalm 37:20;
    Isaiah 34:10

song of Moses (Revelation 15:3)—Exodus 15

Armageddon (Revelation 16:16)—Judges 5:19; 2 Kings 23:30;
    2 Chronicles 35:22; Zechariah 12:11

nations depicted as prostitutes (Revelation 17; 19:2)—
    Exodus 34:15; 2 Chronicles 21:13; Jeremiah 3:1-5; Ezekiel 16

fall of Babylon (Revelation 17–19)—Isaiah 13; see also Ezekiel 37
    (the fall of Tyre)

Gog and Magog (Revelation 20:8)—Genesis 10:2; Ezekiel 38–39

new heaven and new earth (Revelation 21)—Isaiah 65:17; 66:22;
    Ezekiel 48

river of water and tree of life (Revelation 22:1-2)—Genesis 2:9;
    3:22; Ezekiel 47:1-12

Only by becoming familiar with the stories, images, and symbols of the Jewish Bible can we make sense of Revelation, for the Old Testament provides the colors and brushes with which the sweeping images of the apocalypse are painted.

Another interesting point is that the prophecy of Revelation was to be fulfilled "soon." We read of that which "must soon take place " (1:1). Those who take it to heart are blessed "because the time is near" (1:3). But how near? Surely John wasn't saying that the world was going to come crashing down sometime in the second century—or was he?

Once again, Old Testament background information helps enormously. Daniel 8:26, written in the sixth century BC, summed up a prophecy that referred to "the distant future." It was fulfilled in the second century BC—about 365 years later. If you told me an eclipse would occur in the late twenty-fourth century, I might find that interesting, but I would hardly begin preparing for the big day. Daniel's prophecies pertained to the distant future, so they were to be sealed up (Daniel 12:2-4). But the fulfillment of Revelation is near, so it must *not* be sealed up (Revelation 22:10). Like Jesus' prophecy about the destruction of Jerusalem, the fulfillment was to be soon (Matthew 24:34).

This is not to say that there aren't eternally valid lessons and principles in the book of Revelation. The judgment of the great harlot—the beast—shows that no one insults the Lord with impunity. Judgment will follow. But the judgment of the apocalypse was to take place in a particular historical context—the next few generations of the Roman Empire—so we cannot ignore history and jump to the end of the world. That was not the primary purpose for which the Apocalypse was written.

We may always read the Apocalypse with a focus on eternity, but we mustn't forget that its immediate application was to Christians in the Roman Empire. Suffering Christians needed encouragement in their present situation, not the distant future. Telling them, "Don't worry, in 2000 years the bad guys will be punished" would hardly have been comforting. Assuring them that their persecutors would be called to account, on the other hand, would have been encouraging.

How did Rome suffer for its contempt toward Christ and his people? It suffered literal plagues, internal rot, and external attack. The invincible city was sacked multiple times before its final fall in AD 476.[4] Rome's persecution of the church would continue for another two centuries. John's point was never that Rome would be stopped in its tracks immediately, but that God was with his people and that the oppressor would not get away with its godless actions. Long before Rome's definitive collapse, its injustice was made clear to all, and the righteous cause of the saints was obvious to the watching world. Millions joined the Christian cause. Revelation speaks of two cities. Rome was nothing but a cheap harlot. God was on the side of the New Jerusalem, which was also pictured as the bride of Christ. With every man and woman who made Jesus Lord, the wickedness of Rome was rebuked and God's word was confirmed.

The Third Key: Understanding Apocalyptic Literature

Finally, the Apocalypse is cast in the mold of Old Testament apocalyptic. This ancient genre appears in various sections of the Old Testament, though it became more popular between 200 BC and AD 200. Revelation actually includes three genres: The entire message is called a *prophecy* (1:3; 22:7,10,18-19), and chapters 2–3 contain seven *letters*, but it is the genre of *apocalyptic* to which we now turn.

Often employed by the prophetic writers, apocalyptic especially spoke to the hearts of the people in times of turmoil, oppression, and hopelessness. The word denotes unveiling, the pulling back of the curtains in order to reveal what is truly going on in the heavenly realms. In times of stress, God's people increasingly looked ahead to a time when God would enter our world, ushering in a glorious future. Evil would be requited, good rewarded, all things fulfilled. Christians in fact believe that this is precisely what has already begun to take place through the entrance of Jesus Christ into our world, both literally and spiritually.

In this genre, local problems, such as persecution, warfare, and oppression, are seen in cosmic terms. The following description may help.

> Apocalyptic speech is lurid in its colours and very often violent in its tone. It strikes the imagination and grabs hold of the mind. Who, having read it, can forget the seven-headed sea beast or the scarlet prostitute on its back? Whose mind does not boggle over the falling of the stars and the rolling up of the heavens? Apocalyptic speech is vivid and easily remembered. It appeals to our imagination. It is the language of conflict and victory. It is the language used when God smites the oppressor and vindicates his people. It is the language of crisis if not of persecution.[5]

Here is a sampling of examples of biblical apocalyptic: Isaiah 24–27; 33–35; Ezekiel 3; 38–39; Daniel 2; 7–8; Joel 3:9-17; Zechariah 12–14; Matthew 24; Mark 13; Luke 21:5-36; and all of Revelation. There are scores of examples of extrabiblical apocalyptic literature, both Jewish (including 1 Enoch, 4 Ezra, and the Apocalypse of Abraham) and Christian (such as the Apocalypse of Peter, Shepherd of Hermas, and Revelation of Bartholomew).[6]

The two most familiar apocalyptic passages for most readers are Matthew 24 (with parallels in Mark 13 and Luke 21) and the book of Revelation. Jesus foretold the destruction of Jerusalem, which took place at the hand of the Romans in AD 70. In doing so, he chose the language of apocalypse. Many readers of Matthew 24 fail to see that there was a fulfillment within one generation of the oracle itself. As Jesus predicted, everything he described would take place *in that generation* (Matthew 24:34). If it had to be fulfilled literally, then his prophecy was a failure. But if he was using the stock images of apocalyptic, there is no reason to deny that the sun was (metaphorically) darkened, that the Lord came against Jerusalem through the Roman army, or that he gathered his elect from the four winds when believers heeded Jesus' prophecy and fled the city.

Modern readers do not understand the genre and frequently imagine apocalyptic prophetic passages refer to political events in their own time. They have things backward because they have forgotten to *reverse* the rules of interpretation. In normal prose, we take everything literally unless forced to do otherwise. In apocalyptic, we take everything figuratively unless forced to do otherwise. Here are some features of apocalyptic.

- A struggle between cosmic powers of good and evil, typically in times of oppression, upheaval, and chaos, leading to a transformative future that is typically surreal, fantastic, and awe inspiring.

- Cryptic imagery that is rarely interpreted.[7] Prophetic imagery about future events often pertains not necessarily to the end of the world, but rather to ending points in history (such as the ends of lives, eras, or nations).[8]

- Typically imaginative, stylized, and creative depictions of past, present, and future events in coded language.

- An unveiling of previously unknown information, often by a man who sees into the spiritual world by means of dreams or visions.

- A phantasmagorical cast of angels who deliver messengers, exotic animals with supernatural qualities and abilities, uniquely acting astronomic bodies, awesome phenomena and natural disasters, cosmological anomalies, and composite beings.

- Symbolic numbers (such as 7 churches, 1000 years, and 144,000 saved in heaven).

- Gematria (alphanumeric code spellings), like 666.

Paradigm Shift

To read apocalyptic, many people must make a paradigm shift. When an American rents a car in countries where people drive on the left, everything feels backward at first. But eventually, drivers get used it. Or think of making the shift from U.S. measurements to metric (pounds to kilos, yards to meters). When my wife, who is European, moved with me to the United States, she had to stop using the more logical metric system and revert to the U.S. measures.

And yet I believe most people in effect *do* understand how to read apocalyptic. Consider specimens of modern apocalyptic—the Lord of the Rings or Narnia books. No one tries to find Frodo's Shire on a contemporary map or asks why Aslan is able to talk. Such questions belie the understanding of the questioner. Everyone knows that the story can only go one way: Things will get worse before they get better, but in the final showdown, evil will be vanquished.

The Bottom Line

What is the bottom line of Revelation? Using the three keys of interpretation, we discover a message as timely now as it was then.

- The church is on a collision course with the state.
- Things may get worse before they get better.
- God is in control, for Christ holds the keys to history.
- The oppressor will be vanquished and the saints vindicated.

A Quick Review

Revelation, with its grand and polytechnic depictions of the ultimate spiritual battle and its cosmic sweep of biblical history, crowns the writings not only of the New Testament but of the whole Bible. The pieces come together; the picture is complete.

Its message: Despite appearances to the contrary, God has absolute control over history and will vanquish his enemies sooner or later. In Revelation this great message is conveyed by means of the apocalyptic genre. With the assistance of three keys—a little knowledge of history, a solid knowledge of the Old Testament, and an appreciation of apocalyptic—we are able to read the book with relative ease. We shouldn't be derailed from faithful living by sensationalistic interpretations. If you want a précis of Revelation, how about this? God is in control—the victory has been won—so get ready!

᠅

We have surveyed the entire Bible—not only its historical background, literary genres, and story line, but most importantly, its eternal and life-giving message. Let us join the saints through the ages who truly had something to die for because they had Someone to live for. They knew the One who holds the keys of history.

APPENDIXES

For an even more solid overview of the Bible, you can find these four helpful tools online:*

Appendix A: You Can Read the Bible in a Year

Appendix B: Ten Bible-Reading Tips

Appendix C: Teaching *A Quick Overview of the Bible* in a Small Group or Class

Bibliography

---

* www.douglasjacoby.com/view_article.php?ID=6264.

NOTES

Chapter 2: A Story in Four Dimensions

1. The Lausanne Covenant, section 2. Available online at www.lausanne.org/all-documents/lop-3. html.

Chapter 3: Tongues, Translation, and Transmission

1. The Aramaic portions of the Old Testament are Genesis 31:47; Ezra 4:8–6:18; 7:12-26; Jeremiah 10:11; and Daniel 2:4–7:2.

2. Bible versions fall on a spectrum. The more literal versions (the NASB, for example) tend to render words or phrases in the original language the same way every time they appear, taking little license to reword or paraphrase. They may even retain the word order of the original language in the target language. Loose (or less literal) versions (such as the Living Bible and the Message) tend to be paraphrases. The problem with the more literal versions is that they are often wooden, stiff. The fault of the paraphrases is that they do little actual translation work and often reflect the theological bias of their creators. The most popular versions (such as the HCSB and NIV) typically try to strike a balance between strict and loose, wooden and wooly, sacrificing some accuracy for readability. Some of the translations in this third category are more literary versions (including the NEB and JB), which aim to create works of fine literature, even though not all the original biblical documents were works or refinement. In fact, most of the Bible is written in the language of ordinary people.

3. *Amanuensis* is the technical term for the professional who wrote the letter at the speaker's dictation.

4. *Paschal Letter of Athanasius,* AD 367.

Chapter 4: Introducing the Old Testament

1. See also Matthew 5:17-20; 12:39-42; Mark 12:35-37; Luke 4:17-21; 16:16-17.

2. Nahum is a short form of Nehemiah, which means "comfort of Yahweh."

3. The chapter numbers were not added (or standardized) until the late Middle Ages. They are usually credited to thirteenth-century church leaders, but I've personally read Bibles two centuries older with chapter numbers already supplied. The verse numbers weren't inserted until the mid-sixteenth century. Though they are useful for reference, they are not inspired, even though numerical coincidences delight many persons who hunt for mystical patterns.

Chapter 6: God's Universal Purpose: All Nations

1. This quote is from Menahoth 43b-44a in the Gemara (a commentary on the Mishnah, which forms the second part of the Talmud).

Chapter 7: History and Geography

1. If 1 Kings 6:1 is intended to be a literal 480 years, we arrive at the traditional date of 1446 BC. But 1 Kings 6:1 may be symbolic, and 1290 BC is better attested archaeologically.

Chapter 8: Religions of the Ancient Near East

1. We meet Baal in Judges 2:10-13; 3:7; 10:6; 1 Kings 18:16-40; 2 Kings 10:18-28; 21:1-9; Numbers 25:1-5; Jeremiah 2:8,23-25; 7:9; 19:5; 23:13; 32:29,35; Hosea 2:8,13,17; 9:10; 11:2; and Zephaniah 1:4.

2. These include the Greek (Roman) divinities Apollo (Apollo), Aphrodite (Venus), Athena (Minerva), Hera (Juno), Poseidon (Neptune), Ares (Mars), Hephaestus (Vulcan), Hades (Pluto), and Dionysus (Bacchus).

Chapter 9: Genesis: The Primeval and Patriarchal Periods

1. As for Abraham, Terah's line includes not just Abraham but a large number of the important characters in Genesis. As for Joseph, keeping in mind that Genesis is written for Jews and from a Jewish perspective, it is proper that the ten generations not go beyond Jacob, the father of the 12 tribes. In this way, the accent is left on Jacob's generation—Israel—thus setting the stage for the Exodus, which, after all, involved more than the "half-tribes" of Ephraim and Manasseh (originally the two sons of Joseph).

Chapter 10: Exodus and the Law

1. Perhaps this was suggested by Genesis 6:3, but even there it was to symbolize a maximum, an ideal age that only the most virtuous of men could reach. In fact, Moses is the *only* person in the Bible, fittingly, who was said to have lived 120 years (Deuteronomy 34:7). In a similar way, 110 years of age—the age when both Joseph (Genesis 50:26) and Joshua (Joshua 24:29) died—was probably more indicative of their godly character than of their actual age at death.

2. Moreover, if the plague was carried by rats, yet another deity is shown to be bankrupt—Bastet, depicted as a cat, one of whose responsibilities was protecting Egypt from infestations of vermin.

3. Amazingly, very few Scriptures describe Passover celebrations, and yet several Passovers are intricate parts of the spiritual renewal of the nation after periods of apostate abandonment of God and disobedience to his Law (such as those under King Hezekiah in 2 Chronicles 30 and King Josiah in 2 Chronicles 34-35).

4. *Shema'* is the Hebrew name for Deuteronomy 6:4, which along with verse 5 probably make the two most recited verses in the Bible, particularly by faithful Jews who repeat it several times a day: "Hear, O Israel: The LORD our God, the LORD is one. Love the LORD your God with all your heart and with all your soul and with all your strength."

5. Consider the writings of Ignatius and "Barnabas," writer of the *Epistle of Barnabas*. Both interpret Sabbath as a Jewish legal requirement no longer required for Christians. The second writer spiritualizes the Sabbath, as does the writer of the canonical book of Hebrews (4:9).

   If, then, those who had lived in antiquated practices came to newness of hope, no longer keeping the Sabbath but living in accordance with the Lord's Day, on which our life also arose through him and his death...(Ignatius, *Magnesians* 9:1).

   Finally, he says to them, "I cannot bear your new moons and Sabbaths." You see what he means: "It is not the present Sabbaths that are acceptable to me, but the one that I have made; on that Sabbath, after I have set everything at rest, I will create the beginning of an eighth day, which is the beginning of another world." This is why we spend the eighth day in celebration, the day on which Jesus both arose from the dead and, after appearing again, ascended into heaven (*Epistle of Barnabas* 15:8-9).

Chapter 11: The Conquest, Confederation, and Monarchy

1. The word Jew (Judean) comes from the name Judah. Thus one could make the argument that true Jews were members of the southern tribes, not the northern ones.

Chapter 12: Prophets False and True

1. Abraham Joshua Heschel, *The Prophets* (Peabody, MA: Hendrickson, 1962), p. 16.

2. Here are two texts that evince this viewpoint.

   Thus there was great distress in Israel, such as had not been since the time that prophets *ceased* to appear among them (1 Maccabees 9:27 RSV, from about 100 BC; see also 4:46; 14:41).

   From Artaxerxes to our own time the complete history has been written but has not been deemed worthy of equal credit with the earlier records because of the failure of the exact succession of the prophets. ...We have not an innumerable multitude of books among us, disagreeing from and contradicting one another, but only twenty-two books [the same 39 books in the Hebrew Bible/Christian Old Testament—several Old Testament books were combined, most notably the 12 minor prophets], which contain the records of all the past times; which are justly believed to be divine... (Flavius Josephus, *Against Apion* 1:8, from about AD 95).

3. Acts 1:5,22; 10:37; 11:16; 13:24-25; 18:25; 19:3-4.

Chapter 13: The Exile and Return

1. Compare Leviticus 26:29; Deuteronomy 28:53-57; 2 Kings 6:29; Jeremiah 19:9; Ezekiel 5:10.

2. Note that the body of a believer is another temple—a temple in which the Holy Spirit dwells (1 Corinthians 6:19-20).

Chapter 15: The Intertestamental Period

1. One of Herod the Great's sons, Archelaus (Matthew 2:22), had been ruling, but due to his harshness and the subsequent danger of a popular revolt, his leadership was rescinded.

2. The Roman Empire lasted until the fifth century in the west (centered in Rome), and until the fifteenth century in the East (centered in Constantinople—modern Istanbul in Turkey).

3. *Baba Batra* 4a; *Shemot Rabba* 36:1.

4. Protestants err if they claim—as I used to—that the Apocrypha were added to the Bible in the sixteenth century. They were part of the Latin Bible around the year 400, so they had been present for more than a millennium. During the Counter-Reformation, when the Catholic Church was cleaning house and also taking stock of its beliefs, it declared the Apocrypha inspired and imposed severe penalties for regarding it as less than fully authoritative. Technically speaking— and to its credit—the Catholic Church held them to be *deuterocanonical* (second-order Scripture), as opposed to protocanonical, like the 66 books of the Bible. Although the Protestant reformers assigned the Apocrypha only secondary status, they included the Apocrypha in their new translations, including the original King James Version. They could not bring themselves to consider these works inspired, but neither could they bring themselves to remove them completely.

5. This is significant because it is a misunderstanding of the fire and worms of Isaiah 66:24. They do not eternally torment their victims; they consume insentient corpses. The same doctrine, which became the view of the medieval church, is found in Sirach 7:17 and 4 Maccabees 9:9. And yet it is not at all certain that Jesus endorsed the apocryphal view of hell.

6. To learn more, please read my article "The Apocrypha: Second Thoughts." Available online at http://www.douglasjacoby.com/view_article.php?ID=256.

Chapter 17: History and Geography

1. New Testament and early Christian discoveries include the excavations at Caesarea Maritima,

Caesarea Philippi, Capernaum, Bethsaida, Beth Shean (Scythopolis), Ephesus, Pergamum, Rome, and Jerusalem, to name only a few; the Caiaphas ossuary; the Gallio inscription; the Erastus pavement; the skeletal remains of a crucified man; first-century tombs; the synagogue at Capernaum; the Soreg Inscription; the Pilate Stone; the Pool of Siloam; the Alexamenos Graffito; and references to Jesus and the primitive church in Josephus, Suetonius, Tacitus, Thallus, Pliny the Younger, the Talmud, Lucian, and other writings. These are some of my favorites, and the list is in no way complete.

2. Their discussions were recorded in the Mishnah (which was codified in about AD 200), and the Mishnah itself was expanded through generations of rabbinical studies and discussions. These findings were written down in a series of books that became the Gemara. The Gemara and Mishnah were combined to create the Talmud in about AD 500.

3. We see the word as *kaisar* in Greek, *caesar* in Latin, *czar, tzar,* or *tsar* in Russian, *kaiser* in German, and so forth.

4. This includes the Psalms of Solomon 17:26-3, the Dead Sea Scrolls (CD 19:9b-11), the Sibylline Oracles (3:652-795), and the Pseudepigrapha (1 Enoch 48:8-10; Testament of Judah XVII: 5-6).

Chapter 18: Jesus Christ

1. *Jewish Antiquities* 17.6.4.

2. This was the same title that was given to Herod (an Idumean) by the Roman Senate when they restored him to power in 39 BC. Herod had jealously protected that title for himself ever since.

3. This is according to John. Matthew, Mark, and Luke telescope his ministry into a one-year format.

4. In the Law, see Genesis 3:15; 49:10; Deuteronomy 18:15-18. In the Prophets, see 2 Samuel 7:14; Micah 5:2; Daniel 9:24-26; Isaiah 2:2-4; 7:14; 9:1-6; 11:1-10; 42:1-9; 49:5-7; 52:13–53:12; 61:1-3; Ezekiel 34:11-16,33; Malachi 3:1-2. In the Writings, see Psalms 2; 45; 69; 110.

5. For example, see Acts 2:25-28; 2:34-35; 4:11,25-26; 8:32-33; 13:33-35.

6. Targum Jonathan, by Jonathan ben Uzziel, a disciple of Hillel.

7. *Sanhedrin,* 98b.

8. The interchange between Rashi and his fellow rabbis is well known. See http://jewishroots.net/library/prophecy/isaiah/isaiah-53/what-rabbis-said-2.html.

Chapter 19: The Gospels

1. It is interesting that a good case can be made that the author of John, "the disciple whom Jesus loved," is actually Lazarus (Matthew 26:56b; John 11:3,5,35-36,38; 12:2,9-11).

2. Most scholars pin Mark to about AD 65. A minority give John the distinction of being the oldest—and this is possible—but most say Mark came first. Matthew and Luke, which made use of Mark as a source (sometimes using many of the sentences in Mark verbatim), were penned in the years just before or after AD 70. John, though displaying impressive knowledge of Palestine in the period before AD 70, is considered to have been written at the end of the century, sometime in the 90s.

3. The Greek word *bios* is the equivalent of the Latin word *vita,* as in Plutarch's *Lives.*

Chapter 20: Acts

1. For example, *Res Gestae Divi Augusti* (The things done by the divine Augustus) was a Latin funerary inscription, nearly 40 paragraphs in all, praising Augustus Caesar. This was a sort of imperial propaganda. Not to say the biblical Acts is propaganda, but it shares the broader genre.

2. We find another noteworthy example of broken-down barriers in Acts 2 (Pentecost), where Babel (Genesis 11:1-9) is reversed. Instead of being divided and "talking past one another," in Christ we are united, understanding one another.

3. In addition, overly emphasizing the *fruit* of commitment (seen in verses 43-47) is inverted, for fruit results naturally from the *root* (verses 41-42). Leaders overly focused on the bottom line create a sort of "Christian pragmatism" in which the tail is wagging the dog and the organic spontaneity of the church is stultified.

Chapter 21: The Apostle Paul

1. Eusebius, *Church History* 3.30.1.

2. John 13:16; Acts 14:4,14; Romans 16:7; 2 Corinthians 8:23; Philippians 2:25.

3. Quite possibly Paul spent these years in Nabatea.

4. 1 Corinthians 15:9; 2 Corinthians 12:5,10; Ephesians 3:8; Philippians 2:3-4; 1 Timothy 1:15— passages written about AD 55, 56, 58, 60, and 63, respectively. See also 2 Corinthians 12:1-10.

5. Saul could easily be called a "young man" at the time of Stephen's martyrdom (Acts 7:58) because he was not yet 40.

Chapter 22: Other Letters

1. 2 Corinthians 3:1-3; 2 John 12; 3 John 13; see also Jeremiah 36:18.

2. Codex W, from about AD 400, at the Smithsonian; the Gothic Codex Argenteus, also from about AD 400, at Uppsala University, Sweden; and Codex X, from about AD 900, at the Munich University Library.

Chapter 23: The Apocalypse

1. Those who insist that Revelation must be fulfilled in our generation—not to say the end *couldn't* come at any moment!—may be guilty of impatience, akin to the student in history class who thinks the lessons are boring ("How does this apply to me?"). He doesn't mind watching the news because he considers that relevant. Unless he is in the moment, he cannot pay attention and doesn't see the point. But surely there is more to learn from history than there is from current events, which after all form only a minuscule portion of history as a whole. Moreover, if anything, history shows us that all predictions of the end of the world up to now are wrong. Yes, one day somebody might get it right, but that will be only because of dumb luck, not because he is wiser than his predecessors.

2. By the way, all seven are sites of interesting archaeological explorations. Ephesus is my favorite.

3. His low self-esteem was not helped by his baldness. He was highly sensitive about this (he took to wearing wigs), and Suetonius tells us (in *Life of Domitian* 18:2) that eventually he wrote a book titled *On the Care of Hair*.

4. The eastern capital, Constantinople, survived all the way to 1453.

5. Jim McGuiggan, *The Book of Revelation* (Dallas: Star Bible Publishers, 1976), 14.

6. Here is a more complete list. Jewish apocalyptic: 1 Enoch, Testaments of the 12 Patriarchs, Psalms of Solomon, Assumption of Moses, Apocalypse of Baruch, 4 Ezra, Apocalypse of Abraham, Prayer of Joseph, Book of Eldad and Modad, Apocalypse of Elijah, 2 Enoch, Oracles of Hystapses, Testament of Job, Testament of the 3 Patriarchs, Sibylline Oracles. Christian apocalyptic: the Apocalypse of Peter, Testament of Hezekiah, Testament of Abraham, Vision of Isaiah,

Shepherd of Hermas, 5 Ezra, 6 Ezra, Apocalypse of Paul, Apocalypse of John, Apocalypse of the Virgin, Apocalypse of Sedrach, Apocalypse of Daniel, the Revelation of Bartholomew.

7. Exceptions to the rule are 1:13 (Christ), 1:18 (the golden lampstands), 1:20 (the seven stars), 12:9 (the dragon), 17:9 (the seven hills), and 17:18 (the prostitute). These images are interpreted.

8. Some images serve only as flourishes for dramatic effect. See 6:12-14; 9:7-11.

MORE GREAT HARVEST HOUSE
BOOKS BY DOUGLAS A. JACOBY

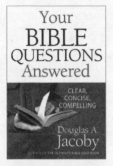

Your Bible Questions Answered

Douglas Jacoby believes that pursuing answers about the Bible and God's truth is healthy for a thriving faith. With encouragement and clarity, he tackles the questions of greatest interest to Christians like you to help you grow in relationship with God and with others.

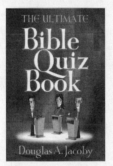

The Ultimate Bible Quiz Book

Who led a rebellion against Moses and Aaron?
Who was Jeremiah's secretary?
What was Peter's father's name?

These questions and countless more fill these entertaining one-page quizzes, with answers on the following page. Categories include important people in the Bible, books of the Bible, and many others.

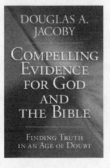

Compelling Evidence for God and the Bible

In an age of doubt, it's rare to find Christians who can speak clearly and boldly about the reasons for their faith. This easy-to-read apologetics work gives you solid reasons why the Christian faith is not only true but also reasonable.

To learn more about other Harvest House books
or to read sample chapters, log on to our website:

www.harvesthousepublishers.com

HARVEST HOUSE PUBLISHERS

EUGENE, OREGON